Austen:
Austen:
Austen:
Blake: SOUTHAM
Charlo
Emily
Browni   Other Poems   J. R. WATSON
Bunyan   's Progress   ROGER SHARROCK
Byron: 'Childe Harold's Pilgrimage' & 'Don Juan'   JOHN JUMP
Chaucer: Canterbury Tales   J. J. ANDERSON
Coleridge: 'The Ancient Mariner' & Other Poems   ALUN R. JONES & WILLIAM TYDEMAN
Congreve: Comedies   PATRICK LYONS
Conrad: 'Heart of Darkness', 'Nostromo' & 'Under Western Eyes'   C. B. COX
Conrad: The Secret Agent   IAN WATT
Dickens: Bleak House   A. E. DYSON
Dickens: 'Hard Times', 'Great Expectations' & 'Our Mutual Friend'   NORMAN PAGE
Donne: Songs and Sonets   JULIAN LOVELOCK
George Eliot: Middlemarch   PATRICK SWINDEN
George Eliot: 'The Mill on the Floss' & 'Silas Marner'   R. P. DRAPER
T. S. Eliot: Four Quartets   BERNARD BERGONZI
T. S. Eliot: 'Prufrock', 'Gerontion', 'Ash Wednesday' & Other Shorter Poems   B. C. SOUTHAM
T. S. Eliot: The Waste Land   C. B. COX & ARNOLD P. HINCHLIFFE
Farquhar: 'The Recruiting Officer' & 'The Beaux' Stratagem'   RAYMOND A. ANSELMENT
Fielding: Tom Jones   NEIL COMPTON
Forster: A Passage to India   MALCOLM BRADBURY
Hardy: Poems   JAMES GIBSON & TREVOR JOHNSON
Hardy: The Tragic Novels   R. P. DRAPER
Hopkins: Poems   MARGARET BOTTRALL
James: 'Washington Square' & 'The Portrait of a Lady'   ALAN SHELSTON
Jonson: 'Every Man in his Humour' & 'The Alchemist'   R. V. HOLDSWORTH
Jonson: Volpone   JONAS A. BARISH
Joyce: 'Dubliners' & 'The Portrait of the Artist as a Young Man'   MORRIS BEJA
Keats: Narrative Poems   JOHN SPENCER HILL
Keats: Odes   G. S. FRASER
D. H. Lawrence: Sons and Lovers   GAMINI SALGADO
D. H. Lawrence: 'The Rainbow' & 'Women in Love'   COLIN CLARKE
Marlowe: Doctor Faustus   JOHN JUMP
Marlowe: 'Tamburlaine the Great', 'Edward the Second' & 'The Jew of Malta'   JOHN RUSSELL
    BROWN
Marvell: Poems   ARTHUR POLLARD
Milton: 'Comus' & 'Samson Agonistes'   JULIAN LOVELOCK
Milton: Paradise Lost   A. E. DYSON & JULIAN LOVELOCK
O'Casey: The Dublin Trilogy   RONALD AYLING
Osborne: Look Back in Anger   JOHN RUSSELL TAYLOR
Peacock: The Satirical Novels   LORNA SAGE
Pope: The Rape of the Lock   JOHN DIXON HUNT
Shakespeare: A Midsummer Night's Dream   ANTONY W. PRICE
Shakespeare: Antony and Cleopatra   JOHN RUSSELL BROWN
Shakespeare: Coriolanus   B. A. BROCKMAN
Shakespeare: Hamlet   JOHN JUMP
Shakespeare: Henry IV Parts 1 and 2   G. K. HUNTER

Shakespeare: *Henry V* MICHAEL QUINN
Shakespeare: *Julius Caesar* PETER URE
Shakespeare: *King Lear* FRANK KERMODE
Shakespeare: *Macbeth* JOHN WAIN
Shakespeare: *Measure for Measure* G. K. STEAD
Shakespeare: *The Merchant of Venice* JOHN WILDERS
Shakespeare: *'Much Ado About Nothing' & 'As You Like It'* JOHN RUSSELL BROWN
Shakespeare: *Othello* JOHN WAIN
Shakespeare: *Richard II* NICHOLAS BROOKE
Shakespeare: *The Sonnets* PETER JONES
Shakespeare: *The Tempest* D. J. PALMER
Shakespeare: *Troilus and Cressida* PRISCILLA MARTIN
Shakespeare: *Twelfth Night* D. J. PALMER
Shakespeare: *The Winter's Tale* KENNETH MUIR
Shelley: *Shorter Poems & Lyrics* PATRICK SWINDEN
Spenser: *The Faerie Queene* PETER BAYLEY
Swift: *Gulliver's Travels* RICHARD GRAVIL
Tennyson: *In Memoriam* JOHN DIXON HUNT
Thackeray: *Vanity Fair* ARTHUR POLLARD
Trollope: *The Barsetshire Novels* T. BAREHAM
Webster: *'The White Devil' & 'The Duchess of Malfi'* R. V. HOLDSWORTH
Wilde: *Comedies* WILLIAM TYDEMAN
Woolf: *To the Lighthouse* MORRIS BEJA
Wordsworth: *Lyrical Ballads* ALUN R. JONES & WILLIAM TYDEMAN
Wordsworth: *The Prelude* W. J. HARVEY & RICHARD GRAVIL
Yeats: *Poems, 1919–35* ELIZABETH CULLINGFORD
Yeats: *Last Poems* JON STALLWORTHY

Medieval English Drama PETER HAPPÉ
Elizabethan Poetry: Lyrical & Narrative GERALD HAMMOND
The Metaphysical Poets GERALD HAMMOND
Poetry of the First World War DOMINIC HIBBERD
Thirties Poets: 'The Auden Group' RONALD CARTER
Comedy: Developments in Criticism D. J. PALMER
Drama Criticism: Developments since Ibsen ARNOLD P. HINCHLIFFE
Tragedy: Developments in Criticism R. P. DRAPER
The English Novel: Developments in Criticism since Henry James STEPHEN HAZELL
The Language of Literature NORMAN PAGE
The Pastoral Mode BRYAN LOUGHREY
The Romantic Imagination JOHN SPENCER HILL

CASEBOOKS IN PREPARATION INCLUDE

Beckett: *'Waiting for Godot' & Other Plays* JOHN RUSSELL BROWN
Defoe: *'Robinson Crusoe' & 'Moll Flanders'* PATRICK LYONS
Dickens: *'Dombey and Son' & 'Little Dorrit'* ALAN SHELSTON
T. S. Eliot: *Plays* ARNOLD P. HINCHLIFFE
Pinter: *'The Caretaker' & Other Plays* MICHAEL SCOTT
Sheridan: *Comedies* PETER DAVISON

Poetry Criticism: Developments since the Symbolists A. E. DYSON
Post-Fifties Poets: Gunn, Hughes, Larkin & R. S. Thomas A. E. DYSON
Shakespeare: Approaches in Criticism JOHN RUSSELL BROWN
The Gothick Novel VICTOR SAGE

O'Casey

The Dublin Trilogy

The Shadow of a Gunman
Juno and the Paycock
The Plough and the Stars

A CASEBOOK

EDITED BY

RONALD AYLING

M

MACMILLAN

First published 1985

Published by
Higher and Further Education Division
MACMILLAN PUBLISHERS LTD
Houndmills, Basingstoke, Hampshire RG21 2XS
and London
Companies and representatives
throughout the world

Typeset by
Wessex Typesetters
Frome, Somerset

Printed in Hong Kong

British Library Cataloguing in Publication Data
O'Casey, The Dublin Trilogy: The Shadow of a
gunman, Juno and the paycock, The plough and
the stars: a casebook.—(Casebook series)
1. O'Casey, Sean—Criticism and interpretation
I. Ayling, Ronald   II. Series
822'.912   PR6029.C33Z/
ISBN 0-333-27964-6
ISBN 0-333-27965-4 Pbk

To Joanna and James Turner
with deep affection

CONTENTS

General Editor's Preface   7

Introduction   8

Part One: The Dublin Trilogy

DAVID KRAUSE: O'Casey's Anti-Heroic Vision   (1960)   29
RAYMOND WILLIAMS: 'O'Casey – The Rhetoric and the
Reality'   (1968)   41

Part Two: *The Shadow of a Gunman*

1 Comment and Reviews

JOSEPH HOLLOWAY, Journal (1923), p. 49 – LADY GREGORY, Journal
(1923), p. 49 – SEAN O'CASEY, Autobiography (1949), p. 51 –
LENNOX ROBINSON (1924), p. 51 – P. S. O'HEGARTY (1924), p. 52.

2 Critical Studies

WILLIAM A. ARMSTRONG: History, Autobiography and *The
Shadow of a Gunman*   (1960)   54
RONALD G. ROLLINS: O'Casey and Synge – The Irish Hero as
Playboy and Gunman   (1966)   62
BERNICE SCHRANK: 'You needn't say no more' – Language
and the Problems of Communication in *The Shadow of a
Gunman*   (1978)   67

Part Three: *Juno and the Paycock*

1 Comment and Reviews

JOSEPH HOLLOWAY, Journal (1924), p. 83 – LADY GREGORY, Journal
(1924), p. 84 – SEAN O'CASEY (1953 & 1955), p. 86 – W. J. LAWRENCE
(1924), p. 87.

2 Critical Studies

LAURENCE OLIVIER: Meditations on *Juno and the Paycock* (1966) 90

HERBERT GOLDSTONE: 'The Need for Community' (1972) 92

JACK MITCHELL: 'Inner Structure and Artistic Unity' (1980) 99

ERROL DURBACH: Peacocks and Mothers – Theme and Dramatic Metaphor (1972) 111

MICHAEL W. KAUFMAN: Structural Design (1972) 121

Part Four: *The Plough and the Stars*

1 Comment and Reviews

GABRIEL FALLON (1961), p. 133 – LADY GREGORY, Journal (1925–26), p. 134 – SEAN O'CASEY (1960 & 1964), p. 138 – BRIGID O'HIGGINS (1926), p. 141.

2 Critical Studies

ROBERT G. LOWERY: Prelude to Year One – Sean O'Casey before 1916 (1976) 144

WILLIAM IRWIN THOMPSON: Easter 1916 – O'Casey's Naturalistic Image (1967) 154

VINCENT C. DE BAUN: O'Casey and the Road to Expressionism (1961) 165

RONALD AYLING: Character Control and 'Distancing' Effects (1970) 171

BOBBY L. SMITH: 'The Game of Chance' (1978) 188

JACK LINDSAY: *The Plough and the Stars* Reconsidered (1976) 190

Select Bibliography 199

Notes on Contributors 201

Acknowledgements 204

Index 205

GENERAL EDITOR'S PREFACE

The Casebook series, launched in 1968, has become a well-regarded library of critical studies. The central concern of the series remains the 'single-author' volume, but suggestions from the academic community have led to an extension of the original plan, to include occasional volumes on such general themes as literary 'schools' and genres.

Each volume in the central category deals either with one well-known and influential work by an individual author, or with closely related works by one writer. The main section consists of critical readings, mostly modern, collected from books and journals. A selection of reviews and comments by the author's contemporaries is also included, and sometimes comment from the author himself. The Editor's Introduction charts the reputation of the work or works from the first appearance to the present time.

Volumes in the 'general themes' category are variable in structure but follow the basic purpose of the series in presenting an integrated selection of readings, with an Introduction which explores the theme and discusses the literary and critical issues involved.

A single volume can represent no more than a small selection of critical opinions. Some critics are excluded for reasons of space, and it is hoped that readers will pursue the suggestions for further reading in the Select Bibliography. Other contributions are severed from their original context, to which some readers may wish to turn. Indeed, if they take a hint from the critics represented here, they certainly will.

A. E. DYSON

INTRODUCTION

The Shadow of a Gunman, the first of Sean O'Casey's plays to be performed, was given its première by the Abbey Theatre, Dublin, in April 1923. *Juno and the Paycock* appeared on the same stage in March the next year, to be followed by *The Plough and the Stars* early in February of 1926. From then until the present time, the three plays that are the focus of this Casebook have remained, consistently, the most successful and the most often revived dramatic works in O'Casey's native city.

Their immediate and persisting popularity has not been confined to Ireland. *Juno and the Paycock* and *The Plough and the Stars*, in particular, are very often performed in other English-speaking countries and, in more recent years, have had marked theatrical success in Europe, especially in West and East Germany. *The Shadow of a Gunman* has been overshadowed by its two immediate successors throughout its stage history outside Ireland. It was the last of the trilogy to be seen in London, for instance, and was immediately, and unfavourably, compared with the other two works, which reviewers, unaccountably, took to have preceded it in order of composition. More recently, however, the work has begun to receive critical acclaim somewhat similar to that accorded the other two dramas. *The Shadow of a Gunman* really came into its own in 1980 when important and critically well received stage revivals in England and Ireland comprised a significant part of celebrations commemorating the centenary of Sean O'Casey's birth.[1] Over the past sixty years, indeed, though prominent critics and reviewers have lambasted each of the three plays as strongly as others have praised them, the practical efficacy of all three as vehicles for stage performance has been, again and again, convincingly demonstrated.

Prominent among the more effective theatrical attributes shared by all three plays, though in varying degrees, are the many opportunities they present for good actors and actresses to create memorable stage personalities – even in a piece like *The Plough and the Stars*, which primarily embodies the drama of the group rather than of the individual – and for them to involve audiences in tragic as well as comic experience, often in bewildering succession and, indeed, sometimes both at the same time. The plays realise in a variety of dramatic styles – utilising naturalistic stage settings and a realistic slum idiom as well as vaudeville clowning, farcical music-hall routines and expressionistic stylisation – civil strife and guerrilla warfare on a scale that has become horrifyingly brutal as well as widespread in modern times. At the same time, as several contemporary critics were quick to observe on the initial appearances of the trilogy in London (at different times in the mid-1920s), the pervasive Dublin slum idiom in O'Casey's hands allows ample play for poetic dialogue and hilarious verbal effects heard but seldom on the English stage – especially in plays of 'low life' or in the speech of working-class men and women – since the days of the better Jacobean dramatists.

It is not true to claim, as various commentators have done, that O'Casey was the first playwright to realise Dublin tenement life and characters on stage. No-one before or since, however, has made greater creative use of proletarian Irish speech patterns, though a number of subsequent dramatists have effectively followed him in this direction – notably Brendan Behan in the Dublin context and John Boyd in a Belfast environment. Indeed, though O'Casey the proletarian playwright received a good deal of critical attention and some unwanted publicity in England in the 1920s precisely for his (and his stage characters') slum origins, it was not until the late 1950s and early 1960s that the racy tenement idiom and class orientation of his work could be seen to have influenced British playwriting. Arnold Wesker, John Arden, Brendan Behan and Henry Livings, among others, have spoken of their indebtedness to him. Even if it be conceded that their plays would have seen the light of day in some form or another whether or not their authors had known O'Casey's writings, they (and many other contemporary British playwrights) were certainly encouraged and stimulated by his bold and resourceful practice thirty years earlier. Moreover, it could be argued that, though the English theatre remained resolutely upper middle-class and predominantly cocktail-party orientated until the 1960s, the success of O'Casey's Dublin trilogy in England as well as in Ireland in the 1920s and 1930s silently prepared the way for an indigenous working-class (and, in some cases, regional) drama in the British Isles in recent years as much as (if not more than) the earlier theatrical successes of the so-called Manchester School led by Stanley Houghton and Harold Brighouse during the Edwardian era.

The Shadow of a Gunman, initially entitled *On the Run*, was written in the eight months' period between March and November of 1922. On 9 October 1922, eight days before the play was submitted to the Abbey Theatre, O'Casey reported substantial progress on the script, telling

Lennox Robinson (who was to direct its Dublin première) that 'the draft of the first act is finished and most of the second. . . . It deals with the difficulties of a poet who is in continual conflict with the disturbances of a tenement house, and is built on the frame of Shelley's phrase, "Ah me, alas, pain, pain ever, forever".' Submitting the typescript on 17 November, the playwright wrote to the same correspondent: 'I have just completed "On The Run". It is a tragedy in two acts – at least I have called it so.' The Abbey's three directors were all away from Dublin at this time; even so, it is strange that the playwright had to wait over three months for their decision which, when it came, was the result of a reading by only two of the three. Robinson's letter, dated 26 February 1923, told O'Casey:

I am very glad to say that Mr Yeats likes your play 'On The Run' very much and we shall try and put it on before the end of our season. Lady Gregory hasn't read it yet but I am sure her opinion of the play will be the same as Mr Yeats. The play will need a little cutting here and there. I like it very much myself.

The fifth play by O'Casey to be submitted to the Abbey Theatre and the first of them to be accepted, *The Shadow of a Gunman* opened on Thursday, 12 April 1923 for a meagre run of three evening performances and a matinée on Saturday 14 April, the last day of the 1922–23 Abbey season. The opening performance (which Lady Gregory thought 'went very well', according to Joseph Holloway, an early unofficial historian of the Abbey) was not well attended, but business picked up through the week until the final performance saw 'house full' notices displayed at the Abbey for the first time in many years. Hugh Hunt, in his semi-official history of the Abbey Theatre (1979), has described in some detail its parlous financial situation at this time.[2] Theatre-going in Dublin had been seriously curtailed in the immediately preceding years of guerrilla warfare, especially in that period during the Anglo-Irish 'Troubles' in which the authorities had imposed an evening curfew. This lasted from February 1920 until July 1921; but many Dubliners, for their own safety, kept indoors at night for a much longer period. Moreover, the Civil War (background to *Juno and the Paycock*) broke out on 28 June 1922, with heavy fighting for many months afterwards between the Pro-Treaty and Anti-Treaty groups of Irish Nationalists.

Hard hit by this, the Abbey Theatre was on the verge of bankruptcy in 1923. From this only the great popular success of O'Casey's plays was to rescue it in the next few years. When his first play was staged for four performances, however, the Abbey's account was 'so heavily overdrawn that the bank refused to cash its cheques',[3] and the playwright was given the choice of being paid immediately, from cash received at the door, or having to wait for a cheque until such time as

the theatre's bank balance was again in credit. (O'Casey's response –
and the rude surprise he received when he did obtain his first royalties
– are related in the autobiographical passage[4] reprinted in the present
collection.)

Things were indeed unpropitious then for a first play in Dublin.
Though the Civil War had passed the peak of its ferocity, few ordinary
citizens could yet know that the worst was over, and bombing raids
and reprisals still plagued the daily life of the nation's capital. Hardly
a night went by without the sound of explosions and gunfire echoing
somewhere in the city. The Abbey directors, understandably
apprehensive about the violent 'noises off' during the raid in Act II of
The Shadow of a Gunman, thought it necessary to print a warning in the
play's programme assuring the audience that the lorry sounds and
rattle of machine-guns were merely harmless stage effects. Lennox
Robinson tells us in his autobiography, 'if we had not done this the
audience might have fled in terror from the theatre'.[5] To complicate
matters, the Abbey had itself been under armed guard (as we learn
from Lady Gregory's *Journals* in an excerpt republished in the present
collection) since 25 March, in the month preceding *The Gunman's*
première there – hardly an atmosphere conducive to theatre-going.
The sentries had been posted as a precaution against threatened
reprisals by Republican forces (the Die-Hards or Irregulars in *Juno
and the Paycock*), angered by the Abbey's refusal to close its doors when
ordered to do so by them as a sign of disapproval of the acceptance of
the Anglo-Irish Treaty by the provisional Irish Free State government.

The armed guard was no empty rhetorical gesture: the Abbey had
been the only theatre to remain open on this occasion and, as W. B.
Yeats was a newly created Senator actively supporting the infant and
still embattled Free State government, threats to the theatre could not
be treated lightly. The plot of *The Shadow of a Gunman* was in itself a
warning against taking such things too lightly, and the grim reality of
terrorism and counter-terrorism in action – outside the play as well as
within it – was illustrated as early as Sunday, 15 April (one day after
The Shadow of a Gunman had ended its run) when Lady Gregory
recorded in her *Journals*:

In Casey's play there were harmless explosions . . . [but] real ones were not far off for on
Friday Perrin told me that a land mine had been put that morning by armed men who
held up the caretaker, in the picture house 'Olympia' close to the Abbey. But the fuse
had burned out without exploding it.[6]

Staged for a run of no more than four performances at the very end of
the Abbey's 1922–23 season, *The Gunman* still managed to gain a good
deal of publicity in the press. Reviewers were intrigued by the slum

origins of the playwright as well as by the highly topical nature of the play itself, though there was little in the way of outright critical acclaim for the artistry of the piece. Hugh Hunt has rightly observed:

When *The Shadow of a Gunman* opened on Thursday, 12 April 1923 . . . neither the size of the audience, nor the critics, suggested that anything unusual had occurred to change the fortunes of the rapidly declining Abbey. Only the critic of the *Evening Herald* saw in it the work of genius.[7]

That critic spoke of the audience 'squirming with laughter and revelling boisterously in the satire', adding 'not for a very long time has such a good play come our way. It was brilliant, truthful, decisive.'[8] As one might expect from the emphasis on Dublin character types by members of the Abbey Theatre company, then at one of the highest points in its history as an acting ensemble, the reviewer was impressed particularly by O'Casey's characterisation and what he (and subsequent Dublin commentators) thought of as realism: attributes which afterwards came to be used as sticks with which to beat more stylised characters and non-naturalistic elements in his later drama: 'His characters were as perfect and his photography, for one really felt his men and women [in *The Gunman*] were but photographs, was nothing less than the work of genius.'

This critic was the only one who was willing to accord the playwright any such mark of recognition. What may be regarded as a more representative response to O'Casey's first play is to be found in Joseph Holloway's private summing up in his journal on 12 April: 'Out of the crudeness of this first-acted play . . . truth and human nature leaped and won the author a call at the end.' Audiences at the first performances similarly revelled in the Dublin dialogue and character types – particularly those of Shields, Grigson and Owens – and no doubt got vicarious thrills as well as the familiar shock of recognition from experiencing the Black-and-Tan raid and the IRA ambush at close quarters while yet being at a safe remove in the theatre. The topicality of the piece was an especial delight, but it led to a common belief, in Dublin and elsewhere, not only that this aspect was the major reason for its popularity, but that once this ephemerality had passed the play would almost certainly cease to have relevance for theatregoers and critics.

A short one-act fantasy for which the author never had much regard, *Cathleen Listens In*, was O'Casey's next play to be staged by the Abbey, on 1 October 1923. According to his own autobiographical account (in *Inishfallen, Fare Thee Well*), what he regarded as the dismal first-night failure of this political extravaganza led him to return straight home and begin work on his subsequent major drama. Subtitled 'a tragedy in three acts', *Juno and the Paycock* was an immediate smash-hit with Dublin audiences.

Submitted to the Abbey on 3 January 1924, it was accepted within a fortnight, given a short and hurried rehearsal period, and first publicly performed on 3 March. The number of people who had to be turned away during the first week's run led to a decision by Lady Gregory and W. B. Yeats (recorded in one of the excerpts from her *Journals* reprinted in this collection) to retain the work in the repertoire for a second consecutive week: the first time in their little theatre's then twenty-year-old existence that this procedure had been followed. In more recent years, particularly in the long years of 'exile' from 1951 to 1966 in the large Queen's Theatre, the Abbey has continued the duration of a play's run after the first week, sometimes for several months at a time. In the much larger theatre, with substantially greater overheads to pay, this policy was often necessary in order to maximise immediately receipts from a popular or topical success. But in the first three decades of the Abbey's existence there was a consistent policy of changing the repertoire after a week's run, however popular a piece might be, and then bringing the more successful ones back within a few weeks. The success of *Juno and the Paycock* thus broke the mould, though as a matter of artistic principle plays were never given long runs until long after Yeats's death in 1939. However, as far as O'Casey was concerned, he had at last achieved, financially, what he had hoped for – but in which he had been cruelly disappointed – from the production of his first play at the Abbey. In his own words, he 'had come into his fortune of twenty-five pounds, after waiting more than a year for it'.[9]

Critical approval of the play in Dublin was by no means universal, as we have been reminded by Gabriel Fallon and Hugh Hunt. Their books provide evidence of contemporary dislike of the play's mixture of tragedy and comedy, and of the inclusion of the final drunken scene (the article by W. J. Lawrence reprinted in the present collection is fairly representative in this regard), as well as disapproval in Cork and Limerick in addition to Dublin of the supposed 'immorality' of the work.[10] However, its public appeal has never waned in its native city, where over the past six decades it has remained the second most popular play in the Abbey's repertoire (the first being *The Plough and the Stars*); Michael O hAodha has rightly claimed that, in this respect, *Juno and the Paycock* 'was O'Casey's only unqualified success at the Abbey'.[11]

The publishing and stage histories of the work, moreover, show it to be O'Casey's most popular drama in the world outside Ireland. The

London firm of Macmillan, O'Casey's publishers throughout his playwriting career, had signed a contract for its publication (with *The Shadow of a Gunman* in a volume to be entitled *Two Plays*) the month before it was first staged, but it did not appear in print until 10 February 1925. Since then it has been very often reprinted. Unlike many of O'Casey's plays, it was not revised after publication, although the acting version printed by Samuel French in 1932 included a number of cuts in dialogue as well as a good many additions to the stage directions. These changes were approved by the playwright, who supervised this stage edition and no doubt incorporated actual theatrical details into it. However, as he did not use any of these changes in the many further editions of *Juno and the Paycock* that he subsequently supervised and proofread, it is surely valid to say that, from a literary point of view, he did not revise the text after its first publication. Theatrical producers may still find the stage version to be of value, however, and no doubt the critical views of many of them (and of some critics, too) are based on their knowledge of that version which, though but little altered from the usually received one, has several significant minor changes, including omission of the poem quoted by Mary Boyle towards the end of the play as well as a different song for Maisie Madigan in the second act 'party scene'.

Juno and the Paycock continues to sell well in paperback and hardbound editions, and it is often a set-text in schools and universities in many English-speaking countries. Theatrical performances by professional and amateur companies are frequent (indeed hardly a week goes by without a production of the play), and here interest extends well beyond the English-speaking world. There are at present in print at least twenty-six translations in fourteen languages. About the play there is, perhaps, more critical agreement than about any other of O'Casey's works, though writers have been divided about its structure and form. It has come in for some heavy criticism, which was most intense from late 1925 among several English reviewers of the first London production. But other eminent drama critics, like James Agate, Ivor Brown and Desmond MacCarthy, were enthusiastic in their appreciation, and the play won the prestigious Hawthornden Prize for the best work of creative fiction published in Britain in 1925.

A further practical breakthrough came about in April 1966 with the critical success of Sir Laurence Olivier's production of the play for the National Theatre in London. Beforehand, there had been considerable trepidation; a number of prominent reviewers wondered aloud how well the work would stand up to reinterpretation in the context of contemporary theatrical taste and a largely non-Irish cast. The anonymous commentator in the *Times Educational Supplement* for 10 June 1966 summed up such doubts as well as their practical rebuttal:

Ten years ago the status of O'Casey's early plays seemed permanently assured. In his *Trends in 20th Century Drama*, Frederick Lumley observed only that these 'masterpieces are too well known to invite approval at this late date'. Four years ago, in *Twentieth Century Drama*, Bamber Gascoigne spoke of these 'rich' and 'warm-hearted farces' as if their quality could never be called in question. But then came the Abbey Theatre's unfortunate participation in the international season at the Aldwych [in 1964]. The masterpieces looked inflated, frowsty, provincial. Was O'Casey at his early best only a 'regional dramatist' after all? Was his work fading with the moods and modes of its time? Sir Laurence Olivier's production of *Juno and the Paycock* at the National Theatre answers resoundingly in the negative. He has taken no great liberties, but the total effect of all the small touches – in place, in the freeing of characters from cliches or attitudes, in bringing forward the profoundly unfunny aspects of Captain Boyle and Joxer – is not merely the rescue of the play from false piety but its redefinition as a sustained masterpiece of bitter dramatic irony that easily defies categorization in conventional terms. What emerges is no mere farce, but an anti-tragedy of timeless validity.

The playwright Hugh Leonard expressed the general critical consensus when he declared that, on this occasion, the play came through 'triumphantly as a masterpiece': a view that was substantially reinforced fourteen years later by the even more resounding success of the Royal Shakespeare Company's production at the Aldwych Theatre, mounted as part of the celebrations marking O'Casey's centenary year. As Juno Boyle, Judi Dench won the award for the best performance by an actress on the London stage in 1980; it was a well deserved honour that O'Casey himself would undoubtedly have approved.

After *Juno and the Paycock*, O'Casey wrote two one-act plays: *Nannie's Night Out* (staged at the Abbey on 29 September 1924) and *The Cooing of Doves*. The latter work, consisting of a series of quarrels in the bar of a Dublin public house, was originally rejected by the Abbey but incorporated into the next major drama by O'Casey to be staged there.

That work was *The Plough and the Stars*, described by its author as 'a tragedy in four acts', and written between October 1924 and August 1925. O'Casey had thought of the play some time earlier, as is shown in a letter of 22 July 1924 to Lady Gregory, where he speaks of continuing work on *Nannie's Night Out*, then nearing completion, but not having yet begun to write 'the more ambitious play' to which he had already given the eventual title based on the banner of the Irish Citizen Army. In a further letter written sometime in October 1924, he told the same correspondent that he was 'anxious to start work on

"The Plough and the Stars" which, dealing with Easter Week, will bring to our remembrance "old unhappy, far off days [sic], and battles long ago" '. By 23 October 1924 he had definitely commenced, but ill-health and eyestrain were hampering its progress. Joseph Holloway confided to his journal for 1 February 1925 that he had been told by Gabriel Fallon that Act I of the play was finished 'and the second of the other two mapped out'. It sounds from this as though his informant thought of it as a three-act drama at that stage; and, indeed, O'Casey may have been planning it along those lines until he conceived the idea of incorporating that earlier one-act play, *The Cooing of Doves*, into it as its virtually self-contained second act.

The typescript was submitted to the Abbey on 13 August 1925. With highly favourable reactions from the three most important directors, it was a foregone conclusion that the drama would be accepted for production, and on 9 September he was able to tell his London publisher:

You may be interested to hear that a new four act tragedy of mine – 'The Plough and the Stars' – has been accepted by the Abbey Theatre, and that Mr Yeats, Lady Gregory and Mr Robinson think it a fine play, possibly the best work I have yet done.

However, this fifth work of his to be accepted by the Abbey had to wait much longer between acceptance and first performance than any of the other four had done. The reasons were two-fold. First (and most important), there were a great number of back-stage bickerings and some opposition to it at the Board of Directors level and from among the actors. These differences, which occurred before as well as after the play went into rehearsal, took some time to resolve. Secondly; the Abbey's leading lady, Sara Allgood, was away in England in the autumn of 1925, taking part in a season of plays promoted by J. B. Fagan. When one of these failed at the box office, *Juno and the Paycock* was substituted at fairly short notice. With the actress in her by this time familiar title role, it opened in London on 16 November 1925. O'Casey had written one of the leading parts in *The Plough* for Miss Allgood, and no doubt the Abbey thought it worth while holding back the new play for a while to see whether the English production of *Juno and the Paycock* would close in time for its leading lady to return to Dublin and play Bessie Burgess in the world première of *The Plough and the Stars*.

The back-stage intrigues and boardroom conflicts that Lady Gregory's *Journals* describe in amusing detail (extracts are reprinted in this volume) were far more significant in holding up the start of rehearsals. Indeed, even after rehearsals had commenced it looked at one point as though the new play would not reach the theatre's boards, for its author formally withdrew it – on 10 January 1926 – when he learned of opposition to the text of the work from several leading members of the company. On that date he wrote to Lennox Robinson:

The play is (in my opinion) a deadly compromise with the actual; it has been further modified by the Directors but I draw the line at a Vigilance Committee of the Actors.

Changes were then made to the cast, with Eileen Crowe being removed from a role to whose dialogue she had made objections; Ria Mooney stood firm in holding on to the part of Rosie Redmond, despite pressure from some members of the company; and rehearsals went on as before.

The modifications made at the request of the directors that O'Casey speaks of in his letter of 10 January were mostly very minor cuts to the dialogue together with the deletion of the bawdy song at the end of Act II. These changes were made to placate George O'Brien, while denying that government representative on the theatre's board the more radical cuts and alterations that he wanted in Act II. Whether the then newly granted government subsidy, so badly needed by the Abbey, was ever in danger is uncertain. Today, all that we can be sure is that Lady Gregory and W. B. Yeats felt that it was threatened. Indeed, it was at this point that the two sole surviving founders of the Abbey made the characteristically courageous decision that, even were their action to bring about the withdrawal of the government's subsidy, they must stoutly resist any and every form of censorship by its representative. Their resistance was wholly successful. O'Brien withdrew his demands completely, only digging in his heels over the supposedly bawdy song – which the other directors had already planned to jettison, offering its deletion to him as a sop to cover their otherwise firm resistance to his demands.

Meanwhile, O'Casey rewrote much of the love scene in Act I (all the board members were agreed on its weakness), telling Lady Gregory on the first of November 1925: 'I have altered the love scene ... and the alteration has eliminated any possibly objectionable passage.' However, even with the cuts and the changes and the collapse of internal resistance to the production at the Abbey, the battle was not yet over. There can be little doubt that the supposedly secret 'back stage' objections to the introduction of a prostitute into the second act of the play got about outside the theatre in the weeks before the play's stage première and helped contribute to the initial atmosphere of hostility that, in some quarters, greeted the first week's performances. Thus, though the censors were largely stifled within the Abbey's management board and the acting company, subsequent ructions were stimulated by strong rumours sweeping Dublin, in advance of its public presentation, that the new play would provoke protest and violence.

O'Casey himself feared that there might be public objections to the work, but his fears concerned, not its sexual or moral nature, but its political and social implications – that is, its fierce satire of a revolution undertaken for what were to him the wrong social reasons, with veiled implications of what a revolution might justifiably be fought for. (His contentious views on Easter Week, nationalism and the Irish struggle for independence have been the subject of many critical essays, represented in the present collection by contributions from Brigid O'Higgins, David Krause, Robert G. Lowery, William Irwin Thompson and Jack Lindsay, as well as from O'Casey himself.) It seems quite clear that, in 1926, the author was himself caught off-guard by public demonstrations against the sexual side of the play. As with objections to Synge's *In the Shadow of the Glen* and *The Playboy of the Western World* some twenty years earlier, the puritanical outrage was only the most immediate and on-the-surface expression of a deep-seated political and moral unease. Synge and O'Casey both hit hard at a fundamental moral hypocrisy and self-deceit in the societies they depict. Audiences were deeply upset by what they saw, but initially reacted against only the most superficial characteristics, which were in each case the sexual implications apparent in the action and in some of the dialogue. Both playwrights were called upon to defend and discuss relatively unimportant matters when in reality much more significant issues were (silently) involved, and this deflection of moral responsibility must have contributed substantially to the depression suffered by both authors on the occasions when initial performances of these plays provoked public outcries.

The Plough and the Stars opened at the Abbey Theatre on Monday, 8 February 1926. It was almost certainly the most eagerly awaited play in the history of the Irish theatre. Its author was by then the most popular playwright in the Abbey's repertoire and word had got about that the subject of his new drama was the Easter Rising of 1916. All tickets for the opening night, as well as for some of the following nights, were sold out shortly after the play was advertised.

Enthusiastically received on the first three nights, muted objections to the play began to be evident at the second performance. On the third night, according to Joseph Holloway, a 'sort of moaning sound was to be heard' from the pit during the Rosie Redmond episodes and 'when the Volunteers brought in the flags to the pub' in the second act. Holloway, who had disliked the play from the time he saw a dress rehearsal the week before, delightedly recorded in his diary that, during the Thursday night's performance, 'a great protest was made . . . [which] ended in almost all the second act being played in dumb show and [with] pandemonium afterwards'. According to the diarist the protest was organised by some of the women whose husbands had been active in the Easter Week Rising of 1916, including well-known figures such as Mrs Tom Clarke and Mrs Sheehy Skeffington, both of them among those made widows by the event. Holloway, thoroughly partisan in his account, was indignant that some of the players were very rough 'to some ladies who got on the stage, and threw two of them into the stalls'. His diary continues:

One young man thrown from the stage got his side hurt by the piano. The chairs of the orchestra were thrown on the stage . . . and some four or five tried to pull down half of [the] drop curtain and another caught hold of one side of the railing. Then a man came on and begged the audience to give the actors a hearing, and they did and Mac [F. J. McCormick] said he wished the actors should be treated distinct from the play etc. and his speech met with applause. The play proceeded in fits and starts, with the whole house in a state of excitement.[12]

An hilarious description of the riots on the fourth night is provided in the dramatist's autobiographical *Inishfallen, Fare Thee Well*, and an interesting and equally subjective account is to be found in Gabriel Fallon's memoir, *Sean O'Casey, The Man I Knew*.

The Abbey was guarded by a large contingent of police for the rest of Thursday night and the last two days of the week's run. The protests, thereby largely muffled inside the theatre itself, then spilled over into the pages of the leading Irish newspapers and periodicals. For the first time (in what would prove to be many such controversies over his dramatic writings) O'Casey was called upon to defend his drama, publicly as well as privately. *The Plough* was savagely attacked in the correspondence columns of Dublin journals for many weeks; the author defended it in letters to the *Irish Times*, the *Irish Independent* and the *Voice of Labour*. He was also called upon to speak in a public debate on the play which took place on 1 March 1926, shortly before he left Dublin to help promote the London production of *Juno and the Paycock* and to receive there the Hawthornden Prize awarded to that very play but a few weeks earlier.

Though *The Plough and the Stars* has long since outlasted the many acrimonious onslaughts launched upon it by people representing many different viewpoints and vested interests, surviving to become the playwright's most popular play in his native city and one of the best loved works in the Abbey Theatre repertoire, the bitterness which the controversy engendered in the playwright was deep and long-lasting. In the years since its première the play has received a great deal of critical attention, especially since the 'epic theatre' of

Bertolt Brecht – with which O'Casey's drama has at times been
compared – began to receive critical recognition in the English-
speaking theatre from the mid-1950s onwards. Ideological considerations, however, have prevented its acceptance by many critics
who might have been thought to be favourably disposed towards its
political and social orientation. The intricacies of these disputes are,
among other things, the subjects of essays by Robert G. Lowery and
Jack Lindsay in the present volume. Generally speaking, however,
The Plough and the Stars and *Juno and the Paycock* – usually in that order,
nowadays – are the most highly regarded of O'Casey's dramas; that is
true, critically, and their stage history shows that judgement to be
valid theatrically as well.

If it be more a matter of convenience than accuracy to use 'trilogy' as a
term descriptive of O'Casey's first three full-length plays, it is even so
one that has been gaining favour in O'Casey criticism. In the present
context, moreover, it is especially useful as a title for this Casebook.
Trilogy or not, it nonetheless remains in many ways rewarding to
approach *Juno and the Paycock* together with *The Plough and the Stars* and
The Shadow of a Gunman as a cycle of political and social plays
conceived on something of an epic scale and deeply tinged by an
overall tragic vision: a 'trilogy' similar in some respects to Shakespeare's cycle comprising *Richard II*, *Henry IV* (two parts), and *Henry
V*, or even the earlier one of *Henry VI* (three parts) and *Richard III*. In
each series individual plays, though self-contained and complete in
themselves, are more meaningful in conjunction with the other plays
relating to their particular cycle, and, together with them, add up to a
panoramic view of a country in a state of crisis. Of course Shakespeare's plays are more consciously shaped as chronicles of an age, a
particular period in history, than are O'Casey's. Starting to write at a
time when there was an immense popular demand for history plays,
Shakespeare took an evolving genre, that only a few years earlier had
been little more than crude two-dimensional representation of
historical and legendary figures, and widened the social context to
embrace many different levels of society and regional ways of life. At
the same time, while he humanised and individualised his narrative
sources, Shakespeare depicted history with an awareness that a moral
design was to be discerned in it. Beginning from the opposite end, as it
were, O'Casey wrote of the lives and struggles of ordinary men and
women at a particular time of social upheaval, and in the process gave
the drama something of an epic compass, realising a social and

political content that is far wider and deeper than is apparent at first sight.

In chronological order of the subject-matter, *The Plough and the Stars* (1915–16), *The Shadow of a Gunman* (1920) and *Juno and the Paycock* (1922) cover the most momentous events in recent Irish history, not from the point of view of the political or military leaders, but from that of the ordinary people unwillingly caught up in the indiscriminate savagery and recrimination of civil war and revolution. It is as though Ralph Mouldy, Peter Bullcalf, Francis Feeble and their families were at the centre of the dramatic action (with Bardolph, Nym and Doll Tearsheet as minor characters) instead of Prince Hal and Hotspur. In this respect, of course, O'Casey is being realistic in writing about Irish history from the point of view of his own experience and realising (in however heightened a manner) people with whom he was intimately familiar.

In O'Casey, as in Shakespeare's history plays, certain recurrent themes are uppermost: the inter-action of public and private drama, the horror of civil strife and anarchy in the state, and, likewise in both, a continuing debate on the ambiguous demands of justice and order in society. The Elizabethan playwright, conveniently distanced in time (but not relevance) from the events he chronicled, was provided with a firm moral as well as political pattern by the Tudor historians whose writings provided his main sources. The Irish author, writing in close proximity to the events he chronicled, naturally lacked so elaborate or consistent a narrative framework and the consequent opportunities for cross-reference within plays and from one play to another; yet even so he does succeed in imposing a sense of unity on the Dublin trilogy. This cohesion is maintained by a grim ironic vision of the destructive forces in society, a compassionate concern for the resultant human suffering, a highly idiosyncratic comic technique, and purposeful thematic patterning common to each of these dramas.

Moreover, it could be argued that, although O'Casey had no Holinshed or Hall to fall back upon, he could (and did) draw upon a massive store of patriotic writings, ballads, speeches and fables which were – he knew – known to and popular with a wide cross-section of Irish society. Again and again, in examining his writings, we are confronted by an astonishing richness of local associations and national folklore, and by a multiplicity of references derived from literary and oral traditions of thought, all cleverly adapted for their specific contemporary relevance. This textual density is the product of more than forty years' immersion in the everyday life and ways of thought of Dublin working-class people, of more than a quarter of a century's acquaintance with the oral sources and copious writings associated with the nationalist and labour movements centred in Dublin, and an extensive knowledge of English and Gaelic literature.

Throughout his life O'Casey enriched the surface texture of his writings with a diverse selection of quotations, references and clichés drawn from both popular and learned sources, using them for a variety of effects, though most often for satire or irony. In *Juno and the Paycock*, for instance, the quotations – usually given by Joxer – are deliberately commonplace examples culled from Burns, Macaulay, Scott, Thomas Moore's *Melodies*, popular proverbs and Irish songs and ballads. Indeed, the use of allusion on such an extensive, if mostly unobtrusive, scale is comparable – though in the Dublin trilogy at a consistently popular, vernacular level – to the poetic practice of Ezra Pound, T. S. Eliot and other modern writers. In *The Waste Land*, say, many lines and phrases are borrowed (either directly or adapted) from the work of other writers, and yet the poem – in its parts as in the whole – has a distinctively personal flavour. Of Eliot's technique in this respect G. S. Fraser says: 'This use of allusion and concealed quotation enables him to set the present and the past in perspective, and to exhibit ironically the decay of past standards in present-day life.'[13]

Though O'Casey's method developed quite independently, it served similar purposes to those described by Fraser. Indeed, the irony works both ways in his case, for certain values of the past are criticised at the same time that their contemporary relevance is questioned. This is particularly true of conventional (that is, chivalric) notions of heroism, of martial glory and chauvinism. Legendary heroes and heroines are introduced at various times but always in a context that undermines the usually accepted valuation of them. Juno Boyle is introduced to us by her husband, who complains of her nagging: 'Tisn't Juno should be her pet name at all, but Deirdre of th' Sorras, for she's always grousin'.' We may smile ruefully at the joke which reduces the tragic Celtic heroine to a termagant, but later we are to recognise that in a sense beyond Boyle's understanding Juno is indeed a genuinely tragic figure comparable with her classical Roman namesake. Later when Bentham hears of her pet name (which has its own relevance, of course, for the Roman goddess is renowned not only for her beauty but for having to put up with a recalcitrant 'spouse' and with the troubles of her offspring) he exclaims: 'Juno! What an interesting name! It reminds one of Homer's glorious story of ancient gods and heroes.' But the rising inflection in his voice is soon brought down by Boyle's prosaic and uncomprehending explanation: 'Yis, doesn't it? You see, Juno was born an' christened in June; I met her in

June; we were married in June, an' Johnny was born in June, so wan
day I says to her, "You should ha' been called Juno", an' the name
stuck to her ever since.'

The anti-heroic attitude is buttressed by a formidable assortment
of weapons. In *Juno and the Paycock*, for example, the despicable toady
Joxer Daly is one of the author's main agents for working this effect.
He is always ready with a made-to-measure, custom-worn quotation
to fit any occasion, whether it be a celebration of military bravery
(Boyle's imaginary deeds in Easter Week), or of marital valour, or of
life at sea. The satire works on various levels: for one thing, there is the
credibility gap between what is said and the speaker himself; there is
the frequent inappropriateness between what is said and the situation
to which it refers; and there is the contrast, too, between what is
resolved by the characters being satirised, and what in fact they do.

One obvious example that covers all these aspects is the histrionic
quotation from Macaulay's 'Horatius' (in his *Lays of Ancient Rome*)
which acts as the climax of Joxer's response to Boyle's announcement
that he is going to stand up to his wife:

Them sentiments does you credit, Captain; I don't like to say anything as between man
an' wife, but I say as a butty, as a butty, Captain, that you've stuck it too long, an' that
it's about time you showed a little spunk. How can a man die betther than facin' fearful
odds, For th' ashes of his fathers an' the temples of his gods?

The quattrain is beautifully incongruous on every count from
subject-matter to mathematical facts! The sentiments themselves are
not only undermined by the character of the man who utters them and
by that of the man to whom they are addressed but by the subsequent
actions of the two men, who, as soon as they hear a woman's voice on
the landing, drop all pretence of resistance in panic-stricken flight.
Elsewhere, the drunken Joxer declaims 'Chains an' slaveree' as he
collapses on Boyle's bed (O'Casey would expect audiences to know
this well-known poem by Burns, and to see the squalid parallel to the
poet's invocation: 'Welcome to your gory *bed*, / Or to victorie'); and,
in the same episode, quotes from Scott's *The Lay of the Last Minstrel*:
'Breathes there a man with soul . . . so . . . de...ad . . . this . . . me . . .
o...wn, me nat...ive l...an'!' Boyle at the same time is speaking about
his imaginary exploits in Easter Week, with 'Commandant Kelly' of
the Irish Volunteeers dying in his arms. Scott's lines, in their full
context, throw further calumny upon the ignoble pair of hypocrites.
Boyle's 'homecoming' here (to a place despoiled of everything that
makes a home, from furniture to people and affection) is glanced at in
the poem. The exile 'As home his footsteps he hath turned' is full of
patriotic feelings; but there is a curse on any wretch ('concentred all in
self') who does not share these generous feelings. Living, such a one is

fated to lose all renown; dead, he shall be 'unwept, unhonour'd, and unsung.' Coming immediately after the real sufferings of Mrs Boyle, the poetic attitudes are seen to be empty rhetorical gestures in themselves and surrogates, not inspirations, for action. While the traditional ethical values and poetic expression of the epic lay are found to be quite inappropriate to the actions of the men who invoke them, they nonetheless throw into relief the really heroic attitudes of Juno Boyle herself.

O'Casey in fact is never wholly anti-heroic even in his most pessimistic moments. There is always someone worthy of esteem, always a hint that, despite all appearances to the contrary, there is in unlikely places and people much genuine bravery and self-sacrifice. His writings imply that a good deal of traditional literature, largely concerned with noble heroes and martial feats, has often celebrated courage and self-sacrifice in the wrong people and circumstances; at the same time we are left in no doubt that there is a good deal of positive human endeavour (generally ignored in pre-Modernist literature) that is really worthy of poetic celebration. Juno Boyle is, after all, aptly named: she does assume universal significance by the end of the play and can rightly be regarded as the 'goddess' or symbol of womankind and marriage.

To approach the Dublin trilogy as political drama on an epic scale need not reduce the critical effect or importance of its component parts, nor should it restrict their significance to the level of documentary reportage – one only has to think in terms of Shakespeare's histories or, say, Brecht's *Mother Courage and Her Children*, with which drama O'Casey's work has much in common. Instead, it is a useful way of viewing the plays in an enlarged focus, for to evaluate *Juno and the Paycock* solely in terms of domestic tragedy (as James Agate did when he described the play 'as much a tragedy as Macbeth, but it is a tragedy taking place in the porter's family')[14] is seriously to diminish the work. It *is*, of course, a domestic tragedy, but it is much more besides, and if judged only as the tragic story of the Boyle family then it will compare unfavourably with many lesser plays. *The Plough and the Stars* is even less rewarding from a dramatic point of view if approached in terms of conventional tragedy, rather than as one of a cycle of plays realising formal variations on certain recurrent political and social themes. Certainly each part of the trilogy would gain immeasurably were they to be performed, successively, in repertory. Yet, though the Abbey Theatre has staged each of the three plays several hundred times, they have never been presented as a cycle – not even in Dublin, where one might well expect such an experiment to be undertaken.

NOTES

1. Two productions of *The Shadow of a Gunman* were particularly important during the O'Casey centenary celebrations: the Royal Shakespeare Company's presentation that opened at The Other Place in Stratford-on-Avon on 26 March 1980 and that by the Abbey Theatre, Dublin, opening on 8 May the same year.

2. Hugh Hunt, *The Abbey: Ireland's National Theatre, 1904–1979* (New York, 1979).

3. Ibid., p. 134.

4. S. O'Casey, *Inishfallen, Fare Thee Well* (London, 1949), pp. 178–9.

5. Lennox Robinson, *Curtain Up: An Autobiography* (London, 1942), p. 139.

6. *Lady Gregory's Journals: Volume One, 1916–1925*, ed. Daniel J. Murphy (Gerrards Cross, Bucks., 1978), p. 447.

7. *The Abbey*, p. 122.

8. *Evening Herald* (Dublin), 13 April 1923.

9. *Inishfallen, Fare Thee Well*, p. 180.

10. Fallon, *Sean O'Casey, The Man I Knew*, pp. 23–5; Hunt, *The Abbey*, p. 123.

11. *Irish Times*, 1 April 1980.

12. *Joseph Holloway's Abbey Theatre: A Selection from his Unpublished Journal, Impressions of a Dublin Playgoer*, ed. Robert Hogan and Michael J. O'Neill (Carbondale & London, 1967), pp. 253–54: entries for 10 and 11 February 1926.

13. G. S. Fraser, *The Modern Writer and His World* (London, 1953), p. 44; this passage is slightly changed in the revised edition of 1964: see p. 49. For further discussion of O'Casey's practice in this regard, see my article, 'Popular Tradition and Individual Talent in Sean O'Casey's Dublin Trilogy', *Journal of Modern Literature*, II (1972), 491–504; reprinted in *Sean O'Casey: A Collection of Critical Essays*, ed. Thomas Kilroy (Englewood Cliffs, 1975), pp. 77–90.

14. *Sunday Times* (London), 22 November 1925.

PART ONE

The Dublin Trilogy

David Krause   O'Casey's Anti-Heroic Vision
(1960)

. . . An anti-heroic vision of life provides the unity of theme and the diversity of character and action in O'Casey's first four plays: *The Shadow of a Gunman* (1923), *Juno and the Paycock* (1924), *The Plough and the Stars* (1926) and *The Silver Tassie* (1928). . . . Here we . . . centre our attention upon the first three plays which are similar in technique as well as theme, and may be said to form a tragi-comic trilogy.

The first three plays are initially linked by the fact that they are all pacifist plays in which the main characters are not the National heroes actually engaged in the fighting but the noncombatants in a city under military siege – a tragic experience which has by [our later day] become terrifyingly familiar to too many people in all parts of the world. O'Casey's 'open city' is Dublin during the Irish War of Independence; the setting of *The Gunman* is 1920 during the guerrilla warfare between the insurgent Irish Republican Army and the British forces, mainly the ruthless Auxiliary troops known by their uniforms as the Black and Tans; the setting of *Juno* is 1922 during the Civil War between the Irishmen who supported the Free State Settlement and the die-hard Irish Republicans who rejected partition; the setting of *The Plough* is 1916 during the Easter Rising against the British. The action in each succeeding play is built around an ever-expanding radius of involvement. In the first play the conflict arises when a poet and a pedlar inadvertently become involved in the war; in the second play a whole family is caught in the cross-fire of the battle; and in the third play all the people in the tenements are trapped by the war that now covers the whole city which is in flames at the end of the play.

In all these plays the theme revolves around a series of illusions of heroism which point to the basic conflict. Donal Davoren in *The Gunman* thinks he is a lofty poet, his neighbours think he is a brave gunman 'on the run'. But he is actually a 'shadow' of a poet, a 'shadow' of a gunman – a shadowman who doesn't know who he is. All the tenement-dwellers in the play suffer from a variety of dreams and deceptions which serve as contrasts to Davoren's self-deception and self-discovery. When his neighbours mistake him for an IRA gunman he foolishly encourages the deception and vainly enjoys it, especially when he is with the impressionable Minnie Powell – 'the Helen of Troy come to live in a tenement' – who has fallen in love with the romantic image of the poet-gunman she thinks he is. But Davoren isn't much of a poet either, for most of the time he sighs like a 'stricken deer' trying to flee from the stupid 'herd', trying to isolate himself from

his neighbours and the war in order to write his sentimental verses in
a watered-down imitation of Shelley. Throughout the play he
indulges his mock-heroic fancies as masquerading gunman and
romancing poet, with the result that his vanity and detachment defeat
him and lead to the tragic death of Minnie Powell.

Davoren tries to see himself as a dreamy poet who 'lives on the
mountain-top'. O'Casey had borrowed Davoren's romantic idealism
from Louis Dubedat's creed in Shaw's *The Doctor's Dilemma*: the belief
in 'the might of design, the mystery of colour, and the belief in the
redemption of all things by beauty everlasting'. Davoren repeats
these words when he tries to escape to his mountain-top, but the
world in which he lives will not allow him to assume the romantic
attitudes of the grandiloquent and dying Dubedat. It is only the shock
of Minnie Powell's death that makes Davoren see himself and his
world with terrifying clarity.

It is his droll pedlar friend Seumas Shields who really understands
the chaotic world in which they are trapped. Seumas understands
that poetic and patriotic poses will not help, even though he is in his
own way just as ineffectual as Davoren, for he is a lazy, blustering,
amiable coward who resorts to the efficacy of prayer or the comfort of
his bed when trouble comes. Yet he understands and is the ironic
Chorus character in the guise of a bumbling clown, a wise-fool who
sees the truth. He has better reasons than Davoren for not becoming
involved in the war since he was once active in the Irish Republican
movement but left it when the fanatical nationalism and the terror of
indiscriminate bloodshed began to destroy the people it was supposed
to save. Seumas makes this point in an episode which thematically
links the plays of the trilogy.

SEUMAS: I wish to God it was all over. The country is gone mad. Instead of counting
their beads now they're countin' bullets; their Hail Marys and paternosters are
burstin' bombs – burstin' bombs, an' the rattle of machine-guns; petrol is their holy
water; their Mass is a burnin' buildin'; their De Profundis is 'The Soldier's Song', an'
their creed is, 'I believe in the gun almighty, maker of heaven an' earth' – an' it's all
for 'the glory o' God an' the honour o' Ireland'.
DAVOREN: I remember the time when you yourself believed in nothing but the gun.
SEUMAS: Ay, when there wasn't a gun in the country; I've a different opinion now when
there's nothin' but guns in the country – an' you daren't open your mouth, for
Kathleen ni Houlihan is very different now to the woman who used to play the harp
an' sing 'Weep on, weep on, your hour is past', for she's a ragin' divil now, an' if you
only look crooked at her you're sure of a punch in th' eye. But this is the way I look at
it – I look at it this way: You're not goin' – you're not goin' to beat the British Empire
– the British Empire, by shootin' an occasional Tommy at the corner of an occasional
street. Besides, when the Tommies have the wind up – when the Tommies have the
wind up they let bang at everything they see – they don't give a God's curse who they
plug.

DAVOREN: Maybe they ought to get down off the lorry and run to the Records Office to find out a man's pedigree before they plug him.

SEUMAS: It's the civilians who suffer; when there's an ambush they don't know where to run. Shot in the back to save the British Empire, an' shot in the breast to save the soul of Ireland. I'm a Nationalist meself, right enough – a Nationalist right enough, but all the same – I'm a Nationalist right enough; I believe in the freedom of Ireland, an' that England has no right to be here, but I draw the line when I hear the gunmen blowin' about dyin' for the people, when it's the people that are dyin' for the gunmen! With all due respect to the gunmen, I don't want them to die for me.

For Seumas as for the women in *Juno* and *The Plough*, for Juno Boyle and Nora Clitheroe, life is more sacred than patriotic slogans; human realities are more meaningful than fanatical abstractions, particularly when in the name of the national honour the revolution devours its own children. When Juno's son Johnny, who had his hip crippled in the Easter Rising and lost an arm fighting with the IRA in the Civil War, boasts about the sacred 'principles' and insists he would sacrifice himself again for Ireland, she promptly offers her opinion about such heroics.

JOHNNY: I'd do it agen, ma, I'd do it agen; for a principle's a principle.

MRS BOYLE: Ah, you lost your best principle, me boy, when you lost your arm; them's the only sort o' principles that's any good to a workin' man.

Juno sees life in terms of the essential human situation – bread on the table and love in the heart; these are the only realities that have any meaning for her and she fights for them without any heroics. And when she loses her son, when Johnny is finally shot, she follows Mrs Tancred and keens the heart-breaking lament of the universal mother for a dead son.

MRS BOYLE: . . . Maybe I didn't feel sorry enough for Mrs Tancred when her poor son was found as Johnny's been found now – because he was a Die-hard! Ah, why didn't I remember that then he wasn't a Diehard or a Stater, but only a poor dead son! It's well I remember all that she said – an' it's my turn to say it now: What was the pain I suffered, Johnny, bringin' you into the world to carry you to your cradle, to the pains I'll suffer carryin' you out o' the world to bring you to your grave! Mother o' God, Mother o' God, have pity on us all! Blessed Virgin, where were you when me darlin' son was riddled with bullets, when me darlin' son was riddled with bullets? Sacred Heart o' Jesus, take away our hearts o' stone, and give us hearts o' flesh! Take away this murdherin' hate, an' give us Thine own eternal love!

But the men go on sacrificing themselves for principles and the 'murdherin' hate' continues. In the second act of *The Plough*, Commandant Jack Clitheroe and two of his comrades, after listening to the speeches about 'the sanctity of bloodshed . . . and the exhilaration of war', drink a toast to Ireland before they go out to battle. The stage directions indicate that 'they speak rapidly, as if unaware of the meaning of what they say. They have been mesmerised by the fervency of the speeches'.

CLITHEROE: You have a mother, Langon.
LIEUT. LANGON: Ireland is greater than a mother.
CAPT. BRENNAN: You have a wife, Clitheroe.
CLITHEROE: Ireland is greater than a wife.

But the mothers and wives of Ireland think otherwise, and in the third act when the pregnant Nora Clitheroe returns from a desperate search for her husband, she replies for all Irish women, for women of all countries who lose their men in wars.

NORA: I could find him nowhere, Mrs Gogan. None of them would tell me where he was. They told me I shamed my husband an' th' women of Ireland be carryin' on as I was —They said th' women must learn to be brave an' cease to be cowardly—Me who risked more for love than they would risk for hate – My Jack will be killed, my Jack will be killed! He is to be butchered as a sacrifice to th' dead! . . . An' there's no woman gives a son or a husband to be killed – if they say it, they're lyin', lyin', against God, Nature, an' against themselves! . . . I cursed them – cursed the rebel ruffians an' Volunteers that had dhragged me ravin' mad intó th' sthreets to seek me husband! . . . An' he stands wherever he is because he's brave? No, but because he's a coward, a coward, a coward! . . . I tell you they're afraid to say they're afraid—Oh, I saw it, I saw it, Mrs Gogan—At th' barricades in North King Street I saw fear glowin' in all their eyes—An' in th' middle o' th' sthreet was somethin' huddled up in a horrible tangled heap—His face was jammed again th' stones, an' his arm was twisted round his back—An' I saw they were afraid to look at it—An' some o' them laughed at me, but th' laugh was a frightened one—An' some o' them shouted at me, but th' shout had in it th' shiver o' fear—I tell you they were afraid, afraid, afraid!

Juno and Nora are against war not Ireland. As wives and mothers they realise there can be no victory in war for them if they lose their men and homes. They repudiate war and the illusion that the soldiers alone are the chief sufferers, the illusion that the soldiers die bravely and beautifully for their country, the illusion that the women willingly send their men out to die. For centuries romantic Irishmen had nurtured these illusions by celebrating in poems and stories the glorious deeds of rebel patriots who kissed their beloved colleens farewell and went off to sacrifice themselves for a greater love, Kathleen ni Houlihan. But now O'Casey was mocking all these illusions by looking at the brutality of war through the realistic eyes of working-class Irishwomen instead of through the haze of sentimental patriotism.

This is O'Casey's underlying theme; and yet his anti-heroic vision of life encompasses infinitely more than an argument against war and the illusions of Irishmen. Because he is sceptical about rampant heroism, he is at heart more concerned about the individual nature of his people than the causes they are heroic about. He creates a unique and diversified world, a human comedy, as well as an incisive theme. Once he establishes his controlling theme he moves freely and even discursively around it, playing tragi-comic variations on it, developing it broadly through an ensemble of characters rather than closely through a few central characters. The structural pattern of his plays is loose not tight, contrapuntal not dialectical.

O'Casey's world is chaotic and tragic but his vision of it is ironically comic. It is in this war-torn world of horrors and potential tragedy that he finds the rowdy humour which paradoxically satirises and sustains his earthy characters: they are the victims of their follies yet they revel in their voluble absurdities. And it is clear that O'Casey himself enjoys his people no less for their follies, as he intends his audiences to enjoy them. There is a sharp tone of outrage in his Daumier-like portraits of life in the slums of a beleaguered city, and this tone becomes even stronger in his later plays, but he was not dramatising case histories. His plays do not follow the documentary principles of Naturalism – of Hauptmann's *Weavers* or Galsworthy's *Strife*. Low comedy is not one of the handmaidens of Naturalism. Even when he is in a serious mood O'Casey is likely to be satiric not solemn, poignant not pathetic. And when the tragic events or consequences of war and poverty become most crucial he will open up the action and counterbalance the incipient tragedy with a music-hall turn or a randy ballad or a mock-battle. While everyone awaits a terrifying raid by the Black and Tans in *The Gunman* the well-oiled Dolphie Grigson parades into the house spouting songs and biblical rhetoric in drunken bravado. Just when Mrs Tancred is on her way to bury her ambushed son in *Juno* the Boyles have launched their wild drinking and singing party. While the streets ring with patriotic speeches about heroic bloodshed in *The Plough* the women of the tenements have a free-for-all fight about respectability in a Pub.

This pattern of ironic counterpoint is maintained as a tragi-comic rhythm throughout the plays. For each tragic character there are comic foils who constantly bring the action round from the tragic to the comic mood; for Davoren there is Seumas Shields, for Juno there is the 'Paycock', for Nora there is Bessie Burgess. Actually, Bessie and Nora exchange roles in the last act of the *Plough* when the mad Nora is reduced to ironic babbling and the previously sardonic Bessie achieves tragic dignity. For all the mock-heroic clowns in the plays there is a retinue of boisterous drunkards, liars, cowards, braggarts, parasites, hypocrites, viragos, and snobs; in *The Gunman* there is Tommy Owens, Mr and Mrs Grigson, Mr Mulligan, Mrs Henderson, Mr Gallogher; In *Juno* there is Joxer Daly, Maisie Madigan, Needle Nugent; in *The Plough* there is Fluther Good, Peter Flynn, the Covey, Mrs Gogan, Rosie Redmond. In a turbulent world crowded with these broadly comic and satiric characters it is not surprising to find that the comic spirit often dominates the action. But O'Casey

would have it so precisely because the humour in his plays reveals a
native vigour and shrewdness in his characters which ironically
becomes a means of survival in a shattered world. It is this attitude
which keeps his plays from becoming melancholy or pessimistic. His
humour saves him and his characters from despair. In the midst of
anti-heroic laughter there can be no total catastrophe. Where there is
suffering and death no happy endings are possible, but where there is
also laughter life goes on.

War and poverty create the terrible conditions that force O'Casey's
people to reveal their resourcefulness in wild scenes of tragi-comic
irony in which the grotesque laughter seems to mock at death. For
instance, the third act of *The Plough* is set among the crumbling
tenements during the week of the Easter Rising; now the speeches
about 'the glory of bloodshed' in the previous act have been
transformed into a terrible reality. The streets are a battlefield and the
sickening whine of bullets fills the air. The British gunboat *Helga* has
begun to shell the city. The hysterical Nora Clitheroe collapses after
her unsuccessful attempt to find her husband at the barricades. The
shrivelled little Mollser, unable to get proper food or medical care, is
dying of tuberculosis. Lieutenant Langon is carried in dying of a
stomach wound. And in the midst of this chaos O'Casey presents the
looting of the shops by the ragged and hungry slum-dwellers who
scramble amid bursting bombs and bullets to grab the only trophies
that have any meaning for them – food and clothing. These people
have been deprived of the bare necessities for so long that those who
are not shot stagger away from the shops overburdened with luxuries
and strange assortments of ridiculous items. Rushing in with a new
hat, a box of biscuits, and three umbrellas, Bessie Burgess sets the
tone of humour amid horror with her breathless announcement:

They're breakin' into th' shops, they're breakin' into th' shops! Smashing windows,
battherin' in th' doors, an' whippin' away everything! An' th' Volunteers is firin' on
them. I seen two men an' a lassie pushin' a piano down th' sthreet, an' th' sweat rollin'
off them thryin' to get it up on th' pavement; an' an oul' wan that must ha' been seventy
lookin' as if she'd dhrop every minute with th' dint o' heart beatin', thryin' to pull a big
double bed out of a broken shop-window! I was goin' to wait till I dhressed meself from
th' skin out.

With this call to action the Covey soon reels in carrying a huge sack of
flour and a ham, and Fluther, as might have been expected, comes in
roaring drunk after having launched a raid on a Pub. Bessie is about
to go out for another haul with a neighbour's pram when she is
intercepted by the eager Mrs Gogan, and the two women rage at each
other in a mock-battle over which of them has the proper right to use
the pram for looting. Their intentions with the pram are equally set on

plunder, yet both women assume an indignant legal attitude, characterised by Mrs Gogan's sense of outrage: 'Moreover, somethin's tellin' me that th' hurry of inthrest you're takin' in it now is a sudden ambition to use th' pram for a purpose that a loyal woman of law an' order would stagger away from.'

The comic absurdity of this fight between two viragos over the jurisdiction of the pram, like the similar brawl in the Pub in the previous act, when contrasted with the fighting at the barricades, irreverently mocks the 'holiness' of the war. The heroes at the barricades are deflated by this profane farce in which the pram and the looting take precedence over patriotism, and thus the anti-heroes of the tenements become heroes by comic proxy.

But before long these anti-heroes begin to earn their ironic heroism. The two women finally go off together with the pram, and as the intensity of the war increases a significant change occurs among these people. Although they all continue to quarrel and 'twart' each other with reckless delight, they also begin to unite against what they gradually recognise as their common enemy – the war. Fluther, before he gets drunk, risks his life to find Nora and bring her back safely from the fighting area. The sharp-tongued but compassionate Bessie Burgess – who grows larger in stature as the play progresses and might finally be said to earn the role of main hero, as the Juno of this play – silently gives the suffering Mollser a bowl of milk, helps the prostrate Nora, whom she has so bitterly abused, into the house, and then risks her life in the machine-gunned streets trying to get a doctor for Mollser, the daughter of her favourite sparring-partner, Mrs Gogan. And in the last act, when Mollser has died and the disconsolate Nora has lost her baby prematurely, all the people in the house take refuge in Bessie's attic flat. It is Fluther again who dodges the bullets to make arrangements for the burial of the two children, and it is Bessie who nurses the deranged Nora through three sleepless days and nights, only to be shot trying to protect Nora. Finally it is Ginnie Gogan who carries on and takes Nora down to Mollser's empty bed.

In this manner the women who are the main victims of the war rise to become the main heroes. This pattern is repeated in all the plays as some of the women die for their neighbours and others live to rebuild a new life out of the ruins. Minnie Powell dies trying to save Donal Davoren, and Bessie Burgess dies trying to save Nora Clitheroe; Juno Boyle and Ginnie Gogan endure everything. This is the only kind of untainted heroism that O'Casey recognises. These women are his Ireland. They are not the patriotic Ireland that made an exhilarating epiphany of the ritual of bloodshed. They are not the romantic

Ireland that idealised Kathleen ni Houlihan of the beautiful green fields and the harp. They are not the sweet blushing colleens whose fabled existence is exalted in the guise of the Stage Irishwoman. They are the Ireland of tenacious mothers and wives, the women of the tenements – earthy, shrewd, laughing, suffering, brawling, independent women. O'Casey found them in the Dublin slums, but they have their counterparts in Synge's peasant women, like Pegeen Mike in *The Playboy of the Western World* and Mary Byrne in *The Tinker's Wedding*; in Joyce's Molly Bloom; in Yeats's Crazy Jane; in the eighteenth-century Brian Merriman's peasant girl of 'The Midnight Court'.

Juno Boyle has the name of a classical heroine, and she has many of the qualities of that Roman goddess, but O'Casey uses the allusion in such a way as to give her the heroic stature of her namesake and the earthy reality of a Dublin housewife of the tenements. When Bentham hears her name he is reminded of the 'ancient gods and heroes', however, the Captain explains how she got her name: 'You see, Juno was born an' christened in June; I met her in June; we were married in June, an' Johnny was born in June, so wan day I says to her, "You should ha' been called Juno', an' the name stuck to her ever since".' Furthermore, O'Casey was aware of the fact that the classical Juno was always associated with peacocks, the patron birds who are often near her or draw her chariot, but he used this aspect of the legend in a completely ironic way by giving his Juno a peacock of a husband who takes his name from the common association of strutting vanity. Thus, the 'Paycock' becomes Juno's parasite not her protector.

The women in O'Casey's plays are realists from necessity, the men are dreamers by default. The men are frustrated and gulled by dreams which they are unable and unwilling to convert into realities. And as if in mock-defence of those dreams they revel in their romanticising and bragging and drinking. In *John Bull's Other Island* Shaw may have gone to the root of the Irishman's curse when he made Larry Doyle pour out his embittered confession: 'Oh, the dreaming! dreaming! the torturing, heart-scalding, never . . . satisfying dreaming, dreaming, dreaming, dreaming! . . .'

O'Casey's Irishmen suffer from the symptoms of this outcry, and as a result there is an undercurrent of tragedy in the plays. But most of O'Casey's Irishmen possess the grotesque symptoms without Larry Doyle's awareness of them, and as a result there is also an abundance of comedy in the plays. Herein lies one of the many differences between tragedy and comedy: the tragic figure becomes truly tragic when he is able to see his own image; the comic figure becomes absurdly comic when he is unable, or pretends to be unable, to see his own image. When the women in O'Casey's plays finally see themselves and their world clearly they become tragic figures, like Juno Boyle and Bessie Burgess. Of the men, only Davoren as the self-confessed 'poltroon' makes Larry Doyle's discovery, at the very end of the *Gunman* after he has fully indulged his aery dreams, but he is the only non-comic character in the play.

There is, however, one unique figure who dominates all three plays, the mock-heroic character who proudly wears his motley and is satisfied to see as much of himself and the world as he expediently chooses to see. This character is first formulated in Seumas Shields in the *Gunman*, and he is fully developed in Captain Jack Boyle in *Juno* and Fluther Good in the *Plough* – those two falstaffian rogues who epitomise the triumphant anti-hero.

Captain Jack Boyle may lack the girth of Captain Jack Falstaff, but he has the same flamboyant humour and glorious mendacity, the ingenious sense of self-indulgence and self-preservation. Both men are bragging scoundrels whose disrespect for the truth stems not only from an instinctive love of licence but from an empirical conviction that a virtuous life invariably leads to dullness and an heroic life often leads to death. Falstaff can point to a corpse on the battlefield and say, 'there's honour for you', or counterfeit death because 'The better part of valour is discretion, in the which better part I have saved my life'. Boyle, living like Falstaff in a time of Civil War when men's lives are valued cheaply, sets too high a price on his own sweet skin to care about honour or become involved in the fighting. And he has his counterfeit game for saving himself from the deadly virtues of work: he automatically develops a powerful pain in his legs at the mere mention of a job. When Jerry Devine goes looking for him in all the Pubs with news of a job, his discretionary wrath erupts and protects him: 'Is a man not to be allowed to leave his house for a minute without havin' a pack o' spies, pimps an' informers cantherin' at his heels? . . . I don't want the motions of me body to be watched the way an asthronomer ud watch a star. If you're folleyin' Mary aself, you've no pereeogative to be folleyin' me.' (*Suddenly catching his thigh.*) 'U-ugh, I'm after gettin' a terrible twinge in me right leg!' Furthermore, Boyle has what he considers a good reason to regard a man like Devine with suspicion: 'I never heard him usin' a curse word; I don't believe he was ever dhrunk in his life – sure he's not like a Christian at all!'

Captain Boyle's account of his adventures on the sea has that comic touch of fantastic imagination which characterised Captain Falstaff's version of his exploits on Gadshill. Juno Boyle knows her husband for the 'struttin' paycock' that he is, and she pointedly explains his seafaring record: 'Everybody callin' you "Captain", an' you only

wanst on the wather, in an oul' collier from here to Liverpool, when
anybody, to listen or look at you, ud take you for a second Christo For
Columbus!' But this fact does not prevent the 'Captain' from telling
his 'buttie' Joxer what it was like to be an adventurous sailor on the
high seas.

BOYLE: Them was days, Joxer, them was days. Nothin' was too hot or too heavy for me
   then. Sailin' from the Gulf o' Mexico to the Antanartic Ocean. I seen things, I seen
   things, Joxer, that no mortal man should speak about that knows his Catechism.
   Often, an' often, when I was fixed to the wheel with a marlin-spike, an' the wins
   blowin' fierce an' the waves lashin' an' lashin', till you'd think every minute was
   goin' to be your last, an' it blowed, an' blowed – blew is the right word, Joxer, but
   blowed is what the sailors use—
JOXER: Aw, it's a darlin' word, a darlin' word.
BOYLE: An' as it blowed an' blowed, I often looked up at the sky an' assed meself the
   question – what is the stars, what is the stars?
JOXER: Ah, that's the question, that's the question – what is the stars?

A clever parasite full of comic platitudes, the ingratiating Joxer is a
perfect foil for the braggart Captain; he spaniels at the Captain's heels
most of the time, but he too sees as much of himself and the world as it
is profitable for him to see. Joxer is capable of reversing the game and
fooling the Captain when he has something to gain. Together they
insulate themselves from the world of terrible realities by living in an
illusory world of fantasies and drunken bravado. O'Casey satirises
them unsparingly for the shiftless rascals that they are, yet because he
also sees the amusement of a universal frailty in them – they are fools
not knaves – he is able to laugh with as well as at their hilarious
mischief. And audiences laugh with as well as at them because they
too recognise the common frailties of man in the Boyles and Joxers of
this world – Boyle the universal braggart-warrior, Joxer the universal
parasite-slave, both of them derived from the well-known clowns of
Roman and Elizabethan comedy. It is also possible that many men
are more than amused by the 'paycock's' game and secretly envy the
Captain and his 'buttie' their merry pranks. The average man who
realises he cannot cope with his besetting problems on an heroic scale
may well have an unconscious desire to get rid of his problems entirely
by emulating the Captain in his irresponsible and therefore irresistible dreaming and singing and drinking. A frustrated non-hero might
if he dared forsake his responsible suffering and seek the uninhibited
pleasures of a clowning anti-hero; however, he probably settles for the
vicarious pleasure of sitting in a theatre and watching a Captain
Boyle thumb his red nose at responsibility. Much is made of the
frustrated clown who yearns to play Hamlet, but the average man is
more likely a frustrated Hamlet who if he had the strength of his

weakness would cheerfully assume the role of an uninhibited Falstaff or Boyle.

The women in O'Casey's plays may be uninhibited creatures, too, but they always remain close to the realities of life and when there is a call for responsible action they put aside self-gratification and act. Even Juno has her fling. When the Boyles have their wild party Juno joins the celebration on borrowed money and time, and after the mourning Mrs Tancred interrupts them, Juno temporarily agrees with the Captain and remarks that maybe Mrs Tancred deserved to lose her Die-hard son. But when her own son is killed, when her daughter is seduced, Juno assumes her burdens; she repeats Mrs Tancred's prayer and rejects the Captain. When her daughter cries out against a God who would allow such tragic things to happen, Juno replies: 'These things have nothin' to do with the Will o' God. Ah, what can God do agen the stupidity o' men!' and she abandons the Captain. When Prince Hal becomes King he assumes the burdens of state and rejects the dissolute Falstaff.

> I know thee not, old man: fall to thy prayers:
> How ill white hairs become a fool and jester!
> I have long dream'd of such a kind of man,
> So surfeit-swell'd, so old, and so profane.
> But being awak'd, I do despise my dream.

In a somewhat similar manner, Juno, being awake, forsakes all dreams and rejects her foolish jester of a husband. Her elegiac prayer brings her to a condition of tragic awareness.

Yet O'Casey does not end the play with Juno. Maintaining the anti-heroic theme and contrapuntal rhythm of the whole work, he concludes on a tragi-comic note by contrasting Juno's heroic condition with the Captain's mock-heroic condition. For it is his play as well as Juno's; together they represent the tragi-comic cycle of O'Casey's world; together they reveal the ironic cross-purposes of life. As Juno and Mary leave to start a new life, the Captain and Joxer stagger drunkenly into the barren room, roaring patriotic slogans as they collapse in a state of semi-coherent bravado. It is a final scene of horrible humour. The Captain remains the 'struttin' paycock' in his glorious deterioration; even in his drunken raving he remains a magnificently grotesque anti-hero. Juno must reject him, yet we can forgive him, for he maintains his falstaffian spirit to the end.

Fluther Good is also drawn in the falstaffian mould, but he is sufficiently different from Captain Boyle to emerge with the stamp of his own individuality. He too is a roistering fellow, a drinking and bragging clown, but he is more impetuous than the Captain, more

aggressive and daring, in his guarded way. He is more of a blustering
gamecock than a 'struttin' paycock'. He has more stomach for a fight
than the wily Captain, though his fighting is discreetly confined to
rhetorical invective. He has no trouble annihilating little Peter Flynn
– that ridiculous 'patriot' clad in the full-dress uniform of a National
benevolent association – when 'oul' Pether' brags about never having
missed a pilgrimage to Bodenstown to the shrine of Wolfe Tone. But
he has to 'sing on the high notes' of his ignorance when he gets into a
shouting contest with the clever Covey [a 'covey' is Dublin slang for a
'smart aleck'] who dumbfounds Fluther with materialistic catechisms
from his vade-mecum, Jenersky's *Thesis on the Origin, Development
and Consolidation of the Evolutionary Idea of the Proletariat*, a tome
which understandably fills the Covey with a proletarian fervour
that makes him impervious to the protests of Fluther, patriots and
prostitutes.

And yet the windy Fluther is capable of courageous deeds where
women are concerned, for he is a knight-errant of the tenements – he
rescues pregnant women in distress and defends the honour of
insulted prostitutes. All the women had a good word for Fluther. Mrs
Gogan praises him for risking his life to arrange the decent burial of
poor Mollser: 'An' you'll find, that Mollser, in th' happy place she's
gone to, won't forget to whisper, now an' again, th' name o' Fluther.'
When he gallantly protects Rosie Redmond and her venerable
profession from the 'twarting' Covey, she describes him as a man
'that's well flavoured in th' knowledge of th' world he's livin' in'.
Perhaps Nora Clitheroe, who is constantly in his debt, pays him the
highest compliment when she calls him 'a whole man'.

Taken in his 'wholeness', Fluther the 'well-flavoured' man is a
magnificent mixture of contradictions. He has the heart of a Don
Quixote but the hide of a Sancho Panza. Among the ladies he is a
protector and a peace-maker, but with the men he is full of himself
and his inimitable flutherian wrath, or full of Irish whiskey. His roar
is worse than his bite; he starts more arguments than he can settle; he
rages and boasts, lies and threatens when he is cornered; he swears
abstinence then drowns himself in drink when the shops are looted,
crying 'Up the Rebels' and 'th' whole city can topple home to hell' in
the same drunken breath; he can defend a prostitute's good name,
and then go off to spend the night with her – 'well-flavoured' man that
he is, Fluther knows that there are times when Dulcinea must give
way to Doll Tearsheet.

As a man of many frailties and fine parts, as a prince of buffoonery
as well as errantry, Fluther the Good is the mock-hero of the play. In a
terrible time of war, he is too shrewd to be a patriot, too wise to be an

idealist; yet in his comic anti-heroism he plays the fool for man's sake. In his vitality and humour there is a hope that man may endure.

SOURCE: extract from *Sean O'Casey: The Man and His Work* (London and New York, 1960), pp. 66–80.

Raymond Williams 'O'Casey: The Rhetoric and the Reality' (1968)

. . . Irish history had broken into revolution, a war of liberation and civil war by the time O'Casey began to write for the Abbey Theatre. His first acted play, *The Shadow of a Gunman*, is at once a response to this experience of violence and, in its way, a bitter postscript to Synge's *Playboy of the Western World*. It is set in the crowded, overflowing life of a Dublin tenement house, which is O'Casey's major early setting. The Irish drama, in this sense, has come to town. The turbulent history through which Ireland had been living breaks into these tenements. As a direct action it is on the streets, and the people crowded in the houses react to it, in essential ways, as if it were an action beyond and outside them.

The Shadow of a Gunman is in this sense exact. It is the shadow that falls across a quite other life, but also it is the *Playboy*'s action of a false hero: the frightened sentimental poet Davoren who is built up, by gossip and surmise, into a gunman's reputation:

And what danger can there be in being the shadow of a gunman?

It is the contrast between the bitter action of the history and a feckless deceiving and self-deceiving talk that O'Casey uses as his dramatic point. Men are killed elsewhere, but within the tenement:

No wonder this unfortunate country is as it is for you can't depend upon the word of a single individual in it.

The only victim within the play is the girl Minnie:

DAVOREN: . . . I'm sure she is a good girl, and I believe she is a brave girl.

SEUMAS: A Helen of Troy come to live in a tenement! You think a lot about her simply because she thinks a lot about you, an' she thinks a lot about you because she looks upon you as a hero – a kind o' Paris . . . she'd give the worl' and all to be gaddin' about with a gunman.

It is Minnie who is killed, after a raid on the house; found hiding arms because she believes in Davoren. The bitterness is carried right through, in that Davoren, after her death, can react only in the stereotyped 'poetry' which has been his pretence and his reality: 'Ah me, alas! Pain, pain, pain ever, for ever!' With real killing in the streets, the poverty and the pretence cross to make new inadvertent victims.

This kind of irony, in O'Casey, is very difficult to follow through. The central language of *Shadow of a Gunman* is bare and taut; it is there, in reality, in the crowded life, as a tension with the endless romanticising, boasting, sentimentality; or, again characteristically, with the simple misuse of language by the uneducated, which O'Casey always emphasises, as here in Gallogher's letter: 'ventures to say that he thinks he has made out a Primmy Fashy case.' It is done from the inside, this tenement life, but with an eye on the audience, on external and 'educated' reactions. O'Casey moves from this kind of caricature to a simpler excited naturalism – the endless overflowing talk:

They didn't leave a thing in the kitchen that they didn't flitter about the floor . . .

It is a dramatist speaking at once from inside and outside this rush of life; in *The Shadow of a Gunman* with genuine uncertainty, and using the tension of the farcical and the terrible.

Juno and the Paycock . . . is in the same structure of feeling. The life is seen as farce, with death cutting across it. This can be rationalised, as in O'Casey's late description of *Shadow of a Gunman*, as expressing 'the bewilderment and horror at one section of the community trying to murder and kill the other'. But this is never, really, what the plays show. What is there is a feckless rush, endlessly evading and posturing, while through it one or two figures – mainly women – take the eventual burden of reality. In *Juno and the Paycock* the dominant action is the talk of Boyle and Joxer: idle talk, with a continual play at importance: the false colours of poverty, which has gone beyond being faced and which is now the endless, stumbling, engaging spin of fantasy. The formal plot is rooted in this, as it might have been in Synge: the false expectation of a legacy, which will alter this world. But what comes, in the real action, is the killing from outside: first Tancred, the Republican fighter, and then Johnny, the son of the house, who betrayed him. The bereaved mothers in each case, and in the same words, call:

Take away our hearts o' stone, an' give us hearts o' flesh! Take away this murdherin' hate, an' give us Thine own eternal love!

It is a deep, convincing, unconnected cry. It is what the mothers feel, in the terrible disturbance of the fighting. But what the play shows is not the 'hearts of stone', it is counterpointing and overriding these moments of intense suffering, the endless, bibulous, blathering talk.

This is, of course, an authentic structure, but it is not that which is usually presented. It is always difficult to speak from outside so intense and self-conscious a culture, but in the end we are bound to notice, as a continuing and determining fact, how little respect, except in the grand gestures, the Irish drama had for the Irish people. It was different when the people were remote and traditional, as in *Riders to the Sea*. But already what comes through the surface warmth of *The Playboy of the Western World* is a deeply resigned contempt – a contempt which then allows amusement – for these deprived, fantasy-ridden talkers. Synge got near this real theme, and O'Casey is continuously dramatically aware of it. But it is a very difficult emotion to control: an uneasy separation and exile, from within the heart of the talk. And because this is so, this people's dramatist writing for what was said to be a people's theatre at the crisis of this people's history, is in a deep sense mocking it at the very moment when it moves him. The feelings of the fighters, in that real history, are not dramatically engaged at all; all we see and hear is the flag, the gesture, the rhetoric. The need and the oppression are silent, or at best oblique in some consequent action. What is active and vociferous is a confusion: the victims trapped in their tenements and abusing or flattering each other. What can be said by the mother, authentically, is 'Take away this murdherin' hate' – a reaction to the fact of a dead son, in whatever cause. But what is primarily and finally said is Boyle's 'The whole worl's in a terrible state of chassis' – the authentic confusion translated into a refrain and a verbal error; the error and inadequacy of this people. It is strange, powerful, crossgrained: a tension worked out, in full view, in this unusual kind of play: the facts of farce and the facts of killing.

The crisis of O'Casey's drama is the working-out of this complicated emotion. What is at issue, always, is the relation between the language of men in intense experience and the inflated, engaging language of men avoiding experience. It is a very deep disturbance, which I suppose comes out of that confused history. But what seems to me to happen, as O'Casey goes on, is the hardening of a mannerism which overrides this crucial and difficult distinction. *Juno and the Paycock* is powerful and unforgettable because the distinction is dramatised, in the loose but authentic form which alone, within naturalism, could express it. *The Plough and the Stars* has resemblances to this, and in fact moves nearer the action that would finally have to be faced if this endless paradox – the reality of suffering and the pathetic winking confusion – was to be directly explored. But there is a change in the language, a development from the earlier plays but now exceptionally self-conscious, as if always with an eye on the audience:

It would take something more than a thing like you to flutther a feather o'Fluther.

Is a man fermentin' with fear to stick th'showin' off to him of a thing that looks like a shinin' shroud?

Phrases like this have been repeatedly quoted as an 'Elizabethan' richness; but they are, in their origin and development, and where successful in their direct dramatic use, the consistent evidence of poverty: of a starved, showing-off imagination. I remember reacting very bitterly against them, and against the repeated tricks of colour – the naming of colours – which O'Casey carried to the point of parody. But the real point is more complex. Through all the early plays, it is the fact of evasion, and the verbal inflation that covers it, that O'Casey at once creates and criticises: Boyle and Joxer, or again Fluther, are in the same movement engaging and despicable; talking to hold the attention from the fact that they have nothing to say. Yet then the manner spills over, into a different dramatic speech. It flares, successfully, into the shouted abuse of the overcrowded people, as here in *The Plough and the Stars*:

BESSIE: Bessie Burgess doesn't put up to know much, never havin' a swaggerin' mind, thanks be to God, but goin' on packin' up knowledge accordin' to her conscience: precept upon precept, line upon line; here a little, an' there a little. But thanks be to Christ, she knows when she was got, where she was got, an' how she was got; while there's some she knows, decoratin' their finger with a well-polished wedding-ring, would be hard put to it if they were assed to show their weddin' lines!

MRS GOGAN: Y' oul' rip of a blasted liar . . .

This almost formal rhetoric, in the daily quarrels, connects with the more difficult use: the almost habitual showing-off. But it is critically different from what looks like the same manner applied to intense feeling, as in Nora in *The Plough and the Stars*:

While your little red-lipp'd Nora can go on sittin' here, makin' a companion of th' loneliness of th' night . . .

. . . It's hard to force away th' tears of happiness at th' end of an awful agony.

The paradoxical force of the language, endlessly presenting and self-conscious, at once to others and to the audience, drives through the play, but not as richness: as the sound, really, of a long confusion and disintegration. A characteristic and significant action is repeated: while the men are dying, in the Easter rising, the people of the tenements are looting, and lying about themselves. It is an unbearable contrast, and it is the main emotion O'Casey had to show: of nerves ragged by talking which cannot connect with the direct and terrible action. The use of random colour, of flags, of slogans, of rhetoric and comic inflation, of the sentimental song, of reminiscences of theatre (as in Nora repeating the mad Ophelia) is a rush of disintegration, of catching at temporary effects, which is quite unique: in a way, already, the separated consciousness, writing from within a life it cannot accept in its real terms yet finds endlessly engaging and preoccupying: the structure of feeling of the self-exile, still within a collective action, which can be neither avoided nor taken wholly seriously; neither indifferent nor direct.

Those three Abbey plays – *Shadow of a Gunman*, *Juno and the Paycock*, *The Plough and the Stars* – are a substantial but increasingly precarious achievement. The emotion is so difficult, so deeply paradoxical, that no simple development was possible. As it happened, O'Casey went away: all his remaining plays were written in exile, and there was a turning-point in his life when the Abbey Theatre, stupidly and unjustly, rejected *The Silver Tassie*. We have already seen the paradox, when the connection with Irish life and theatre was direct. That essential tension might have worked out differently, in a continuing contact. As it was, O'Casey went on elaborating his unusual forms: in a way released, in a way deprived. . . . It is to the Abbey plays that we still go back, but watchfully, moved and involved and yet without sentiment: seeing what happened, what so strangely happened, as the rhetoric and the reality collided, memorably, and then lurched away singing, gesturing, suffering.

SOURCE: extracts from *Drama from Ibsen to Brecht* (London, 1968), pp. 147–51, 153.

PART TWO

The Shadow of a Gunman

The Shadow of a Gunman

Première: 12 April 1923, Abbey Theatre, Dublin.

First London production: 27 May 1927, Court Theatre.

First New York production: 30 October 1932, Martin Beck Theatre
(by the Abbey Theatre company on tour).

1. COMMENT AND REVIEWS

Joseph Holloway   (1923)

Thursday, April 12, 1923: . . . I saw a film picture, Zane Grey's *Roaring U.P. Trail* at the Grand Central before going on to the Abbey and slipping into a front seat in the stalls just as *The Shadow of a Gunman* was beginning.

The scene was a room in a tenement in Dublin during the period of May 1920, and it proved a bitingly sarcastic study of many types of character during that stirring period of our history. . . . The author, Sean O'Casey, set himself out to character sketch rather than to write a well-knit-together play. What it lacked in dramatic construction, it certainly pulled up in telling dialogue of the most topical and biting kind, and the audience revelled in the telling talk. . . . McCormick was in his element as 'Seumas Shields', and his creation became a memorably humorous one, as was Dolan's 'Tommy Owens' also. Both Carolan and Fallon put in splendid studies, and May Craig as 'Mrs Grigson', who could talk the hind leg off an ass, was quite convincing.

Out of the crudeness of this first-acted play by the author, truth and nature leaped and won the author a call at the end. During the second act, Mr W. B. Yeats sat a few seats away from me and applauded vigorously the play and the author. . . .

SOURCE: extracts from *Joseph Holloway's Abbey Theatre*, edited by Robert Hogan and Michael J. O'Neill (Carbondale, Ill., 1967), pp. 215–16.

Lady Gregory   (1923)

April 15, 1923: At the Abbey I found an armed guard; there has been one ever since the theatres were threatened [by the Republican Die-Hards during the Civil War] if they kept open. And in the

Green-room I found one of them giving finishing touches to the costume of Tony Quinn, who is a Black-and-Tan in the play, and showing him how to hold his revolver. *The Shadow of a Gunman* was an immense success, beautifully acted, all the political points taken up with delight by a big audience. Sean O'Casey, the author, only saw it from the side wings the first night but had to appear to make his bow. I brought him into the stalls the other two nights and have had some talk with him.

Last night there was an immense audience, the largest I think, since the first night of *Blanco Posnet* [in 1909 at the Abbey]. Many, to my grief, had to be turned away from the door. Two seats had been kept for Yeats and me, but I put Casey in one of them and sat in the orchestra for the second. I had brought Casey round to the door before the play to share my joy in seeing the crowd surging in. . . .

I forget how I came to mention the Bible, and he asked 'Do you like it?' I said, 'Yes. I read it constantly, even for the beauty of the language.' He said he admires that beauty, he was brought up as a Protestant but has lost belief in religious forms. Then, in talking of our war here, we came to Plato's *Republic*, his dream city, whether on earth or in heaven not far away from the city of God. And then we went into the play. He says he sent us a play four years ago, *The Frost in the Flower*, and it was returned, but marked, 'not far from being a good play'. He has sent others, and says how grateful he was to me because when we had to refuse the Labour one, *The Crimson in the Tri-colour*, I had said, 'I believe there is something in you and your strong point is characterisation.' And I had wanted to pull that play together and put it on to give him experience, but Yeats was down on it. Perrin [Secretary to the Abbey Theatre] says he offered him a pass sometimes when he happened to come in, but he refused and said, 'No one ought to come into the Abbey Theatre without paying for it.' He said, 'All the thought in Ireland for years past has come through the Abbey. You have no idea what an education it has been to the country.' That, and the fine audience on this our last week [of the 1922–23 season], put me in great spirits.

SOURCE: extracts from *Lady Gregory's Journals, 1916–1930*, edited by Lennox Robinson (London, 1946), pp. 70–3.

Sean O'Casey   (1949)

A Retrospect

. . . The first night of his first play had gone very well indeed, and Sean had been congratulated by all the actors. But he was troubled with vexation of spirit when he was told that the play was to run for three nights only, and this vexation was sharpened when the Secretary of the theatre added the information that there was but thirteen pounds received for the night. However, the second night's receipts jumped to thirty pounds, and the last night to over fifty, which meant the first full house for the Abbey Theatre for many a long night. Sean smiled benignly at the Secretary when he was told the theatre would have no money in the bank till the guarantors sent in their guarantees; but, if Sean so desired, he could be paid from the cash received at the door, instead of in the usual way by cheque. Full of shy vanity, with a grand wave of the hand Sean told the Secretary he wasn't to bother, and that he'd willingly wait for the cheque.

When it came, it was less than four pounds. Less than four pounds! And he had bargained in his mind for twenty, at the least. And, if the receipts hadn't jumped up at the end, he'd have had but half of that amount. Dimly he began to realise that the Abbey Theatre would never provide a living. It was a blow, a bitter disappointment. . . . What he had got wouldn't even pay what he owed. The amount didn't extend even to the purchase of a book. What was he to do? One thing, and one thing only – go forward. He had put his hand to the plough, and he wasn't the one to look back. He would start a new play that very night. . . .

SOURCE: extract from O'Casey's autobiography, *Inishfallen, Fare Thee Well* (London and New York, 1949), pp. 177–8.

Lennox Robinson   (1924)

. . . the most remarkable of our new dramatists is Mr Sean O'Casey. He tried, with little success, to write plays in which he pursued a moral idea; he only completely found himself when he was content to act as a reporter. But it is reporting of the highest kind, almost of genius. He captures to perfection the life of the Dublin slums, shaping and altering it so little for the stage that the characters in his plays often bear the same names as they do in real life. His *Shadow of a Gunman* had an instant success last April, but as a great deal of it expressed the anti-bellicose sentiments of civilians during the Anglo-Irish war, I thought that much of its success might be due to the fact that the author was giving expression to the audience's feelings with regard to our civil war, which at that time was still being waged. But in days of peace the play has the same success – it filled the theatre all last week – which I must attribute to its veracity. It can hardly be classed as a realistic play, for it is so little arranged, so little 'constructed' – and realistic plays seem always to depend for their effect so much on construction and selection of incident and character. I am curious to see it play before an audience which will not recognise it for the pitiless photograph it is, curious to see how it will stand that test. . . .

SOURCE: extract from article in the *Observer*, 10 Feb. 1924.

P. S. O'Hegarty   (1924)

'A Drama of Disillusionment'

Until quite recently Mr O'Casey's *Gunman* had eluded me, through being on only when I happened to be unable to go and see it, but a couple of weeks ago I did manage to get in. After seeing it my main thought was that it seemed hardly worth anybody's while attempting to record recent Irish history in sober prose, seeing that it was being done brilliantly by the artists. And not alone brilliantly, but in true historical perspective, for Mr O'Casey records things as they were, but records them with that air of detachment and disillusionment which the historian aims at; he is usually wise after the event, and so is Mr O'Casey. If he had written his play three years ago it would have been full of noble heroes and bloody ruffians, whereas now it is full of human beings, the only unnatural and unbelievable characters in it being those of the gunman hero and of the Auxiliary ruffian. The gunman is a real shadow, while the Auxiliary, in many respects a true portrait, is spoiled by the cheap touch of his sudden exit from the stage when informed that there is whiskey on the premises.

There is little or no dramatic idea in Mr O'Casey's play, but there is good character drawing and tremendous power of observation. It is a gramophone record of the Dublin accent and the Dublin tenement and the Dublin poor, all illumined by the Terror and sharpened and defined by it. It is not the whole Terror, I agree, because it does not give, and it does not attempt to give, the heroic side of it, the way life felt to the men on the run and to those who helped them. But it does give what life looked like to the common people of Dublin, between the devil of the Auxiliary's pistol and incendiary bomb and the deep sea of the Irish Volunteer's home-made bomb. That is why it draws the crowd. It tells everybody what *they* thought while the two armies shot up each other and made life hideous for people who wanted to go about their business and live a normal human life. It gets back at the heroes. It is a play of disillusion for a people who have been disillusioned, and can take their disillusionment without bitterness. . . .

The dramatists keep pace with the nation. In the old untroubled days we were angry with them because they did not show us a life in Ireland like the life that came to us out of foreign plays. They only showed us what was in us. Now that strange and terrible things have come to us, they show them to us. And that is one of the necessities for a cure. We are finding ourselves out – the first step on the road to sanity and health.

The new drama is a drama of disillusionment – but of great promise.

SOURCE: extract from article in the *Irish Statesman*, vol. II, no. 4 (7 June 1924).

2. CRITICAL STUDIES

William A. Armstrong   History, Autobiography
and *The Shadow of a Gunman*   (1960)

Sean O'Casey is said to prefer his first major work, *The Shadow of a Gunman*, to his next play, *Juno and the Paycock*. To many of his readers, however, *The Shadow of a Gunman* has seemed much more limited, local, and topical in appeal. Passing judgement on O'Casey's achievement in this play in *The Nineteenth Century and After* (April, 1925), Andrew E. Malone has declared that 'his characters are taken from the slums of Dublin, and his theme is little more than a commentary upon the warlike conditions of the city during the year 1920'. One purpose of this article is to suggest that this verdict is a deceptive half-truth. O'Casey certainly does provide a realistic cross-section of life in a Dublin slum in 1920, and, as will be shown, the play certainly acquires greater significance when it is related to the social and political history of that year. But even where O'Casey's representation is closest to social or historical fact it exhibits a distinctive tone and colouring imparted by his imagination in obedience to a dramatic design. Moreover, a comparison between the play and certain parts of his autobiography, *Inishfallen, Fare Thee Well* (1949) reveals that the personal element in the play is more important than the historical one because it helped to determine its form and the interpretation of life which that form was designed to emphasise.

O'Casey dates the period of his play as May 1920. During this month the bitter struggle between the Crown and the Irish separatist movement known as Sinn Féin ('We Ourselves') reached a critical stage. Before the end of 1919, Sinn Féin and its legislative assembly, Dáil Éireann, had been declared illegal, and Lloyd George had devised his 'Bill for the Better Government of Ireland', which recommended separate parliaments for the six northeastern counties and for the other twenty-six counties of Ireland. This scheme for partition at once intensified the struggle between Sinn Féin and the British Executive in Ireland. After the shooting of a policeman in Dublin on 20 February 1920, a curfew was imposed on the city, making it illegal for any persons other than members of the Crown forces to be in the streets between midnight and 5 a.m. Soon afterwards the curfew period was extended and began at 8 p.m. On

March 24, four days before the Second Reading of Lloyd George's Bill at Westminster, the power of the British Executive was reinforced by the first detachments of a special police force recruited from the toughest ex-servicemen of the First World War. These detachments wore khaki coats with black trousers and black caps and were promptly christened 'the Black and Tans' after a well-known Tipperary pack of foxhounds. To combat these forces, the Irish Republican Army split into small groups of fifteen to thirty men who used guerilla tactics to keep their foes under constant strain. Many of its fighters lived on the run, moving continuously from place to place and seldom sleeping at home. By May 1920, the forces of the Crown were being gradually forced back to their headquarters in Dublin and many Irish Protestants who had previously been strong supporters of the Union with England had become passive spectators of the struggle.

Most of these facts are vividly reflected in *The Shadow of a Gunman* which had an immense local appeal when it was first acted at the Abbey Theatre on 12 April 1923. Its action hinges on the fact that a poet, Donal Davoren, who has recently come to share a Dublin tenement with Seumas Shields, allows himself to be regarded as a gunman 'on the run'. *On the Run*, indeed, was O'Casey's original title for the play and he abandoned it only because a drama of that name already existed. Another character, Maguire, is a real gunman on the run and is killed in a guerilla action not far from Dublin. A third character, Grigson, is an Orangeman and professes loyalty to the Crown, but he is politically passive and assures Davoren that 'there never was a drop av informer's blood in the whole family av Grigson'. While Grigson is out drinking during the curfew period, his wife is worried in case he may be shot by the Black and Tans. Soon after Grigson's safe return, shots are heard in the lane outside and Davoren and Shields are terrified at the prospect of a raid because Maguire has left a bag of bombs in their room. Shields prays that the raiders may be Tommies and not the dreaded Tans.

Discussing the behaviour of the Black and Tans in *The Revolution in Ireland* (1923), W. Alison Phillips primly remarks that 'there is evidence that some of these men – by no means all – brought to Ireland the loose views as to the rights of property which had been current during the war at the front, and helped themselves to what they needed without in these requisitions always discriminating between the loyal and the disloyal'. In the play, Mrs Grigson's description of how the Black and Tans treat her husband puts flesh on the dry bones of this generalisation. To prove his loyalty, Grigson puts a big *Bible* on his table, open at the First Epistle of St Peter, with a pious text on obedience to the King marked in red ink. The representatives of the Crown are unimpressed, however; the Black and Tans fling Grigson's *Bible* on the floor, interpret his picture of King William crossing the Boyne as seditious propaganda, and force him to sing, 'We shall meet in the Sweet Bye an' Bye' as they drink his whiskey. After arresting Minnie Powell, who had bravely concealed Maguire's bombs in her room, the Black and Tans raid another house and immediately afterwards are caught in the ambush in which Minnie is killed.

The setting of the play reinforces the strong local interest of these events. The scene represents 'A room in a tenement in Hilljoy Square, Dublin'. There is no such place as 'Hilljoy Square' in Dublin, but the significant combination of 'hill', 'joy', and 'square' and some other details in the play made it pretty certain that O'Casey was representing a tenement in Mountjoy Square, which is situated in the northeastern part of the city and was built between 1792 and 1818 at a time when it was fashionable to live on the north side of the Liffey. By the end of the nineteenth century, however, the south side had again become the fashionable residential area, and many of the fine Georgian houses in Mountjoy Square and the surrounding district had been converted into tenements which were occupied by the poorest citizens. The Georgian architecture of Mountjoy Square and its surroundings no doubt explains why the scene of the play is described as a *Return Room*, in which two large windows *occupy practically the whole of the back wall space*, and why Mr Gallogher and his family are described as the tenants of a 'front drawing-room' and their obnoxious neighbours, the Dwyers, as the tenants of a 'back drawing-room' in a house nearby.

In May 1920, the tenements of Dublin were appallingly over-crowded. In 1913, a Local Government Board Commission recorded that 21,000 families were living in one-room tenements, of which 9,000 were occupied by four or more persons. In O'Casey's play, Mr Gallogher's tenement falls into the latter category for it is occupied by his two children as well as his wife and himself. The complaint which Gallogher makes to Davoren, whom he regards as an important member of the Irish Republican Army, is due to over-crowded conditions of life. Despite his protests, Mrs Dwyer has persisted in allowing her children to keep the hall door open and to use the hall as a playground. 'The name calling and the language' of the Dwyers is 'something abominable' and Mrs Gallogher often has to lock her door to keep them from assaulting her. Gallogher fears that things will get worse when Mr Dwyer, a seaman, comes home, and anxiously petitions the Irish Republican Army for protection.

The quaintly-worded petition which Gallogher brings to Davoren establishes yet another connection between the play and the revolutionary situation in Ireland in May 1920. Early in 1920, the Dáil Éireann began to organise its own police and its own law courts in opposition to those of the Crown. By June, Republican courts had been established in no less than twenty-one counties and the royal judges who went on circuit found no litigants awaiting them. In May and June the pressure of business in the Republican courts became so great that the Dáil was obliged to limit the cases to be heard to those licensed by its Minister for Home Affairs. Against this background, Gallogher's letter of 21 May to the 'Gentlemen of the Irish Republican Army' acquires additional significance. The anomalous legal conditions of the time explain why he carefully excuses himself for having taken out a summons against the Dwyers because 'there was no Republican Courts' at the time when he did so, and why he adds that he did not proceed with it because he has 'a strong objection to foreign courts as such'. He goes on to urge the Republicans to send 'some of your army or police', preferably with guns, to his tenement, for he believes that he has 'a Primmy Fashy Case against Mrs Dwyer and all her heirs'.

O'Casey certainly made abundant use of local geography and history when he wrote *The Shadow of a Gunman*. But his choice of material is selective and his treatment is consistently ironical. There is a visual irony in the very setting in which Shields's meagre, slovenly furnishings clutter a room in a Georgian mansion in a once-fashionable square. The dangers of the curfew period set Mrs Grigson worrying about her absent husband, but they also produce the irony of her canny speculation: 'Do the insurance companies pay if a man is shot after curfew?' In their treatment of Grigson, the Black and Tans are the unconscious agents of the irony of poetic justice because Grigson is a boastful tippler who treats his wife like a skivvy. The Republican Courts were established with the high purpose of saving Ireland from anarchy during a time of great emergency; Gallogher expects them to sort out a tenement squabble. If O'Casey had preserved his original title, *On the Run*, it would have combined irony with topicality since Davoren is an artist 'on the run' in search of peaceful conditions of work, not the dedicated gunman he is taken for. In *The Playboy of the Western World*, the pose so artfully assumed by Christie Mahon stimulates both his imagination and that of his admirers; in *The Shadow of a Gunman*, Davoren's half-hearted pose illustrates only his vanity and evokes only vainglory or self-interest in such characters as Tommy Owens, Grigson and Gallogher. The saddest of the many ironies in the play is that Minnie Powell sacrifices

herself for a versifier whom she regards as a patriot as well as a
poet.

Minnie Powell represents the most positive set of values in *The Shadow
of a Gunman*. These values emerge chiefly from the interaction between
Minnie, Davoren and Shields. A comparison between the play and
the third and fourth sections of *Inishfallen, Fare Thee Well* (1949)
provides good reasons for believing that these three characters had
their origins in certain experiences described by O'Casey in this
autobiography and that he modified and intensified these experiences
to create the contrast between Minnie, Davoren and Shields which is
the main theme of the play.

In his autobiography, O'Casey describes how the behavior of his
brother made it impossible for him to carry on with his creative
writing in their Dublin tenement and how he moved to another
tenement in a different house. This parallels Davoren's move from
one tenement to another so as to be able to work in peace. One night
when O'Casey lay in bed in his new abode the house was raided by
Black and Tans; in the play, Davoren finds himself in the same
predicament. In his autobiography, O'Casey describes 'a volley of
battering blows on the obstinate wooden door, mingled with the crash
of falling glass' which indicated that 'the panels on each side of it had
been shattered by hammer or rifle-butt'. These details are closely
paralleled by the stage-direction in the play: *There is heard at the street
door a violent and continuous knocking, followed by the crash of glass and the
beating of the door with rifle butts*. As O'Casey awaited the entry of the
raiders, he thought of Whitman's lines, 'Come lovely and soothing
death, Undulate round the world, serenely arriving', and pondered
the fact that 'Death doesn't arrive serenely here. . . .' Corresponding-
ly, Davoren recalls Shelley's description of 'the cold chaste moon . . .
Who makes all beautiful on which she smiles', and bitterly reflects
that the moon 'couldn't make this thrice accursed room beautiful'.

At the back of the house described in the autobiography is a 'large
shed that was said to be used as a carpenter's shop' by O'Casey's
neighbor, Mr Ballynoy, a thin, delicate man who was reputed to care
'for no manner of politics'. A similar building appears in the play
when Shields mentions that 'There's a stable at the back of the house
with an entrance from the yard; it's used as a carpenter's shop.'
Shields goes on to suggest that this shop is used for the manufacture of
bombs, but whether this is so is never revealed, and in the play the
passage about it is rather redundant. The carpenter's shop probably
found its way into the play because the Black and Tans discovered

that the shed described in the autobiography contained a large quantity of explosives. These had evidently been manufactured by Mr Ballynoy, who was wounded when he tried to prevent the raiders from entering the shed. As he stands in the lorry after his arrest, Ballynoy's final gesture is one of patriotic defiance: ' "Up th' Republic!" he shouted with the full force of his voice.' This gesture is strikingly paralleled in the play; when Minnie Powell is thrust into a lorry after her arrest, she shouts 'Up the Republic!' at the top of her voice.

Though O'Casey's sympathies were with the Republicans, there were moments when he grew weary of the fighting and contemplated both sides with a jaundiced eye: 'Gun peals and slogan cries were things happy enough in a song, but they made misery in a busy street. . . . The sovereign people were having a tough time of it from enemies on the left and friends on the right. Going out for a stroll, or to purchase a necessary, no one knew when he'd have to fall flat on his belly, to wait for death to go by, in the midst of smoke and fire and horrifying noises. . . . Christian Protestant England and Christian Catholic Ireland were banging away at each other for God, for King, and Country.' In the play Shields re-echoes these bitter sentiments when he exclaims, 'It's the civilians that suffer; when there's an ambush, they don't know where to run. Shot in the back to save the British Empire, an' shot in the breast to save the soul of Ireland. I'm a Nationalist meself, right enough . . . but I draw the line when I hear the gunmen blowin' about dyin' for the people, when it's the people that are dyin' for the gunmen!'

In its modification of the personal experiences and feelings just described, O'Casey's imagination makes Davoren an embodiment of frustrated life, Shields an embodiment of life turned sour and superstitious, and Minnie Powell an embodiment of an ideal fullness of life, in order to create that intense contrast between masculine and feminine nature which is fundamental to his interpretation of human existence. The particular form of Davoren's frustration is that of an artist at odds with society; Shields is a nationalist who has degenerated into abysmal selfishness. The two characters are aptly symbolised by certain properties among the untidy furnishings of their tenement: the self-protective superstition of Shields by the crucifix and the statues of the Virgin and the Sacred Heart on the mantelpiece; the aesthetic aspirations of Davoren by the flowers, the books and the typewriter[1] on the table. Both have catch-phrases expressive of their exaggerated discontents. Shields makes any annoyance, however trivial, an excuse

for invective against the 'Irish People' as a whole, and his misanthropy persistently finds vent in the refrain, 'Oh, Kathleen ni
Houlihan, your way's a thorny way'. Whenever Davoren's attempts
to write are interrupted, he echoes the words of Shelley's tormented
Prometheus, 'Ah me! alas, pain, pain, pain ever, for ever.' Each of
them proudly claims that his creed sets him above fear. According to
Shields, 'No man need be afraid with a crowd of angels round him;
thanks to God for His Holy religion!' and Davoren retorts, 'You're
welcome to your angels; philosophy is mine; philosophy that makes
the coward brave; the sufferer defiant; the weak strong. . . .' A second
later a volley of shots outside reduces both of them to the same state of
abject fear.

For all the mock-heroic effect of his Promethean pose, Davoren is
not an unsympathetic character. Unlike Joyce's Stephen Dedalus, he
is a portrait of the artist as a not-so-young man subject to the
withering effects of poverty, the noise and interruptions of slum life,
and the danger of sudden death in a time of revolution and war. Yet
his aesthetic creed has much in common with that of Dedalus. It is
described at the outset of the play as a devotion to '*the might of design,
the mystery of colour, and the belief in the redemption of all things by beauty
everlasting*'. These phrases are borrowed from Dubedat's climactic
speech in the fourth act of Shaw's *The Doctor's Dilemma*. They are
repeated when Shields maliciously remarks that 'a poet's claim to
greatness depends upon his power to put passion in the common
people', and Davoren bitterly replies, '. . . to the people there is no
mystery of colour. . . . To them the might of design is a three-roomed
house or a capacious bed. To them beauty is for sale in a butcher's
shop. . . . The poet ever strives to save the people; the people ever
strive to destroy the poet.' This is a central issue in the play. It is put to
the test by Davoren's reactions to Minnie Powell.

Characteristically, Davoren is reluctant to admit Minnie when she
knocks gently on his door. But their conversation reveals that this
daughter of the people is an unconscious devotee of all that Davoren
values most; she loves beauty, design and colour in the forms
available to her – the poetry of Burns, the music of Tommy Owens's
melodeon, and the flowers on Davoren's table. What is more, she has
the courage and the feeling of community that Davoren lacks; 'I don't
know how you like to be by yourself', she tells him, 'I couldn't stick it
long.' Davoren forgets his timidity as he joyfully realises that Minnie
embodies his ideals; 'My soul within art thou, Minnie!' he exclaims,
but after she has gone his exaltation gives way to uneasiness as he
ponders the dangers of being 'the shadow of a gunman' to please
her.

Shields's reaction to Minnie exhibits his misanthropy at its worst. She is 'an ignorant little bitch that thinks of nothing but jazz dances, foxtrots, picture theatres an' dress', and would 'give the world an' all to be gaddin' about with a gunman' but would not grieve long if he were shot or hung. As for her courage, 'She wouldn't sacrifice a jazz dance to save a man's life.' Minnie gives the lie to this and to Davoren's assertion that 'the people ever strive to destroy the poet' when she takes the bombs from their room and is killed after being arrested. Shields is unmoved by this sacrifice; he sees in it nothing more than a gratifying confirmation of his superstitious belief that the tapping on the wall was an ill omen. But for Davoren it is a tragic experience which leads him to know his own nature better; he recognises that he is 'poltroon and poet', and it is a measure of his development that in his final lament Shelley's words, 'Ah me, alas! Pain, pain, pain ever, for ever!' no longer sound mock-heroic on his lips. In *A Portrait of the Artist as a Young Man*, Dedalus's aesthetic adventure ends with an inspiring epiphany of beauty; Davoren's ends with a revelation of the moral inadequacy of his creed.

The contrast between Davoren and Shields and Minnie Powell raises *The Shadow of a Gunman* to a tragic level. This major design is reinforced by several lesser but parallel contrasts. Like Davoren and Shields, most of the other men in the play are intent on vanity or self-preservation; only the women show themselves capable of courage and charity like Minnie Powell's. The pathetic Mr Gallogher is under the wing of the immensely maternal Mrs Henderson, who teases him out of his timidity and admires his fantastic prose. Grigson's drinking and boasting flourish at the expense of Mrs Grigson, who lets him have most of their food, *getting just enough to give her strength to do the necessary work of the household*. In the face of danger and death, a moral paralysis afflicts the men, whereas the sympathies of the women expand; Mrs Grigson mourns the death of Minnie and Mrs Henderson is arrested for fighting the Black and Tans. *The Shadow of a Gunman* is skilfully constructed to create a contrast between the masculine and the feminine character as stern as that elaborated in *Juno and the Paycock*. The most significant difference between *The Shadow of a Gunman* and O'Casey's autobiography lies in the substitution of Minnie Powell for Mrs Ballynoy. No less than Yeats's Countess Cathleen and Synges's Deirdre, Minnie Powell treads the thorny way of Cathleen ni Houlihan; Shields's catchphrase is more relevant than he will ever realise. It is this mythopoeic level of meaning which makes *The Shadow of a Gunman* much more than 'a commentary upon the warlike conditions of the city during the year 1920''and brings it into contact with what Yeats called the *anima mundi*, the world of ideal passion, to which the tragic heroine aspires even at the cost of her physical destruction.

SOURCE: article in *Modern Drama*, II (1960), pp. 417–24.

NOTE

1. One is rather surprised to find that the impecunious Davoren owns a typewriter. Like the carpenter's shop, it may have found its way into the play *via* the experiences recounted in *Inishfallen, Fare Thee Well*. In the sixth section of this autobiography, O'Casey records how he managed to acquire a secondhand typewriter by hire-purchase just after the events already described.

Ronald G. Rollins   O'Casey and Synge: The Irish Hero as Playboy and Gunman   (1966)

The Kelt . . . has in his blood an excess of impulsive, imaginative, even fantastic qualities. It is much easier for him to make a fool of himself, to begin with, than it is for people of slower wits and more sluggish temperaments. When you add whiskey to that, or that essence of melancholia which in Ireland they call 'porther,' you get the Kelt at his very weakest and worst.
                              —Harold Frederic, *The Damnation of Theron Ware*

Numerous observers of Irish culture have frequently felt compelled to comment upon two recurrent behavioral patterns in the chaotic and frequently bloody history of Ireland: the imaginative Irishman's obsessive and apparently compulsive need to isolate, admire, and sometimes abuse the heroic personality, and the Irishman's habitual tendency to be attracted to and then tragically deceived by meretricious trappings, especially flamboyant, Byronic attitudinising and fustian. James Joyce once observed: 'The Irish are people who will never have leaders, for at the great moment they always desert them. They have produced one skeleton – Parnell – never a man.'[1] Arland Ussher adds that the Irish apparently have a weakness for 'bravado' and the 'actor-type',[2] William S. Clark concludes that Ireland has had a tendency to 'confuse the fools with the heroes in her long struggle for freedom.'[3] Finally, George Bernard Shaw casts additional illumination upon his countryman's antipathy for the pedestrian personality and the grim, confining real, and the Irishman's special fondness for the romantic and the ideal in this speech by the perceptive Irishman Laurence Doyle in *John Bull's Other Island*:

An Irishman's imagination never lets him alone, never convinces him, never satisfies him; but it makes him that he cant face reality nor deal with it nor handle it nor conquer it. . . . He cant be religious. The inspired Churchman that teaches him the sanctity of life and the importance of conduct is sent away empty; while the poor village priest that gives him a miracle or a sentimental story of a saint, has cathedrals built for him out of the pennies of the poor. He cant be intelligently political: he dreams of what the Shan Van Vocht said in ninety-eight. If you want to interest him in Ireland youve got to call the unfortunate island Kathleen ni Houlihan and pretend she's a little old woman. It saves thinking. It saves working. It saves everything except imagination, imagination, imagination; and imagination's such a torture that you cant bear it without whiskey. . . . At last you get that you can bear nothing real at all; youd rather starve than cook a meal; youd rather go shabby and dirty than set your mind to take care of your clothes and wash yourself; you nag and squabble at home because your wife isnt an angel, and she despises you because youre not a hero; and you hate the whole lot round you because theyre only poor slovenly useless devils like yourself. . . . And all the while there goes on a horrible, senseless, mischievous laughter . . . laugh! laugh! laugh! eternal derision, eternal envy, eternal folly, eternal fouling and staining and degrading. . .[4]

It is precisely these persistent problems – the Irishman's extreme fondness for heroes and heroic speech and action – that interest, perhaps irritate, Sean O'Casey and John Millington Synge in *The Shadow of a Gunman* and *The Playboy of the Western World*, two satiric dramas remarkably alike with respect to character, situation and theme, but not, to be sure, resolution. As a drama ridiculing hypocrisy, reckless bravado and hollow, false conceit, O'Casey's *The Shadow of a Gunman* re-examines a national habit or proclivity which Synge had previously exploited in his comically ironic *The Playboy of the Western World*: the Irish tendency to mistake sham heroes and false patriots for men of real conviction and courage.[5] Indeed, O'Casey's Donal Davoren is a slightly modified Christopher Mahon in a proletarian, rather than a peasant, milieu, whose career, with some significant exceptions, roughly parallels that of Synge's impulsive but rapidly maturing playboy.[6]

Like Christy, Donal is a traveller, a migratory writer, who wanders into a strange place, the peddler Seumas Shields's disorderly tenement room, in search of food, shelter, and quiet safety. Christy has precisely these same needs when he shyly enters the shebeen or public house on a wild coast of Mayo in his flight from his atrocity. We meet both young men, then, when they are travel weary, despondent, and dishevelled in dress. Both young men also manifest similar attitudes as they try to acclimatise with a minimum of friction to their new locales; they are somewhat shy and aloof, immersed in their private reflections, and prone to give abrupt and indirect replies when questioned.

The two Irish lads are likewise quickly mistaken for something which they are not: Christy for a brave, daring fellow who has killed his 'da', and Donal for a calm and intrepid freedom fighter on the run. In both cases, moreover, young women, Pegeen Mike and Minnie Powell, figure prominently in this expanding misconception. Pegeen declares that she can't believe that Christy, with his 'quality' name and noble brow, was always a quiet, docile fellow, toiling stoically in the fields, until the great day that he smote his domineering father with a loy; and Minnie, happy in her wide-eyed adoration, assures Donal that he *is* a gunman on the run who would not hesitate to die for his country.

Christy and Donal are pleased but somewhat dumbfounded by the unexpected turn of events, but both rapidly acquire pride and apparent self-confidence as they receive the compliments of their female admirers and those who flock to pay them tribute. Christy expresses his happy astonishment in this speech at the close of Act I:

CHRISTY: Well, it's a clean bed and soft with it, and it's great luck and company I've won me in the end of time – two fine women fighting for the likes of me – till I'm thinking this night wasn't I foolish not to kill my father in the years gone by.

Donal is equally joyful in his new role as the curtain scene in Act I shows:

DAVOREN: Minnie, Donal; Donal, Minnie. Very pretty, but very ignorant. A gunman on the run! Be careful, be careful, Donal Davoren. But Minnie is attracted to the idea, and I am attracted to Minnie. And what danger can there be in being the shadow of a gunman?

Both playwrights, however, never let us forget that both lads are basically cowardly and indecisive, and that their followers are romantic, gullible dupes in viewing them as they do. In Act I of *The Playboy of the Western World*, for example, a knock at the door causes Christy, who has been boasting of his prowess, to cling to Pegeen in terror; and in Act II of *The Shadow of a Gunman*, moments after Donal has declared that he has no fear of death, a volley of shots outside causes him to stand rigid with violent fear.

In the face of mounting pressure and attention from their admirers, Christy and Donal are incited to elaborate upon their abilities, Christy by embellishing his tale of murder, and Donal by emphasising the calm courage and nonchalance that he manifests in the presence of danger. In Act II Christy delights his rapt listeners with an embellished version of the murder:

CHRISTY (*flattered and confident, waving bone*): He gave a drive with the scythe, and I gave a lep to the east. Then I turned around with my back to the north, and I hit a blow on the ridge of his skull, laid him stretched out, and he split to the knob of his gullet. (*He raises the chicken bone to his Adam's apple.*)

In a similar scene in O'Casey's play, Davoren boasts of his poise gained through experience:

DAVOREN (*delighted at Minnie's obvious admiration, leaning back in his chair, and lighting a cigarette with placid affectation*): I'll admit one does be a little nervous at first, but a fellow gets used to it after a bit, till, at last, a gunman throws a bomb as carelessly as a schoolboy throws a snowball.

It is in the resolutions of the plays – when the heroic fiction must be tested in the destructive element of life itself – that we notice the radical dissimilarities in the careers of the protagonists. In Christy's case his wholehearted reliance upon the capricious affections and hero worship of his followers brings about his rather abrupt downfall and subsequent disenchantment; but, paradoxically, it is this same dependence on the public's hyperbolic image of him that infuses Christy with the strong assurance that he must have to 'transform into reality the illusions about himself which his new acquaintances have inspired'.[7] It is tragically ironic that Christy deceived Pegeen with a lie, a lie that belatedly creates the man she must love and lose. Because of the power of a lie, therefore, Christy is transformed, moving confidently forward as the possible master of all future challenges:

CHRISTY: Go with you is it? I will then, like a gallant captain with his heathen slave. Go on now and I'll see you from this day stewing my oatmeal and washing my spuds, for I'm master of all fights from now. (*Pushing Mahon.*) Go on, I'm saying.

Evaluating this surprise ending, Otto Reinert comments:

By the time Pegeen and the others lose their illusions about him, illusion has turned into reality: Christy has become what the village thought he was, because its belief has become his own. He leaves as the hero of his own glorious fable, timid lout turned 'likely gaffer', bullying his proud father, and rich enough in the promise of his 'romping lifetime' to lose even a girl like Pegeen.[8]

The reverse is true in Donal's case. He has deceived his tenement associates with a lie – with a vain, mock-heroic masquerade – but he cannot, when the time for action arrives, translate this lie into the truth of decisive, courageous action. He lets Minnie die for him. Unlike Christy, the lie does not enable Donal to achieve his self-liberation; he remains the same inept, histrionic and cowardly fellow he was at the beginning. Like Christy, he has deceived his sweetheart with a false face and with false facts, and, ironically, she sacrifices her life for him without ever knowing the truth of the matter. His disgust for himself is quite apparent in his final speech.

DAVOREN: Ah me, alas! Pain, pain, pain ever, for ever! It's terrible to think that little
Minnie is dead, but it's still more terrible to think that Davoren and Shields are alive!
Oh, Donal Davoren, shame is your portion now till the silver cord is loosened and the
golden bowl be broken. Oh, Davoren, Donal Davoren, poet and poltroon, poltroon
and poet.

In ridiculing the foolish pretensions of Donal – and others like
Tommy Owens, another whiskey-sipping hero-follower in the same
play – O'Casey seems determined to accentuate the fact that 'there
can be no revival of hope in their country until Irishmen have shed all
their vain illusions about themselves and have been steeped in the
waters of self-disgust'.[9] Their insatiate desire either to be a hero or
worship one can only lead to sorry confusion and disaster, as O'Casey
indicated in this passage from a letter:

The chasing of the hero is in the play and also the readiness of poor conceited minds to
be chased and honored for a heroism which is often foolish; though, of course, it remains
true to believe that it is good to die for one's country (people, really), should the need
arise. Old Glory is often fluttered for unworthy purposes; but the flag remains a true
and beautiful symbol even when held aloft by the hands of a scoundrel. We have to pay
for vain conceits; and Davoren had to pay for his.[10]

Hence playwrights O'Casey and Synge concern themselves with the
same moral problem in these plays: the difficult and frequently
painful movement by two young men away from wasteful self-
intoxication and toward the waters of self-disgust (Donal) and
self-knowledge (Christy). In the end both make the same overwhelming discovery: it is one's character and conduct – not hasty estimates
by emotional associates – that reveal one's true essence.

SOURCE: article in *Arizona Quarterly*, XXII (1966), pp. 217–22.

NOTES

1. Marvin Magalaner and Richard M. Kain, *Joyce: the Man, the Work, the Reputation*
(New York, 1962), p. 33. For Joyce's bitter reaction to the destruction of this Irish
statesman, see 'Et Tu, Healy' and 'Ivy Day in the Committee Room', two works which
place Parnell, the proud and silent figure, far above the grovelling mass of Irish
politicians and their sycophants.
2. *Three Great Irishmen* (New York, 1957), p. 69.
3. *Chief Patterns of World Drama* (New York, 1946), p. 891. For Yeats's view on the
fickleness of those who followed the great man, see 'Parnell's Funeral' in *Selected Poems of
William Butler Yeats*, ed. M. L. Rosenthal (New York, 1962), p. 152.
4. *Selected Plays of George Bernard Shaw* (New York, 1949), pp. 516–17.
5. The plays of Walter Macken, *Home is the Hero* and *Mungo's Mansion*, also
investigate the Irishman's desire to be or revere the hero. See Saros Cowasjee, *Sean
O'Casey, The Man Behind the Plays* (New York, 1964), p. 22.
6. 'Playboy' has two basic implications: a hoaxer and one adept in games. 'Western

World' is 'an old Irish poeticism for Western Ireland'. See Otto Reinert, *Drama: An Introductory Anthology* (Boston, Mass., 1961), p. 696.

7. Paul M. Cubeta, *Modern Drama for Analysis* (New York, 1955), p. 326.
8. Reinert, op. cit., p. 701.
9. John W. Cunliffe, *Modern English Playwrights* (New York, 1927), pp. 240–1.
10. Letter from O'Casey to this writer, 30 March 1959.

Bernice Schrank   'You needn't say no more':
Language and the Problems of Communication
in *The Shadow of a Gunman*   (1978)

I

From Boyle's repeated comment in *Juno and the Paycock* that 'the whole worl's ... in a terr...ible state o' ... chassis' to the vision of Armageddon in Act II of *The Silver Tassie*, O'Casey explores the theme of breakdown. *The Shadow of a Gunman*, O'Casey's first full-length play to be accepted by the Abbey, reflects the dominant motif of the other early plays. Here too O'Casey examines the manifestations of chaos. The 'troubles', the slum poverty, the religious hypocrisy and the exploitative personal relationships contribute to the overwhelming sense of breakdown in this play.

O'Casey's presentation of breakdown in *The Shadow of a Gunman* is, no doubt, important in itself.[1] It also provides the context for his treatment of language. For some critics, the colourful language of his characters is one of the most remarkable features of an O'Casey play.[2] But language does not float on the surface of an O'Casey play like a layer of cream in a cup of Irish coffee. The language the characters use in *The Shadow of a Gunman* is an integral part of the play's overall vision of chaos.[3]

The characters have one of two basic problems with language. The majority – Gallogher, Owens, Grigson, Seumas and Donal – indulge in meaningless talk. In contrast to the talkers are Maguire and Minnie who act. But Maguire refuses to communicate his true purposes, while Minnie is unable to express herself in her own words. Maguire and Minnie do not adequately explain their actions and, as a result, these actions are open to some very unflattering interpretations. Maguire, in silently leaving the bombs, seems reckless and morally reprehensible. Minnie's 'heroism' in removing the bombs, all

the while believing they belong to Donal, can also be seen as an
unheroic amalgam of illusion, sentimentality and second-hand
patriotism.

From the examples of Gallogher, Owens, Grigson, Seumas and
Donal on the one hand and Maguire and Minnie on the other,
O'Casey demonstrates that words without deeds and the converse,
deeds without appropriate words, are unsatisfactory. Both are
essentially negative responses to chaos which give rise to new
manifestations of breakdown. Both approaches to language will be
examined in turn, beginning with the talkative characters.

II

Gallogher, Owens, Grigson, Seumas and Donal flood the play with a
veritable Niagara of words. The politically and economically hostile
environment of O'Casey's Dublin is more likely to stimulate talk than
to produce constructive action. Should Seumas organise his fellow
pedlars into a union of the unskilled and underemployed? Should
Owens and Grigson really take sides and quite possibly get themselves killed? The point is that the kinds of actions which poverty and
political turmoil suggest to the activist or social reformer – commitment and militancy – are unattractive or dangerous and are never
seriously considered by these characters. All Gallogher, Owens,
Grigson, Seumas and Donal have, then, is talk and they talk
unceasingly to insulate themselves from a destructive reality. By
allowing them to project pseudoselves of heroism and brilliance, their
talk relieves their sense of fear and their feelings of impotence.
Unfortunately it also paralyses them. More than just insulating them,
their talk, idiosyncratic, incoherent and egotistical, isolates them
from meaningful communication with each other and from any hope
of collective action. Thus the various distortions of normal speech
that Gallogher and the others demonstrate, while superficially comic,
are ultimately destructive because they are not only a response to, but
a perpetuation of, the overall chaos.

Gallogher's ineffectual talk characterises the man and his situation
as he is overtaken by the effects of breakdown. The unpleasant truth is
that he is economically, politically and verbally impotent. In seeking
help from the IRA, Gallogher shows how desperate life in Dublin's
tenements can be and how distant that life is from the official channels
of law enforcement. In requesting Donal's intervention, Gallogher
illustrates his own incapacity to act. The situation is in fact doubly
ironic because, by going to Donal who is himself unable to act,
Gallogher demonstrates still further incompetence. Gallogher's utter
powerlessness is summed up in his manner of lodging the complaint.

Gallogher presumably initiates it, but he does not use his own words when he presents it. At first, a parrot-like repetition of Mrs Henderson's comments is the best he can muster. When he breaks free of her linguistic embrace, however, he does not discover his own voice. He proceeds to read his jargon-laden letter which strives for absolute precision through a dense array of misused legalisms and which achieves only bombastic incoherence. Finally, although his parting words to Donal are clearly unrehearsed, they do not so much resemble spontaneous discourse as badly studied affectation. On behalf of himself and his wife, Mr Gallogher thanks Donal for his 'benevolent goodness in interferin' in the matter specified, particula-rated an' expanded upon in the letter, mandamus or schedule, as the case may be'. This hodge-podge of jargon, malapropism and redundancy is Gallogher's unsuccessful attempt to create a super-self by manipulating language. He tries to disguise his powerlessness in pomposity, but the only people he takes in are himself and Mrs Henderson. To everyone else, what he says is so patently a pose that it only emphasises his own impotence. Gallogher's fate is to be forever seeking the attributes of power in language because he cannot alter the basic powerlessness in fact.

Gallogher's verbal distortions are harmless when compared with those of Tommy Owens and Dolphie Grigson. The discrepancy between what these two say and what they mean is so great that their speech comprises a case study in the verbal art of non-communication. Tommy's first words set the pattern of verbal perversion which will characterise his and Dolphie's entire perfor-mance. As Tommy enters in Act I, he observes Donal and Minnie kissing. Yet he insists that he has seen 'nothin' – honest – thought you was learnin' to typewrite – Mr Davoren teachin' you. I seen nothin' else – s'help me God'. Now Tommy knows perfectly well that Donal and Minnie are not 'typewriting', but he deliberately lies in order to curry favour with Donal, the presumed gunman on the run. If, in the process, Tommy converts Donal and Minnie's genuine display of affection into a sordid and dirty secret, trust Tommy not to be unduly concerned. Tommy's disjointed syntax is, moreover, the ideal medium for his perverted comments. By consistently avoiding connectives in his speech, he can jump from 'typewriting' to self-praise to patriotic effusiveness without the slightest nod to the demands of logic and coherence. Furthermore, by suppressing the logical and verbal links, Tommy makes his speech resemble a series of explosions which suggest to the ear what has been plain to the mind, that political disorder and verbal dislocations are related.

For the most part, however, Tommy and Dolphie are not casual

liars. Their lies are usually part of a calculated plan of self-promotion.
As long as it is cheap and fashionable to be patriots, Tommy Owens
and Adolphus Grigson swell with national pride, shout patriotic
slogans and fill the stage with patriotic songs. Their heroic posturing
is based on the odds that their rhetoric will never be tested by
unpleasant facts. Thus, Tommy goes out of his way to establish his
patriotic credentials. He intentionally refuses to understand Donal's
straightforward statement that he 'has no connection with the politics
of the day'. Instead, Tommy chooses to hear in Davoren's disclaimer
a verbal code which confirms Tommy's fantasy that Donal is indeed a
gunman on the run.

> TOMMY: You needn't say no more – a nod's as good as a wink to a blind horse – you've no
> meddlin' or makin' with it, good, bad, or indifferent, pro nor con; I know it an'
> Minnie knows it – give me your hand.
> (*He catches Davoren's hand.*)
> Two firm hands clasped together will all the power outbrave of the heartless English
> tyrant, the Saxon coward an' knave. That's Tommy Owens' hand, Mr Davoren, the
> hand of a man, a man – Mr Shields knows me well.
> (*He breaks into song.*)
> High upon the gallows tree stood the noble-hearted three,
> By the vengeful tyrant stricken in their bloom;
> But they met him face to face with the spirit of their race,
> And they went with souls undaunted to their doom!
> MINNIE (*in an effort to quell his fervour*): Tommy Owens, for goodness' sake . . .
> TOMMY (*overwhelming her with a shout*):
> God save Ireland ses the hayros, God save Ireland ses we all,
> Whether on the scaffold high or the battle-field we die,
> Oh, what matter when for Ayryinn dear we fall!
> (*Tearfully*) Mr Davoren, I'd die for Ireland.

Tommy uses language here not to communicate sincerely-held
beliefs, but to stage an act in which a heroic Tommy Owens plays the
lead. Tommy's metamorphosis from slum dweller to sentimental star
can be traced in the syntax. As the disconnected clauses typical of the
real Tommy Owens become complex and inverted rhetoric, a
platform hero is hatched. Fortunately, the verbiage becomes so
overwrought that Tommy cannot keep it going indefinitely. He soon
collapses into the more natural and disconnected, 'Mr Shields knows
me well', and for a second the real Tommy is back. But the illusory
Tommy regains control of stage centre by bursting into song. From
the moment Tommy grasps Donal's hand until he ends the song, he
creates a verbal routine in which to project a bogus identity many
times removed from his real self.

What Tommy does to language in Act I, Grigson perpetuates in Act
II. Like Tommy, but even more frequently, he refers to himself in the
third person, the unmistakeable sign for the *poseur* infatuated with the

role he is playing. And like Tommy, Grigson fancies himself a hero, 'Dolphus Grigson's afraid of nothin' creepin' or walkin',' and a patriot. Although he is an Orangeman and drinks to 'King William, to the battle av the Boyne . . . an' to The Orange Lily O', he assured Donal, the supposed Republican gunman, of his unswerving loyalty in a burst of confused, intoxicated effusiveness. Grigson's comments here are as short on logical connections and inner consistency as Tommy's are. The syntactic disorder gives the same boost to Grigson's need for self-advertisement, to his penchant for rhetorical flights and to his love of heroic poses that it gives to Tommy Owen's very similar reflexes. For both Tommy and Dolphie, language is a plastic medium that can be moulded to the shapes of their egos and their illusions without the slightest regard for the demands of logic, grammar or reality.

Yet reality finds them out during the raid. When the Black and Tans put pressure on their patriotic sentiments, Tommy and Dolphie collapse into terrified submission. Both the easy bombast and the cringing about-faces are the responses of politically uncommitted characters caught in the middle of warring political factions and overcome with a sense of their own helplessness. Tommy and Dolphie create verbal smokescreens because no other action seems possible and their boasts and songs give them a false but needed sense of security.

The overriding sense of breakdown which encourages Owens and Grigson to develop their own private and idiosyncratic language, moreover, fosters still further breakdown. Their cowardice is a weakness; their reckless misuse of language and their wholesale illusion-mongering are much more serious matters because they intentionally cater to a tenement audience which is already prone to accept illusion for reality. It is understandable that Owens and Grigson resist going to the barricades themselves. It becomes morally damaging when, in glorifying the barricades, they help create the emotional climate that sends Minnie in their place. The talk of Owen and Grigson is not the harmless self-indulgence that Gallogher displays. In itself and, more importantly, in its consequences, it illustrates a very destructive form of breakdown.

Seumas Shields also distorts language. But unlike Tommy and Dolphie who use verbiage mainly to inflate their egos and unlike Gallogher who uses jargon as a defence against his own impotence, Seumas's rhetoric is sometimes intentionally anti-rhetorical. Frequently an ironist of penetration in dealing with others (he is as blind as everyone else in the play to his own failures), Seumas can deflate verbal pretensions with well-turned barbs of his own. His comment on Nationalist propaganda, 'I draw the line when I hear the gunmen blowin' about dyin' for the people, when it's the people that are dyin' for the gunmen', is an effective putdown couched in nicely balanced clauses. He undercuts the romanticism of Donal's poetry with equal ease by reminding Donal of the realities of proletarian life.

But although Seumas understands and criticises the rhetorical affectations of others, he has problems with language himself. His verbal awareness, subtler than Tommy's, Gallogher's or Grigson's, is nevertheless partial and flawed. Through his facile wordiness, which in moments of crisis degenerates into a nervous stutter, he too is caught in the Babel of tongues.

Side-by-side with his sensible observations about propaganda and poetry, Seumas has long-winded, bad-tempered and know-nothing opinions on religion, society and personality. In Act I, many of these opinions take the form of grandiose pronouncements that are, on closer examination, nothing more than glib generalisations. Seumas uses this bloated rhetoric to work off tension that might better be vented in action. Thus when Maguire is late for his appointment in Act I, Seumas relieves his annoyance by denouncing the entire population of Ireland instead of going off to peddle on his own. 'No wonder this unfortunate country is as it is', he complains, ironically providing a good example in his procrastinating speech of the laziness he rails against. Again when the landlord threatens to evict Seumas, Seumas tries to dissolve the problem in words. Twice Donal asks Seumas what he intends to do and, although Seumas can offer no plan of action, he neither exits quickly as he promises, nor remains silent.

DAVOREN: What are we going to do with these notices to quit?
SEUMAS: Oh, shove them up on the mantelpiece behind one of the statues.
DAVOREN: Oh, I mean what action shall we take?
SEUMAS: I haven't time to stop now.

At this point, Seumas ought to rush for the door. He claims he has no time to deal with the matter at hand, yet he stays to denounce the landlord, to wish him and his tenement ill (which is enormously self-destructive in that it is Seumas's room that will be destroyed as Mulligan's 'rookery'), and to sing a song, ending with the self-pitying largeness of 'Oh, Kathleen ni Houlihan, your way's a thorny way'. Then, and only then, does he actually leave. Now this generalisation, like the previous one about 'this unfortunate country' is as irrelevant as it is comforting. Since neither points to specific and remediable problems, even though these problems exist, neither requires any action. The generalisations are, at least in Act I, agents of paralysis.

In Act II, Seumas's pronouncements seem on the whole more

appropriate to the situation than they do in Act I. When he talks of
Ireland as a 'hopeless' country 'gone mad', he acknowledges the
political chaos that has overtaken it. But his pronouncements do not
prepare him for the reality of chaos; quite the reverse. They
incapacitate him, thus reproducing his situation in Act I. As he and
Donal hear the Black and Tans approaching and simultaneously
discover the bag of bombs, Seumas becomes terrified. He expresses
his fear by repeating empty phrases: 'Did I know he was a gunman;
did I know he was a gunman, did I know he was a gunman. Did . . .
Just a moment . . . Just a moment . . . Just a moment.' It is as if
Seumas were trapped in a circle of words. Clearly, wallowing in
generalisations, even accurate generalisations, leaves Seumas verbally and mentally unfit to deal with the raid. But he almost always
talks with little point, he cannot, in moments of crisis, get beyond his
habitual verbal distortion and come to terms with the specific matter
at hand. Worse, at these moments the verbal distortions intensify and
become an overt stutter: repetitious and unmeaning noise which has
ceased to even sound like real speech. Unable to improvise or
verbalise any solution himself, he compounds the chaos by allowing
Minnie to carry off the bombs.

Seumas is all talk until the raid; then ('Just a moment . . . Just a
moment'), language utterly fails him. His fate, like Gallogher's,
Owens' and Grigson's, is to be imprisoned in compulsive non-
communication. They all share the same basic problem with
language: they love empty, endless and ultimately destructive talk.

III

Donal's more skilled use of language ought to offer a positive
counterweight to the distortions of Gallogher, Owens, Grigson and
Seumas. Ostensibly, Donal is a craftsman in words, the poet in
residence. Both Acts open with examples of Donal's poetic skills. The
very first lines of the play are Donal's:

> Or when sweet Summer's ardent arms outspread,
> Entwined with flowers,
> Enfold us, like two lovers newly wed,
> Thro' ravish'd hours –
> Then sorrow, woe and pain lose all their powers,
> For each is dead, and life is only ours.

As poetry, these lines invite and justify Seumas's parody. They are
imitation Romantic and badly done at that. The rhyme of 'hours'
and 'ours' depends entirely on the eye. It is quite likely that the phrase
'only ours' will be heard as 'only hours', an unintended, if subcon-

sciously appropriate, word-play. Donal's lines at the beginning of Act
II are more competent than those in Act I, but they too are highly
imitative, showing the influence of Shelley's 'Epipsychidion', specifically the lines on 'the cold chaste moon, The Queen of Heaven's
bright isles' which Donal quotes just before he composes his own lines
on the moon. But for all Donal's growing poetic competence, his
juxtapositioning of Shelley's lines with his own can only call attention
to his amateurishness.

In the same vein, Donal's habit of alluding to major literary figures
– to Shakespeare and to Milton as well to Shelley – provides another
benchmark for judging Donal's poetic achievement. If Donal's poetry
appears flimsy and imitative in its own right, the literary companion-
ship of Shakespeare, Milton and Shelley can only diminish it further.
Now the last thing the world of *The Shadow of a Gunman* needs,
populated as it is by so many other windbags, is a second-rate,
second-hand versifier.

Donal's persistence in spite of his limited inspiration and Seumas's
acute criticism suggests that poetry serves very intense personal (and
non-poetic) needs for him. In fact, Donal's dedication to the Muse is
an attempt to escape from the chaos that surrounds him. Donal is in
terrified verbal flight from oppressive conditions. The operative word
is 'verbal' because Donal is physically inert. As the other characters
pass across the stage, Donal tends, in striking contrast, to remain
standing or sitting in place. Donal's poetry reflects the inertia of the
poet. It makes nothing happen because it, like Donal, evades reality.
Donal passively hides from life in Seumas's room; Donal's poetry
ignores the existence of Seumas's chaotic room by projecting a fantasy
world of perpetual summer.

And it is not merely the sordid tenement room from which Donal is
trying to escape. Through poetry, Donal hopes to retreat from the
totality of life. The last line of his verse in Act II revealingly states that
'all beautiful and happiest things are dead'. By itself, that line
suggests that Donal is at once horrified and fascinated by death. But
there is other, perhaps more convincing, evidence. As Donal is
finishing his rhyme in Act I, '*a woman's figure appears at the window and
taps loudly on one of the panes; at the same moment there is a loud knocking at the
door*'. The room is besieged by voices at windows and door trying to
awaken Seumas and simultaneously calling Davoren back from his
dream world where 'life is only ours', to the real world where 'life is
only hours'. Donal perceives these invitations to life as an irritation
and a threat. Such interruptions are sure signs to Donal that his
attempts to escape from life are doomed to fail and that he is caught in
the inevitable pattern of human decline. The unintentional Freudian

play on 'hours' captures Donal's flagging sense of life, his fear of growing old, and the degree to which his poetry, such as it is, is being made to pander to his middle-aged insecurities.

Donal's poetry certainly demonstrates a sensitivity to some of the possibilities of language. But insofar as his poetry expresses his fear of life and creates a fantasy world of 'summer' to redeem the impossible conditions of poverty and undeclared war, Donal's poetry does not really set him apart from the other rhetoricians. It is as empty as Gallogher's legal jargon, Owens' and Grigson's patriotism, and Seumas's stutter.

Moreover, Donal's use of poetic language distorts his use of everyday speech. Donal tries to strike the same high tone here that he attempts in poetry. By introducing literary allusions, balance, poetry and a highfalutin' word choice into ordinary discourse, Donal again tries to transform his sordid environment through words. Occasionally, Donal gets out a powerful sentence. For instance, when Seumas complains that nobody has bothered to wake him on time, Donal explodes: 'Why, man, they've been thundering at the door and hammering at the window for the past two hours, till the house shook to its very foundations, but you took less notice of the infernal din than I would take of the strumming of a grasshopper.' The grasshopper image, the internal rhythm and the logical relationship of the parts are all used to good effect. But Donal is also capable of the rhetorical pretensiousness of the following remark to Seumas and Mulligan, the landlord: 'For goodness' sake, bring the man in, and don't be discussing the situation like a pair of primitive troglodytes'. Here the image is 'literary' and weak.

Unfortunately, it is this weak literary style in Donal's speech that predominates. Speaking to Donal, Minnie praises Tommy Owens' melodeon playing. Donal cannot let things go at that. He comments that Tommy is 'a gifted son of Orpheus'. His success at communicating through that classical reference can be gauged by Minnie's response: 'You've said it, Mr Davoren: the son of poor oul' Battie Owens, a weeshy, dawny, bit of a man that was never sober an' was always talkin' politics.' Donal might just as well be talking to himself for all the communicating he has done. But Minnie's lack of comprehension perversely stimulates more verbal fireworks. Donal goes on to call weeds 'wild flowers', 'wild violets', '*Arum maculatum*', 'Wake Robin' and 'Celandines'. Minnie does not understand this gush any better than the reference to Orpheus. Clearly Donal's verbal affectations frustrate communication and isolate him in language. But like Gallogher, Grigson, Owens and Seumas, Donal enjoys misusing language for maximum display. No sooner has Donal

finished naming the weeds than he bursts into poetry in much the
same way that Tommy and Grigson burst into song.

DAVOREN (*he quotes*):

>   One day, when Morn's half-open'd eyes
>   Were bright with Spring sunshine –
>   My hand was clasp'd in yours, dear love,
>   And yours was clasp'd in mine –
>   We bow'd as worshippers before
>   The Golden Celandine.

MINNIE: Oh, aren't they lovely, an' isn't the poem lovely too! I wonder, now, who she
was.

DAVOREN (*puzzled*): She, who?

MINNIE: Why, the . . . (*roguishly*) Oh, be the way you don't know.

DAVOREN: Know? I'm sure I don't know.

MINNIE: It doesn't matter, anyhow – that's your own business; I suppose I don't know
her.

DAVOREN: Know her – know whom?

MINNIE (*shyly*): Her whose hand was clasped in yours, an' yours was clasped in hers.

DAVOREN: Oh, that – that was simply a poem I quoted about the Celandine, that might
apply to any girl – to you, for instance.

Donal's word games turn language into a vehicle for confusion, not a
method of communication.

Clearly, Donal's talk leaves something to be desired. Inasmuch as
Donal does nothing but talk and recite poetry, he lacks the habit of
acting decisively. As long as no action is called for, Donal's rhetorical
displays and romantic poetry seem harmless. But the Black and Tan
raid is the same moment of truth for Donal that it is for Grigson,
Owens and Seumas. Donal finds that he must act and cannot. His
verbal escapism isolates him from reality, renders him impotent and
forces Minnie to act for him. She takes the bag of bombs. Later, Donal
blames himself for Minnie's death, calling himself a 'poet and
poltroon'. But the relationship between Donal as poet and Donal as
poltroon is never as clear to Donal as it should be to the audience:
Donal is a poltroon because he is not the right kind of poet. Unlike his
oft-quoted model Shelley who related poetry to political action in his
life and in such works as *Prometheus Unbound* (a poem, ironically, never
far from Donal's lips), Donal remains a sterile and self-absorbed
manipulator of language.

It would thus be wrong to think that Donal's recognition of his
responsibility in Minnie's death changes him. In death, Minnie is still
grist for Donal's word-mill. The first news of Minnie's death forces
Donal to some measure of self-knowledge as he tells Seumas that the
two of them precipitated the tragic event by their inaction.

DAVOREN: Do you realise that she has been shot to save us?

SEUMAS: Is it my fault; am I to blame?

DAVOREN: It is your fault and mine, both; oh, we're a pair of dastardly cowards to have
let her do what she did.

But Donal's recognition of responsibility does not linger long. His
final words are a return to the *status quo ante*, a triumph of rhetoric over
reality. Minnie's memory and Donal's sense of complicity both fade
as Donal takes stage centre for a final thrust of words.

Ah me, alas! Pain, pain, pain, ever, for ever! It's terrible to think that little Minnie is
dead, but it's still more terrible to think that Davoren and Shields are alive! Oh, Donal
Davoren, shame is your portion now till the silver cord is loosened and the golden bowl
be broken. Oh, Davoren, Donal Davoren, poet and poltroon, poltroon and poet.

Not only are the phrases more measured and poetic here than they
were in the previous exchange with Seumas, but the pronouns of
Donal's previous speech have been translated into nouns. Rather
than Donal expressing himself, Donal the poet is watching Donal the
man expressing himself. And he pulls out all the stops. His favourite
quotation from Shelleys' *Prometheus Unbound*, 'Ah me, alas! Pain, pain,
pain, ever, for ever', is heightened by Biblical allusions to silver cords
and golden bowls. Minnie is mentioned only once at the beginning
which strengthens the feeling that Donal is now chief in Donal's mind.
As Donal's immediate response gives way to aesthetic distancing, as
ordinary discourse becomes highly allusive and alliterative, Donal
refashions Minnie's death into a lament for himself, 'Davoren, Donal
Davoren, poet and poltroon, poltroon and poet'. That this lament is a
more satisfying conclusion to Donal than his straightforward recognition of responsibility is understandable because once again the flood
of words dissipates any need for action.

It is surely ironic and sad that Donal, who has a talent for words,
who is sensitive to prose construction and who appreciates poetic
creation, succumbs to the verbal chaos. Yet neither Donal's poetry
nor his ordinary speech suffers a counterweight to the verbal
distortions of Gallogher, Grigson, Owens and Shields. Donal's
misuse of language may be more sophisticated than the others, but it
ultimately degenerates into the same empty rhetoric. Typical of all of
them is the pattern of words without deeds. They also share the
isolation, the inflation of ego, and the illusions which such a pattern
provokes and sustains. Finally and most importantly, the accumu-
lated weight of all their words and inaction contributed to Minnie's
death.

IV

If Donal, Seumas, Owens, Grigson and Gallogher live in a world of
words, Minnie and Maguire exist in the realm of action. Neither has
much to say. Unlike Donal and his group, Minnie's language is

consistently unaffected and plain. In her conversations with Donal,
the two are often at cross-purposes because Donal insists on 'literary'
words and Minnie cannot understand him. Minnie talks about
'weeds' whereas Donal talks about 'wild flowers'; Donal recites
poetry and Minnie gets the mistaken impression that he has another
girlfriend. When Minnie takes the bombs, she remains true to her
own voice and does so without song, dance or rhetorical show. Minnie
matter-of-factly states, 'I'll take them to my room; maybe they won't
search it, if they do aself, they won't harm a girl', and exits. Maguire,
like Minnie, hardly speaks at all. He flits across the stage, deposits the
bag, and flits off again to meet a bullet at Knocksedan.

That neither Maguire nor Minnie says much does not mean that
what they say or do is inadequate. Maguire's remark about catching
butterflies is a transparent lie, an intentional failure to communicate.
The bag of bombs he casually leaves behind makes the whole
tenement vulnerable during the Black and Tan raid and contributes
to Minnie's death. He never explains his patriotic motivation, so his
own death seems unnecessarily meaningless. In acting without
stating his true purposes, Maguire collaborates in the overall drift to
chaos and destruction as surely as the more talkative and less active
characters.

While Maguire is one of the play's prime movers, a major cause of
the closing plot complications, Minnie reacts. Her last words and
actions are the results of the endless babble, the verbal obstructionism
and the prior actions of others. Thus, when Minnie is arrested, she is
heard *'shouting bravely, but a little hysterically, "Up the Republic"* '. That
Minnie's commonsense approach to language should be channelled
into an empty slogan first spewed out by Tommy Owens in Act I, a
slogan, moreover, that Minnie gives no previous indication of
supporting, is as much a measure of how contagious the verbal
distortions of the others are as of her own fright.

Minnie's actions are no more satisfying than her slogans. Taking
the bombs is a selfless gesture, but it is also an impulsive and
irrational one. Her comment that 'they won't hurt a girl' fails to take
into account the callous nature of the political turmoil. The ruthless-
ness of both sides and the large role accident plays are facts that
Minnie ignores or never really appreciates. So the Black and Tans
arrest her, the IRA open fire at the Black and Tans, and in the
confusion a stray bullet from one side or the other kills Minnie. Her
seemingly decisive and heroic action in taking the bombs is, thus,
compromised by her inability to perceive the consequences of her
actions. Part of her apparent decisiveness is surely based on her lack
of political consciousness.

Yet accident and faulty analysis are only partial determinants of Minnie's fate. As important is the recognition that Minnie's death is the end product of a collective failure – Maguire's, Tommy's, Grigson's, Seumas's, Donal's and the socio-political fabric's – to establish the proper relationship between language, thought and action.

It seems fair to say that, in *The Shadow of a Gunman*, acts divorced from rational and articulate thought are no more meaningful than words without deeds. Neither Minnie nor Maguire sets things right by his/her actions. In fact, Maguire's actions lead to his own and Minnie's deaths. Maguire's wilful silence and Minnie's inarticulate action are further illustrations of the overall language problem in *The Gunman* and just as potent forces for creating chaos as the rhetorical strategies of Grigson, Gallogher, Seumas, Owens and Donal.

V

Thus *The Gunman* offers no solutions to the language problems it dramatises in such careful detail. All the characters have difficulties with language. Their distortions vary greatly and some of their verbal pyrotechnics are hilarious. But a closer analysis proves them all dangerous. The breakdown in communication has dire results: it eventuates in Minnie's death. As one of the most vital characters in the play, her death seems tragically unnecessary. To the degree that the verbal perversions contribute to Minnie's death, they may be viewed as instruments of murder. It is not accidental that Owens's explosive rhetoric and Seumas's stutter sound like guns going off. Yet, it would be unfair to blame the characters entirely for their verbal distortions without noticing that the characters in *The Shadow of a Gunman* are terrified as well as terrifying. They may perpetuate chaos, but they rarely initiate it. They exist in a hostile and chaotic world not of their own making and their verbal manoeuvres are, in one sense, only an unsatisfactory adaptation to that world.

Source: article in the *Irish University Review*, VIII (1978), pp. 23–37.

NOTES

[Reorganised and renumbered from the original – Ed.]

1. Critical opinion is divided on this point. David Krause – in *Sean O'Casey: The Man and His Work* (London and New York, 1960) – treats *The Gunman* as the first example of O'Casey's tragi-comic art. His approach balances the negative aspects of life in the play with the decency of Mrs Henderson and the heroism and sacrifice of Minnie Powell.

Herbert Goldstone – in *In Search of Community: The Achievement of Sean O'Casey* (Cork, 1972) – views the play as a study in the failure of responsibility and commitment. He is thus far less charitable to Minnie Powell than was Krause. These two contrasting views establish the poles within which other critics (for example, Saros Cowasjee) fall. I view the play more negatively than Goldstone does, but I do not pursue the point directly in this paper.

2. Raymond Williams – in *Drama from Ibsen to Eliot* (London, 1952) – has a good deal of fun at the expense of the impressionistic critics who talk vaguely about O'Casey's language. He claims (correctly, I believe) that O'Casey's language is 'widely praised in terms that certainly require scrutiny. The usual adjective is "colourful", and it is not often that a reviewer fails to make a subsequent reference to "Elizabethan richness" ' (p. 169). Williams surely has in mind comments like the following by J. C. Trewin, *The English Theatre* (London, 1948): 'Today we listen to O'Casey as we listen to Synge. Either he speaks as they spoke in the lyric gold of the Elizabethan daybreak, or his words hang like banners on the outward walls. He is not heard as often as we wish, but when he does open his mouth, no man is less a niggard of his speech; words rush from him in a race of metaphor, a tumbling surge' (p. 67).

3. When Raymond Williams scrutinised O'Casey's dramatic language (op. cit., pp. 169–75), he felt the alliteration, the repetitions and the allusions were verbal pyrotechnics without dramatic relevance. Ronald Ayling countered Williams's argument in his 'Introduction' to the volume on *Sean O'Casey* he edited for the 'Modern Judgements' series (London, 1969). Using specific examples like 'Kathleen ni Houlihan, your way's a thorny way' (Seumas's lament in *The Gunman*), Ayling shows how such phrases simultaneously characterise the speakers and illustrate broader issues in the plays. Interestingly, in Raymond Williams's most recent version of his drama survey – *Drama from Ibsen to Brecht* (London, 1968) – published shortly before Ayling's volume, he has reconsidered his position on O'Casey's language. He comments penetratingly that O'Casey's dramatic language contrasts 'the language of men in intense experience and the inflated, engaging language of men avoiding experience' (p. 150). Williams then goes on to quote several of O'Casey's best known alliterative lines and says that they 'have been repeatedly quoted as an "Elizabethan" richness; but they are, in their origin and development, and where successful in their direct dramatic use, the consistent evidence of poverty, of a starved, showing-off imagination' (p. 150). Ayling's and Williams's seminal remarks are the sum total of critical treatment of O'Casey's dramatic language to date. To my knowledge there are no extended studies of any of O'Casey's plays from the point of view of language.

PART THREE

Juno and the Paycock

Juno and the Paycock

Première: 3 March 1924, Abbey Theatre, Dublin.

First London production: 16 November 1925, Royalty Theatre.

First New York production: 15 March 1926, Mayfair Theatre.

A film version, directed by Alfred Hitchcock and starring Sara Allgood, was released by British International Pictures early in 1930 after its first screening in London on 30 December 1929.

1. COMMENT AND REVIEWS

Joseph Holloway   (1924)

Monday, March 3, 1924: . . . 'It is powerful and gripping and all that, but too damned gruesome; it gets you, but it is not pleasant', is the way Dan Maher summed up *Juno and the Paycock*, O'Casey's new play at the Abbey. . . . The last act is intensely tragic and heart-rendingly real to those who passed through the terrible period of 1922. . . . The tremendous tragedy of Act III swept all before it, and made the doings on the stage real and thrilling in their intensity. The acting all round was of the highest quality, not one in the long cast being misplaced or for a moment out of the picture. Fitzgerald and McCormick as 'Captain Jack Boyle' and his bar-room pal 'Joxer Daly', an old Forester, make a splendid pair of workers who never work. Sara Allgood as 'Juno Boyle', with all the worries of trying to keep everything together, was excellent, and in Act III she had great moments of heart-rending sorrow. Arthur Shields, as the haunted, maimed boy 'Johnny', got the right note of dread into his study from the very first, and Eileen Crowe as 'Mary' presented every side of the character cleverly and realistically, and her singing of the duet, 'Home to our Mountains', with her mother at the hooley was deliciously droll. Maureen Delany, as the talkative 'Mrs Maisie Madigan', was most amusing, and Christine Hayden, as the sorrowing mother 'Mrs Tancred', sorrowed for her son most touchingly. . . .

In Act III some in the pit were inclined at first to laugh at the tragedy that had entered into the 'Boyle' family, but they soon lost their mirth and were gripped by the awful actuality of the incidents enacted so realistically and unassumingly before them. As I left the theatre, cries of 'Author, Author!' were filling the air, and I suppose O'Casey had to bow his acknowledgment. He sat with a friend in the second row of the stalls with his cap on all the while, I noticed. He is a strange, odd fish, but a genius in his way. . . .

Thursday, August 14, 1924: . . . I witnessed a strange incident last night in seeing W. B. Yeats and Mrs Yeats being crowded out of the Abbey, and having to seek the pictures to allay their disappointment. O'Casey's play, *The Shadow of a Gunman*, had been staged for three nights with the usual result – that crowds had to be turned away each performance. This and his other play, *Juno and the Paycock*, have wonderful drawing power. The same people want to see them over and over again. . . . And the author stood chatting to me in the vestibule the other night as the audience came thronging in, proud of the fact, but in no way swell-headed, his cloth cap cocked over his left eye, as his right looked short-sightedly at the audience's eager rush. Certainly he has written the two most popular plays ever seen at the Abbey, and they both are backgrounded by the terrible times we have just passed through, but his characters are so true to life and humorous that all swallow the bitter pill of fact that underlies both pieces. . . .

SOURCE: extracts from *Joseph Holloway's Abbey Theatre*, edited by Robert Hogan and Michael J. O'Neill (Carbondale, Ill., 1967), pp. 226, 235–6.

Lady Gregory   (1924)

March 8, 1924: In the evening to the Abbey with W. B. Yeats, *Juno and the Paycock* – a long queue at the door, the theatre crowded, many turned away, so it will be run on next week. A wonderful and terrible play of futility, of irony, humour, tragedy. When I went round to the Green-room I saw Casey and had a little talk with him. He is very happy.

I asked him to come to tea after the next day, the matinée, as I had brought up a barmbrack for the players, but he said, 'No. I can't come. I'll be at work till the afternoon and I'm working with cement, and that takes such a long time to get off.'

'But after that?'

'Then I have to cook my dinner. I have but one room and cook for myself since my mother died.'

He is, of course, happy at the great success of his play, and I said, 'You must feel now that we were right in not putting on that first one you sent in – *The Crimson and the Tri-colour*.[1] I was inclined to put it on because some of it was so good and I thought you might learn by seeing it on the stage, though some was very poor, but Mr Yeats was firm.'

He said, 'You were right not to put it on. I can't read it myself now. But I will tell you that it was a bitter disappointment for I had not only thought at the time it was the best thing I had written but I thought that no one in the world had ever written anything so fine.'

Then he said, 'You had it typed for me, and I don't know how you could have read it as I sent it in with the bad writing and the poor paper. But at that time it was hard for me to afford even the paper it was written on.'

And he said, 'I owe a great deal to you and Mr Yeats and Mr Robinson, but to you above all. You gave me encouragement. And it was you who said to me upstairs in the office – I could show you the very spot where you stood – "Mr Casey, your gift is characterisation". And so I threw over my theories and worked at characters and this is the result.'

Yeats hadn't seen the play before, and thought it very fine, reminding him of Tolstoi. He said when he talked of the imperfect first play, 'Casey was bad in writing of the vices of the rich which he knows nothing about, but he thoroughly understands the vices of the poor'. But that full house, the packed pit and gallery, the fine play, the call of the Mother for the putting away of hatred, made me say to Yeats, 'This is one of the evenings at the Abbey that makes me glad to have been born'.

March 9, 1924: I took cakes to the Abbey, and after the performance gave tea in the Green-room. . . .

I came back there for the evening performance – such a queue, and so many had to be turned away, but we are running on next week and I hope they will come then. Casey was with me, watching them. . . . Then Jack Yeats [the painter, brother of the poet] and his wife came, could get no seat; so we went round to the stage door and when the orchestra stopped we went down and took their chairs. When the mother whose son had been killed, 'Leader of an ambush where my neighbour's Free State soldier son was killed', cried out, 'Mother of Jesus, put away from us this murderous hatred and give us thine own eternal love', I whispered to Casey, 'That is the prayer we must all use, it is the only thing that will save us, the teaching of Christ'. He said 'Of humanity'. But what would that be without the divine atom?

SOURCE: extracts from *Lady Gregory's Journals, 1916–1930*, edited by Lennox Robinson (London, 1946), pp. 74–6.

NOTE

1. [Ed.] *The Crimson in the Tri-colour* was the third, not the first, play submitted to the Abbey Theatre by O'Casey.

Sean O'Casey

I A Retrospect   (1953)

Juno and the Paycock was written many years ago, when strife ruled Ireland and men and women took a sadistic pleasure out of injury to, and the death of, others. Now, after so many years it tires the mind to think of all its stupidity; and although we haven't yet buried the gun, the conscience of man is more flexible towards stretching into a finer sense of brotherhood and co-operation.

All that happened in the play, or almost all, happened in the house where I once lived; a tenement house still standing. Even the young man who was 'found dead on a lonely road in Finglass' lived there and was a friend of mine – I have his photograph here with me now. A terrible thing when romantic youth start shooting each other, all mad for a curious abstract idea of their native land.

I hope the Cockermouth Players may enjoy themselves doing it, and I am fond enough of the play to hope that they may do it well. My best wishes to them.

SOURCE: Programme Note for the Cockermouth Players (Cumberland) production which opened on 3 October 1953.

II On Juno   (1955)

. . . Sorry you didn't like poor Juno. Forgive her for nagging. She had a hard time of it, &, needing help, she got none. It is very hard to be brave (as she was) in the stress of poverty. Hard, after a day's work, to come home & start on regulating & replenishing the home. I know what this is like, having worked for years after my mother's death, then having to come home, had to set about cleaning up, lighting a fire, cooking the meal, before I could say my work was done. To give a lasting sunny disposition in poverty is not possible; the whole damned, rotten system must go, before the good word always comes to the tongue, & the smile shines forth from the eye. The play doesn't 'end on a note of despair'. Read Juno's last fine words to Mary as she & her daughter go forth to begin again. As for the other two – Joxer and Capt. – they are past praying for. 'Ephraim is joined to idols: leave idols alone.' . . .

SOURCE: extract from letter to Mrs Helen Kiok of New York (3 Aug. 1955); reproduced in *Sean O'Casey Review*, III (1976), p. 50.

W. J. Lawrence   (1924)

I doff my hat to Mr Sean O'Casey. He is the realisation of one of my longest-cherished hopes. For many years, practically ever since the opening of the Abbey, I have scanned the horizon anxiously for the looming of that new native dramatist whose powers should enable him to inflame the popular imagination. Synge, for all his transcendency, could not accomplish it: there was something in his chill austerity that repelled the man in the street. All sorts and conditions of writers have since been called to the task, but Mr O'Casey alone has been chosen. His name has only been a few months before the public, and already it is one to conjure with. The spectacle of the Abbey crammed to the doors on the first week in Lent is eloquent of the fascinations of his curiously-composite dramaturgy. He has been the means of showing us (unless, indeed, his unparalleled success is the mere swing of the pendulum) that what the great public hungers after is not poetic or historical drama, not even peasant drama, but the drama of palpitating city life. Democracy has at last become articulate on both sides of the curtain.

Years ago, when the Abbey was in its crudely experimental stage, Senator Yeats, in one of those delightful little impromptus with which he used to favour us between the acts, expressed the opinion that the prevailing dramatic moulds had become outworn, and that we in Ireland would have to break them and fashion moulds nearer to the heart's desire. If he is as strong a believer now as he was then in the necessity to go back to first principles, he, as chief director of the Abbey, should be proud of the vogue of Mr O'Casey's plays. For Mr O'Casey is at once iconoclast and neo-Elizabethan. One cannot place his plays in any recognised category. Nothing in Polonius's breathless, jaw-breaking list applies; and he flouts all the precepts of Aristotle. He lures us into the theatre under the pretext of affording us hearty laughter, which, sooth to say, he most profusely provokes, and he sends us away with tears in our eyes and with the impression of direst tragedy lying heavy on our hearts. None but a neo-Elizabethan could accomplish this, since the secret of juxtaposing and harmonising the comic with the tragic, and thereby throwing the elements of terror and pathos into greater relief, has been lost to the English-speaking stage for over a couple of centuries. Moreover, one-half of the fascination of Mr O'Casey's work lies in its red-hot throbbing contemporaneity, and that too was a prime trait of Elizabethan drama. There are moments in his plays, such as the search of the Black-and-Tans in *The Shadow of a Gunman*, and the haling to death of the crippled informer, Johnny Boyle, in *Juno and the Paycock*, so vivid in the light of recent experience that they transcend all mere theatricality and thrill one to the marrow like matters of personal suffering.

Mr O'Casey will undoubtedly go far, if he can only restrain his keen sense of the theatre and trust more fully to his powers of observation. At present he is apt to play a trifle too much to his audience. Wit he has in abundance, but occasionally his snappy dialogue degenerates into a sort of sublimated music-hall cross-talk. Truth to life is sacrificed for the sake of a cheap laugh. This is much to be deprecated, seeing that he has a Dickens-like eye for quaint characterisation, and has the capacity to make us see what he himself has so well observed. It is probably because of this excessive playing to the likings of his audience that we cannot wholly believe in the existence of his 'Captain' Jack Boyle in his last new play, despite the delights of his perennial Dogberryisms, as delivered with telling effect by Mr Barry Fitzgerald. Though a lineal descendant of old Eccles in *Caste*, this hypocritical shirker is none the less a true type, and, if the machinery now and again creaks, it is not because of any falsity in the fundamental concept of the character, but in its extrinsicalities. With an exponent less dowered with the *ars celare artem* than Mr Fitzgerald, the effects would have been more obvious, but Mr Fitzgerald succeeded in infusing so much vitality into the heartless old wastrel as to make his perennial 'nice derangement of epitaphs' plausible. But, for the matter of that, the acting in *Juno and the Paycock* was of a high, all-round standard of excellence. This may be largely attributed to the fact that since Mr Michael J. Dolan's accession to managerial control there has been none of those flagrant examples of miscasting which formerly imperilled the success of many a new play. As for the rest, Miss Allgood rose to such fine heights of pathos in the harrowing last act that one would fain ask that the play should end with her agonised prayer to the Virgin. This is the natural climax, a climax of rich nobility, leaving the echo in our hearts of the wish for peace on earth and good-will towards men. The drunken epilogue which follows is artistically indefensible, and cannot be characterised otherwise than a painful mistake.[1] In a word, Mr Sean O'Casey has something yet to learn; but, despite its blemishes, *Juno and the Paycock*, running as it does over the entire gamut of the emotions, is distinctly a play to be seen.

SOURCE: article in the *Irish Statesman*, II (15 March 1924), p. 216.

NOTE

1. [Ed.] A number of Dublin citizens agreed with W. J. Lawrence on the aesthetic impropriety of the play's drunken coda. James Agate, reviewing the London première one year later, took a diametrically opposed stand: '*Juno and the Paycock* is as much a tragedy as *Macbeth*, but it is a tragedy taking place in the porter's family. Mr O'Casey's extraordinary knowledge of English taste – that he wrote his play for the Abbey Theatre, Dublin, is not going to be allowed to disturb my argument – is shown by the fact that the tragic element in it occupies at the most some twenty minutes, and that for the remaining two hours and a half the piece is given up to gorgeous and incredible fooling. . . . There are some tremendous moments in this piece, and the ironic close – in which the drunken porter returns to his lodging unconscious of his son's death, daughter's flight to river or streets, and wife's desertion – is the work of a master' (*Sunday Times*, 22 Nov. 1925). The playwright's own view on the matter surfaced in a letter to the actor Cyril Cusack (dated 25 May 1956), commenting on the then recently issued phonograph recording of *Juno*: 'Now I know why I got no record . . . They didn't wish me to realise that the epilogue had been cut out. I was *not* informed of the cut, and it never crossed my mind that such a god-damned stupid thing could be done to spoil a play. . . . The cut from *Juno* is in my opinion the comic highlight (and tragic highlight too) of the play.'

2. CRITICAL STUDIES

Laurence Olivier   Meditations on *Juno and the*
Paycock (1966)

I saw *Juno and the Paycock* when I was just about eighteen, I should
think, at the old Royalty Theatre in Dean Street, which was managed
at that time by the famous actor, Dennis Eadie. I came to play there
myself two or three years later and found all the dressing-rooms to be
clustered underneath the stage. There was one important-looking one
in the middle of the cluster which was unlocked to nobody but Mr
Eadie himself. This might seem like *folie de grandeur* as well as a wicked
waste of space these days, but to the convinced Conservative that I
then was it was all very splendid, right and proper. I would wander
into the dressing-rooms of my colleagues from time to time wondering
how they had been inhabited when 'They' were playing there. 'They'
were my worshipped heroes, Arthur Sinclair (Boyle), Sara Allgood
(Juno), her sister Maire O'Neill – a famous red-haired beauty a few
years previously, but now a raspy-voiced, arms-akimboed Maisie
Madigan – Sydney Morgan (Joxer), Kathleen O'Regan (Mary), and
our present very welcome 'verisimilitude verifier' Harry Hutchinson
(Johnny).[1]

The sad news of Sean O'Casey's death brought an immediate
prompting from our Literary Department to do one of his plays at the
National and *The Silver Tassie* was strongly favoured. I had forgotten it
rather, as we who read an awful lot of plays are prone to do, and read
it again. I liked it well enough but my memory of *Juno* was so strong
that I felt convinced it must be the best of the plays and if we were
going to offer a memorial occasion to O'Casey, nothing but the best
was good enough for him. I also recognised, swiftly and delightedly,
that we had within the company a group of players who in my belief
should be as well cast as any in this generation.

In a repertory theatre where storage space is strictly limited you
can't always do a thing when you think you will and in consequence
this memorial tribute to our great and beloved dramatist is a little late
in the day.

The die having been cast and the lot of producing having fallen
upon me, I realised a little to my dismay as I settled down to read it
that I was actually *reading* it for the first time in my life. The

extraordinarily strong impression that the play had made upon me, the vivid, crystal-clear memories of many of the lines, inflexions, situations, the business and the atmosphere had lived with me for more than forty years, all born from the singular experience of 'assisting' – as the French quaintly put it – at one performance in 1925. In some cases the actors' business which I so vividly remembered was at variance with that described in the text. When I nudged Harry Hutchinson on such things he would think for a bit and then exclaim that I was quite right. Let me say that I am by no means always infallible on such things. I have often treasured for years devoted memories of the way some actor did something or other in a film and years later on reviewing the film have found that it was no such matter; it is simply that the impression made upon me at this one matinée performance so long ago was phenomenally lasting and unwontedly correct.

It is of course hard to be detached about a work for which one feels such very strong devotion, but detachment is one of the things required of a producer and I have tried to be strong with myself.

Realistic would not be quite the right word to describe this piece, nor naturalistic; I think 'life-like' would be nearer the mark. Though there is fantasy in the characters I feel O'Casey wished the play itself to be kept out of that realm. Poetic, of course, it is, but in its time it was felt to be very actual, as naturalistic as you could very well go in the early twenties, with 'good' lines and a generous portion of rhetoric without which no decent author would stretch out his hand towards his pen. It is, in fact, closer to Osborne than to Chekhov. There is no playing about with it, it is all there and it is as clear as daylight what he wants done with it. What is it makes the characters so immediately recognisable and familiar and at the same time so freshly minted, I wonder? The play deals in eternals and there isn't a character who hasn't made a turning-point mistake in his life (though I suppose the worst that poor Jerry has done is to fall in love with Mary).[2]

I would say the first act is about as tight a job as can be read; the second and third acts do loosen up a bit, once or twice a little dangerously, and some exits and entrances are a little rough-shod, making it hard to avoid the suspicion that people who for the action's sake must avoid each other might well have met on the staircase or in the street.

I have taken two small liberties in the staging. Owing to the forty-foot downstage width at the Old Vic the 'tenement room' required by O'Casey presents a bit of a problem. Carmen Dillon and I have therefore lifted from *The Plough and the Stars* the 'front and back drawing-rooms in a fine old Georgian house struggling for its life against the assaults of time and the more savage assaults of the tenants'. I think that perhaps the tempo of the early twenties would probably be a little slow for our pulses these days; also the curtain which is required to fall in the third act to denote the passage of time (and incidentally to clear quite a bit of furniture) is hardly tolerable to us in the sixties and so with only a modicum of skirmishing, I trust I have managed to fix that all right; but the titanic metal of the piece is kept in constant temper by the astonishing volatility of its emotional variations.

Its switchback ride between hilarity and extreme pathos puts me in mind of a definition by Miss Rose Brennan, the Irish singer, of an Irish 'hooley' ('If you're Irish, come into the parlour' is the record O'Casey requires Boyle to put on, so it's all splendidly relevant):

In the middle of all the fun somebody will get up and sing a nostalgic song and before you can say Ballaghaderreen we're all crying in our beer. The whole essence of a hooley is this sudden switch from hilarity to sadness and the equally sudden explosion back to noise, song and laughter.

When I was in Ireland one time I learnt that the homespun or bucolic play was known as a 'pratie' (potato). I think just possibly O'Casey might have described *Juno and the Paycock* as a 'hooley'.

SOURCE: Lord Olivier's Programme Note for the National Theatre production at the Old Vic theatre, April 1966.

NOTES

1. [Ed.] Harry Hutchinson worked with Lord (then Sir Lawrence) Olivier as an assistant to the director for this production of *Juno*.
2. [Ed.] For a less favourable interpretation of Jerry Devine, see the exchange between Paul Banks and Sean O'Casey in the *New English Review* (Sept.–Oct. 1933).

Herbert Goldstone   'The Need for Community'
(1972)

We can all too easily both underrate and overrate *Juno and the Paycock*, the brilliantly amusing but sometimes heart-rending portrayal of the disintegration of a Dublin tenement family, the Boyles. We can underrate the play if we merely think of it as a lively, free-wheeling comedy that suddenly takes a tragic turn at the end. While in some respects the tragedy is forced and sudden, the comedy remains an integral part of O'Casey's vision in which folly, selfishness and moral chaos have grim, tragic consequences. On the other hand, we overrate the play if we assert that its affirmation of responsibility and elemental family love, embodied in Mrs Boyle (Juno), is as sustained or powerful as the irresponsibility and selfishness embodied in Boyle himself (the Paycock). In between these two extremes of judgment, we can still appreciate *Juno* as one of O'Casey's best plays, if only for Boyle himself, one of the greatest comic creations in modern drama and the supreme embodiment of the forces of egotism so important in the play.

Like *The Shadow of a Gunman*, *Juno* also takes place against a war background in which terror and ambush are all too common. This time, however, instead of fighting a common enemy, the English, Irishmen are fighting each other in a civil war. Nor would the civil war seem to make sense because it broke out right after the Irish had signed a peace treaty with England that gave them dominion status and considerable self-determination. But since the treaty did require an oath of allegiance to the British crown, though nominal, and it did not apply to the six counties of Northern Ireland, it did not embody the objectives to which the nationalists had pledged themselves, an Irish Republic and a Republic of all of Ireland. In addition, as historians point out,[1] there were other, more complex reasons having to do, among other things, with the conduct of the negotiations, and poor communication between the Irish delegates in London and their government in Dublin. Whatever the case, a sizable number of nationalists, led by De Valera and much of the Irish Republican Army, felt impelled to oppose the treaty and to refuse to take the required oath of allegiance to King George v. Actually, the reasons are less important than the climate of opinion created by the causes and course of the war.

For the average person and indeed many Irish leaders the causes were vague, since they were complex and ambiguous, despite much debate in the Dáil Eireann (the Irish parliament). In fact, the average person couldn't believe there were any good reasons to explain the tragedy. After all, the very leaders supporting the treaty (who constituted the Irish Free State), insisted that the treaty really did embody, potentially, the Republican ideals to which both sides earlier had pledged themselves. Such an ambiguous situation in which people could either affirm or deny the reality of the war strengthened the Republicans in their conviction that if only the people knew the facts, they would support them. Therefore, the Republicans, though

losing, also felt impelled to pursue their cause. Any deviations from
their camp would have been considered treasonous.

If the causes were ambiguous, the nature and course of the war
were not. It was brutally clear: there were raids and reprisals, similar
to the Black and Tan terror, but probably much more destructive.
Dorothy MacArdle[2] estimates that at one time there were 15,000
political persons in Free State jails; how many under Republican
confinement she does not say. This is not to mention the executions,
injuries and deaths by ambush, on both sides. O'Casey in volume IV
of his autobiography describes one such horrifying incident, which
makes anything in *Juno* tame by comparison. This incident involves a
young Republican bomb thrower who, after a long, hectic chase, is
cornered by three Free Staters led by a Colonel who as a sergeant had
been one of the Republican's buddies in fighting the Black and Tans.
To the very end, the bomb thrower really can't believe what is going
to happen to him:

– Jesus! whimpered the half-dead lad, you wouldn't shoot an old comrade, Mick!
  The Colonel's arm holding the gun shot forward suddenly, the muzzle of the gun,
tilted slightly upwards, splitting the lad's lips and crashing through his chattering
teeth.
– Be Jesus! We would, he said, and then he pulled the trigger.[3]

A war which was so poorly understood and yet so violent, so secret
and yet so open since people in the same building could be killing each
other, could produce national schizophrenia. For one had to be
prepared to live simultaneously in radically different worlds, each of
which seemed both real and unreal.

Besides the similar background of terror, *Juno* also has a plot
structure that depends upon a 'gimmick' and sudden changes of
fortune. This 'gimmick' is an unexpected legacy that dramatically
changes the lives of the Boyles, who have been existing in rancour and
squalor. Captain Boyle, or the Paycock, is a lazy, irresponsible
boaster, even more ingenious in his defences against reality than
Seumas Shields. Mrs Boyle, or Juno, is a shrewd, realistic and
compassionate woman. But she too easily equates her realism with
economic security and lets middle-class, or lace-curtain, gentility
dominate her. Mary, the daughter, is an intelligent, idealistic girl
who, like Minnie, envisions a nobler life than that of the slums. Her
problem is that she likewise identifies this life with middle-class
gentility, although for different reasons than her mother. As for
Johnny, her brother, he is a disillusioned Irish Republican Army
veteran who has informed on one of his comrades. . . . Carried away
by their expectations, the Boyles plunge into debt and put on absurd,
middle-class airs. When it turns out that the law clerk (Mary's fiancé)

who drew up the will made it too ambiguous, the roof falls in on the Boyles. Mary is deserted by her fiancé after she has become pregnant; Juno, together with Mary, walks out on Boyle because he has known for some time that the inheritance was out of the question. Boyle, like Seumas, stubbornly refuses to accept any responsibility for what has happened and retreats into a drunken stupor; and Johnny is killed by his Republican comrades in reprisal.

While Johnny's death certainly has no direct connection with the inheritance fiasco, his disillusionment and betrayal do. Although Johnny does not make his motives too clear, apparently as a mere boy he joined the Irish Republican Army (or a youth organisation with similar purposes) in 1916 because of confused motives. He believed in the cause, though how deeply or knowingly is difficult to tell, and he apparently had the support of his parents and neighbours. Despite the fact that he was wounded in the hip and lost his arm, he remained loyal to the cause for several years. As he remarks to his mother, 'a principle is a principle'. At the time the play begins, however, he seems to have reached the breaking point because, like all the other characters, he found himself undermined by an insidious, corrosive force. This force, to use Boyle's great malapropism, is a 'state o' chassis' or moral chaos, brought on by successive national crises and the stifling, divisive environment. The many conflicting loyalties undermined by the years of fighting, the failure of the average person to understand the issues of the civil war, and the enervating effects of the prejudice and poverty in the environment have demoralised the characters. Consequently, they desperately need something that will provide some structure to their lives. For them conformist pressures or appearances such as material status seem to be the answer. Of course they aren't, since they are just a projection of the most elemental selfish needs. As a result, people have become even more confused, self-centred, and irresponsible than before, though this may not be apparent to them.

Or another way to describe what has happened is to say that there is the appearance of community rather than the substance, and that the need even for appearance is important; but that the consequences for settling for appearance and middle-class materialism are disastrous, at least for the Boyles. When we further remember that O'Casey (as O'Faolain pointed out), associates these particular values with nationalism, we can better understand why the play has such serious consequences.

While the 'state o' chassis' affected every one – and the variety of ways is what is interesting in the play – it affected Johnny Boyle the most. He is traumatised, fearful, reduced to a shell of a person.

Although O'Casey gives us very little to go on, I think we can infer
that Johnny simply couldn't sustain his Republican convictions. This
would have been difficult for anyone, but was accentuated for him
because his neighbours and parents, whose support he needed, came
to regard the Republicans as 'Diehards'. (This apparently was the
state of affairs just before the play opens.) As a result, Johnny had
nothing to believe in and, in bitterness and desperation, began to hate
those forces that made him what he was, his family and the Irish
Republican Army. He fights bitterly with his father who epitomises
the worst in his family and informs on one of his comrades, his
neighbour, Robbie Tancred. Having betrayed Tancred, Johnny
becomes even more self-centred because now he lives in utter fear of
his life. Except for arguing with Boyle, he has no defences, so that he is
reduced to letting his mother treat him like a sick child.

Although Johnny does not appear in very many scenes, he shows us
to what desperate lengths people can go when at best they have only
basic selfish feelings to sustain them, and at worst, they begin to
destroy even these. The fact that Johnny does embody so clearly the
confusion and narrow self-interest with which the play concerns itself
may explain why O'Casey, during rehearsals, used to refer to *Juno* as
the play about Johnny Boyle.[4]

Mary Boyle's problem is one of shallowness in belief. It is true that
Mary can envisage a better life than that of the tenements and she is
determined to try to attain this in some way. Active in her union, she
supports her fellow workers when they go out on strike, even though
her family objects and she jeopardises her own job. Through Bentham,
she hopes to create a more interesting and dignified life than that of
her family or neighbours, which she scorns as materialistic. She
simply doesn't see that she also accepts appearances as an end-all,
except that for her they exist on a higher social plane. Besides being
victimised by her environment, Mary romanticises or idealises her
own self interest and vanity. Ironically, because Mary is finer grained
than most of the others in her environment, she indulges herself more
subtly.

Common sense realism may have its virtues, but *Juno* reveals that
it may also be foolish and destructive. Basically generous and
compassionate, Juno has worn herself out assuming the major family
responsibilities which Boyle has simply ignored. How much waste
this involves is clear from one of the stage directions which
emphasises that under other circumstances she could have been
talented and still good looking. Although she has been heroic, she has
also been somewhat foolish. Not only has she let Boyle take advantage
of her by being so shiftless, but she may even prefer such a situation.

In this way she can exult her importance by exposing Boyle for being so lazy and tricky. But even more important evidence of her foolishness is that, like Mother Courage, Juno simply doesn't realise that she has let the very conditions of life which have victimised her become her ultimate standard of value. Consequently, once Boyle seems to be getting the inheritance, Juno encourages him to be a proper middle-class husband to whom appearance and material security mean everything, and she disclaims any responsibility for what he does.

For Boyle such a disclaimer does not matter. But by accepting such ultimate values, Juno does hurt Johnny. Under the influence of the first, she may have encouraged Johnny to enlist without realising how shallow such motivation actually was. Then, when the going was rough, she ridiculed Johnny for being an impractical diehard, unaware that this could only make his plight all the worse. Nor does she see that both her approval and disapproval of Johnny's patriotism represent two sides of the same coin. For all her sympathy, Juno remains powerless to help Johnny because she can't understand what happened to him.

If Juno bears considerable responsibility for what occurs, Boyle still bears the most precisely because he is so callous and self-centred. Throughout the play he thinks only of himself, even if it is just to cheat his parasitic buddy, Joxer Daly, out of breakfast sausage or to fancy himself a successful business man. As his nickname 'Paycock' suggests, he struts around, enthralled with himself, ever on the alert to wheedle his way out of work and to boast about his imagined exploits. Certainly Boyle's behaviour largely results from his character; how could he be otherwise? Nevertheless, the squalid tenement and the chaos create a strong temptation to escape, if possible. And Boyle has a great talent for such escape. He can shamelessly live off Juno when this is possible; he can always enjoy himself because he has vitality and zest for life; and, if he has to – or chooses to – he can act a role, instinctively knowing how far he can go without being hurt. All Boyle has to do is to know the outward signs and, since he is quick-witted, he can pick these up readily.

I don't mean simply that Boyle likes to act out parts; rather he knows how, chameleon-like, to find an attitude or pose that works for him at a certain moment. At one time, when he wants to condemn the clergy, he affects the Republican attitude that it was the clergy who did Parnell in; another time, when he wants to be properly middle class, he praises the clergy as the backbone of Ireland. Boyle's technique is not unlike that of 'double think' in Orwell's *1984*, except that it is more intuitive and spontaneous.

Boyle, nevertheless, is a more destructive and vulnerable figure than I have indicated. He is more destructive because he has completely failed Johnny as a father. It is not what Boyle has overtly done, but simply the fact that he obviously never cared for his family. Since Boyle was so unwilling to recognise anyone else's identity, it would be difficult for Johnny to have any self or identity of his own. Johnny could also have been so ashamed of his father that he felt driven to believe in something. He could not, however, sustain his belief, since he had no respect for authority figures who would embody the values underlying such belief. From the bitter arguments between Boyle and Johnny, particularly in Act I, it is obvious how little Johnny respects his father – and with good reason.

A comment that crystallises many of the play's implications is one Mary Boyle makes to Jerry, her former boy-friend, when he comes to console her after Bentham has deserted her and the inheritance has failed. Jerry, an earnest, ambitious young labour leader, passionately asserts that he unconditionally forgives Mary and still wants her. But when Mary remains sceptical and hints about her pregnancy, Jerry suddenly becomes unctuous and moralistic. In a flash Mary sees through him. 'Your humanity [Jerry's], is just as narrow as the humanity of the others.' She is not saying that people are inhuman, but simply how callous, opportunistic, and self-centred they have all become.

In emphasising human narrowness as a major theme, O'Casey finds that the family provides a most effective focal point. It can represent the most concrete embodiment of what full humanity can mean; conversely, the failure of humanity becomes most evident within the family situation. In Act I the Boyles exist as a family in name only as they all go their own ways, confused and self-centred. In Act II they seem united only to attain middle-class respectability and material comforts, both of which only accentuate their confusion and self-concern. Then in Act III the Boyles seem destroyed because everything turns against them. Yet precisely at this moment when Mrs Boyle and Mary walk out on Boyle do love and responsibility become a meaningful reality. To Mary's complaint that her child will not have a father, Juno caustically replies, 'It'll have what's far better – it'll have two mothers.' . . .

SOURCE: extract from *In Search of Community: The Achievement of Sean O'Casey* (Cork and Dublin, 1972), pp. 34–42.

NOTES

[Reorganised and renumbered from the original – Ed.]

1. Cf. Dorothy MacArdle, *The Irish Republic* (Dublin, 1951), p. 251 ff.
2. Ibid., p. 279.
3. *Inishfallen, Fare Thee Well*, in *Autobiographies*, vol. II (London, 1963), p. 91.
4. Gabriel Fallon, *Sean O'Casey: The Man I Knew* (London, 1965), p. 24.

Jack Mitchell 'Inner Structure and Artistic Unity' (1980)

At first sight this [play] looks rather like the conventional 'naturalist' family drama of drunkenness and defeat, and it was often enough judged to be such. A closer look, however, reveals a sophisticated inner structure and artistic unity in this supposedly 'photographic' play. The unity of structure brings out a unity of theme. Almost all the characters have, in their relationship to living in the present, something in common. An unwillingness to face reality and grapple with it. Each of them makes an attempt to hide from it, or escape from it, while leaving it socially intact.

First there are the attempts at physically getting out of the slums and the proletariat. For all her proclaimed devotion to the principles of solidarity, Mary makes two such attempts. The first is via the careerist trade-union official, Jerry Devine; the second is via the bourgeois intruder, Bentham, who can outbid Jerry. Both these men corrupt and almost destroy their working-class victim. Mary's native realism is almost obliterated by a half-digested rehash of attitudes imported from Devine and Bentham – 'Jerry says this . . .' or 'Charlie says that . . .' Both her 'outside helps' abandon her in her moment of greatest need. This road, then, leads nowhere.

Some critics would like to see Mary's disaster as a proof that O'Casey was distrustful of all 'general principles' of living. But it is clearly not Mary's 'principle' (class loyalty and solidarity) that is wrong, but that she does not stick to it systematically – a contradiction between theory and practice. This happens because her grasp of principle is too abstract. It is evident in her defence of Johnny when the pragmatic Juno justly attacks his abstract principles – 'He stuck to his principles, an', no matther how you may argue, ma, a principle's a principle.' Clearly there is also a contradiction between one part of Mary's practice and another. We will meet this again. In this case it arises from a lack of sufficient confidence in herself, for she is not only a proletarian but a young woman, conditioned to be dependent on men.

Of the two men involved here, one is an outsider (Bentham) and therefore not an escape-candidate. As far as facing reality is concerned O'Casey puts his own people to shame in the person of this presumed Englishman. Bentham professes a pseudo-scientific spiritualist 'philosophy' – theosophy (scorned by Boyle who has no time for religions), and yet, when Johnny runs out of the bedroom during the party screaming that he has just seen Robbie Tancred's ghost in there, Bentham is the only one with enough courage to go in and report that there's no spirit there. This bourgeois Englishman does not let his absurd philosophy come between him and a sober appraisal of reality. The spirits of the dead, in his case, are kept in their place. This is a contradiction between word and deed of a very different sort, in which the almighty Word is put in its place.

If Bentham's late-bourgeois philosophical principles are corrupt and of no possible use to anyone, it is Jerry's lack of a scientific and principled philosophy which leaves this trade-union official open to corruption. Typical of the play-safe post-Connolly-Larkin leadership of the union, his main aim is to escape by making his career within the union. He succeeds in this personal escape, but at the expense of his fellow workers and his humanity. Jerry does, in his social-democratic way, contribute to a vaguely critical and humanist view of the world. The poem, which Mary heard him quote at a lecture and quotes back at him when he deserts her, voices the tragic paradox of life in class society which lies at the heart of the play: 'An' we felt the power that fashion'd / All the lovely things we saw / [. . .] Was a hand of force an' beauty, / With an eagle's tearin' claw. / [. . .] Like a glowin' picture by a / Hand unsteady, brought to ruin; / [. . .] Like the agonising horror / Of a violin out of tune.' Thus word and deed, insight and action fall apart and the critic becomes a contributor to the alienated reality he criticises.

Johnny's flight from the mad reality which he has helped to create is also, at one level, physical – into the back bedroom, from which he only rarely emerges. This is symbolic of an escapism in him of a much more insidious kind – into abstract Principle, in his case that of the 'Republicans'. These principles, once filled with the democratic life given to them by Wolfe Tone, had dwindled down to a sorry abstraction. As Peadar O'Donnell says, 'The Republican movement was inspired by "pure ideals". In the grip of this philosophy the Republican struggle could present itself as a democratic movement of mass revolt without any danger to the social pattern [. . .] under the shelter of pure ideals the Irish middle-class held its place within a movement it feared.'[1] For someone in Johnny's position these principles appeared as a sacred, finished, total reality, needing no thought and demanding preservation, not change. Within their charmed circle one can live a quasi-heroic life without getting involved in the real problems of one's existence.

What destroys Johnny is principle so abstract that it turns into its opposite – total lack of principle: he betrays his friend and comrade Robbie. Death pushes its way between Johnny and life. Death's coming for him at the end is only the logical conclusion of this process. Death will not allow him to live. It is a fear of the dead Robbie that drives him into a hole. Ireland is rich in dead heroes. As we have seen in *The Shadow of a Gunman* O'Casey sets out to rid his country of this dead weight of heroes, in the veneration of whom his countrymen so often found a convenient substitute for doing anything on their own account. Here, in Robbie and Johnny, he shows that their lives and deaths are heroic, in many cases, only in the romantic and impotent imaginations of the survivors.

This *diktat* of the dead over the living pervades the whole play. There is one moment where the forces of life and reality seem about to achieve a victory – during the party in Act II. They are just going to put a record on the gramophone – in this context partly a symbol of modern living – when they are interrupted by Mrs Tancred passing down to her son's funeral. At last they get the gramophone going only to be interrupted by Needle Nugent, another neighbour, bursting in and demanding whether none of them have any respect for the Irish people's National Regard for the dead, to which Mrs Boyle answers that 'Maybe, Needle Nugent, it's nearly time we had a little less respect for the dead, an' a little more regard for the livin'.' The funeral gets under way, not to the music of the gramophone but to the moaning of a hymn. The celebration of death, romantically decked out, wooes them from their celebration of life:

MRS BOYLE: Here's the hearse, here's the hearse!
BOYLE: There's t'oul' mother walkin' behin' the coffin.
MRS MADIGAN: You can hardly see the coffin with the wreaths.
JOXER: Oh, it's a darlin' funeral, a daarlin' funeral!

This death-dominated, death-dealing reality which Johnny has helped to make, invades his 'castle', winkles him out and destroys him. Thus the Johnny-figure is the mediator between the 'private' context of the Boyle family and the 'public' context of the civil war. They interpenetrate and determine each other, so that the myth

about the separateness of private and public life becomes hard to
maintain. This civil war has not only nothing to do with the real needs
of the people – its negative, destructive nature is partly a reflection, a
product of the weaknesses of the people themselves. So long as they
remain as they are they will not be able to produce, out of themselves,
a true revolution in their own interests. So it is not simply that these
people inhibit their own ability to live as a result of their distorted
relationship to reality. They simultaneously distort social reality
itself, which in its turn breaks in and almost destroys them. They are
responsible for reality. Reality (environment) is not portrayed as
simply something to be contemplated and understood, as something
which determines people, but as human practice, as something
determined *by* the people. This dialectical and revolutionary portrayal of the relationship of man to his environment lies at the very
heart of O'Casey's specific contribution to realism in the drama. . . .
. . . None of the slum-dwellers have (in the main body of the play) an
adequate relationship to reality and experience. None of them are
heroes. All are engaged in some attempt to escape or hide from reality
and their own position and function within it. All these attempts are
doomed. On the surface this has a certain similarity to the contemporary tradition of 'slum naturalism' in bourgeois literature and
drama. These naturalists showed the submerged masses as mere
products and passive victims of environment. Therefore all their
attempts to free themselves are doomed to failure from the start, the
only result of their efforts being that their last state is worse than their
first. The latter is certainly true of the people in *Juno* and several critics
have labelled O'Casey's 'Dublin' plays naturalist. In fact nothing
could be further from naturalism than O'Casey's picture of the
people. He certainly does not underestimate the formative influence
of environment. Of Mary he says in the stage directions, that her
speech and manners have been degraded by her environment and are
marked by the struggle of opposing forces. There are similar remarks
in the stage directions describing Juno, etc. Boyle's distaste for work is
shown as conditioned by the degrading circumstances surrounding
wage labour – 'I don't want the motions of me body to be watched the
way an asthronomer ud watch a star.' Boyle's attitude to work is also
formed by Ireland's history. In a situation where work, the attempt to
improve one's position, was used against one, say in the form of a
raised rent for the poor tenant farmer who had been foolhardy enough
to 'improve' his holding, 'laziness' became a kind of defence-
mechanism.

Nevertheless these people emerge not only as victims but as makers
of the alienated environment. They have an active relationship to

their environment – albeit a negative one under the given conditions. Their efforts to escape fail, not because all efforts are worse than useless, but because they are the wrong kind of efforts. In engaging in them they are making the situation worse. Their 'solutions' are traditional, superannuated self-comforters and attempts at local 'break-outs' which leave the total set-up intact. Their hopes of such break-outs are based on rescue through outside agencies rather than through their own efforts. The affair of the legacy is the point of focus for all this.

The legacy device, the discovery that the poor hero or heroine was, after all, the heir to a fortune, was a favourite *deus ex machina* of bourgeois literature and drama, the Happy End of the well-made play. It was an especially popular plot device in the Victorian melodramas which O'Casey so enjoyed. He takes this convention, as he takes others, and remoulds it to his own purpose. In *Juno* the great expectations do not materialise and there is no happy end. But the real irony is that it is not the non-materialisation of the legacy which hastens the disaster, but the naive assumption that it *will* materialise. This, as we have seen with Juno, aggravates all their most negative features. So the legacy-line in the plot is not merely a means of heightening the tension or of forwarding the plot, as some critics have maintained.[2] It is a focal point for organising the statement of the play, bringing out the fact that the characters all have important weaknesses in common, i.e. that these weaknesses are social rather than individual. The final implication is that the situation would have been even worse (Juno, for instance, might have been corrupted beyond redemption) if the legacy had materialised. Moral: the only thing worse than building false hopes on help 'from above' is if these hopes do not prove false and the 'help' were to come true.

So one is led to the conclusion that Juno is right when she says, 'Sure, if it's not our business, I don't know whose business it is.' They must free themselves. They are continuously moulding reality; it is time they learnt to mould it in their own interests instead of against them. All O'Casey's images infer a) the latent qualities necessary to achieve this, and b) that these qualities themselves are a part of that truly human way of living that one must fight to achieve. It is a measure of the deeply popular nature of O'Casey's realism that he is able to make these potentially world-changing qualities shine through between the lines of his criticism.

They give unfailing stature to the characters from the working people. They are a decisive part of the immanent all-pervading perspective. O'Casey's message is that they must be mobilised *now*. The fact that these potential strengths instead of being a means of liberation are still so often a means of enslavement is an important aspect of the tragedy. What transforms this from a largely abstract perspective into the beginnings of a real, concrete one is that a few characters, here above all Juno, do begin to mobilise them in an effort to move forwards.

The famous contradictoriness or ambivalence of O'Casey's characters is the expression of this inner tension between the two opposite and conflicting possibilities coexisting closely and precariously within these qualities – a tension between the actual and the possible.

The language of these people is the most universal carrier of their 'double' nature.[3] This is concentrated in one word in Boyle's justly famous phrase, 'a terrible state o' chassis'. On the one hand this kind of thing is an expression of the environmentally imposed illiteracy and mental confusion of the characters. On the other it bears witness to their creative, highly individual manipulation of the tool of language. These Irish word-forgers make their own rules and break the old rules. These 'unruly' people have a spontaneously creative approach to English. There is nothing sacrosanct about it for them. They are not inhibited by the weight of literary and academic authority, or their use of it dulled by the meticulous and sobering demands of 'commerce and industry'. It is the absence of this latter influence which makes their speech so 'Elizabethan' rather than the mere historical fact that English was imposed upon them in the time of 'Good' Queen Bess (before English had become castrated in the 'motherland'). They have put their own stamp on the language. Today, in the rhythm and form of almost every phrase, the transforming spirit of the people's old Gaelic tongue has 'subverted' the King's English. So the English language, forced upon them as a means of their enslavement, has been partly transformed into a tool to express *themselves*, their particular receiving-end view of the world. In the word 'chassis' the all-invading aggressive essence of capitalist anarchy is expressed in the anarchic form of the word itself. But let us take a longer passage from the play so that the characters can speak for themselves. It will also give us the opportunity of going on to a wider discussion of the potentially positive side of the conflicting opposites on which the characterisation is based.

The infuriated Boyle is relating to Joxer how Jerry Devine brought him the terrible news that Father Farrell had a job lined up for him (Boyle).

BOYLE: . . . I'm goin' to tell you somethin', Joxer, that I wouldn't tell to anybody else –
the clergy always had too much power over the people in this unfortunate country.
JOXER: You could sing that if you had an air to it!
BOYLE (*becoming enthusiastic*): Didn't they prevent the people in '47 from seizin' the corn,

an' they starvin'; didn't they down Parnell; didn't they say that hell wasn't hot enough nor eternity long enough to punish the Fenians? We don't forget, we don't forget them things, Joxer. If they've taken everything else from us, Joxer, they've left us our memory.

JOXER (*emotionally*): For mem'ry's the only friend that grief can call its own, that grief . . . can . . . call . . . its own!

BOYLE: Father Farrell's beginnin' to take a great intherest in Captain Boyle; because of what Johnny did for his country, says he to me wan day. It's a curious way to reward Johnny be makin' his poor oul' father work. But that's what the clergy want, Joxer – work, work, work for me an' you; havin' us mulin' from mornin' till night, so that they may be in betther fettle when they come hoppin' round for their dues! Job! Well, let him give his job to wan of his hymn-singin', prayer-spoutin', craw-thumpin' Confraternity men!

(*The voice of a coal-block vendor is heard chanting in the street.*)

VOICE OF COAL VENDOR: Blocks . . . coal-blocks! Blocks . . . coal-blocks!

JOXER: God be with the young days when you were steppin' the deck of a manly ship, with the win' blowin' a hurricane through the masts, an' the only sound you'd hear was, 'Port your helm!' an' the only answer, 'Port it is, sir!'

The Captain now launches upon his seafaring fantasy . . . culminating thus:

BOYLE: An', as it blowed an' blowed, I ofen looked up at the sky an' assed meself the question – what is the stars, what is the stars?

VOICE OF COAL VENDOR: Any blocks, coal-blocks; blocks, coal-blocks!

JOXER: Ah, that's the question, that's the question – what is the stars?

BOYLE: An' then, I'd have another look, an' I'd ass meself – what is the moon?

JOXER: Ah, that's the question – what is the moon, what is the moon?

(. . . *the door is opened, and the black face of the* Coal Vendor *appears.*)

THE COAL VENDOR: D'yez want any blocks?

BOYLE (*with a roar*): No, we don't want any blocks!

The salient features of Boyle's language here are concreteness combined with the large rhetorical gesture. His images are markedly mimetic, depicting vigorous bodily actions. He is able to give expression to precise and deep critical insights into society. There is a drive to dramatisation and confrontation. Rhythm, originality, imagination and passion fuse into an aggressive energy. These qualities in Boyle's speech are highlighted by being juxtaposed to Joxer's derivative echoes. Joxer's speech is a blunted tool by comparison.

Boyle and most of the others throw their whole personality into this prodigal and prodigious talking. All the force, revolt and inventiveness which should by right find its main field of realisation in deeds, is poured into the *word*. This too, bears witness to the frustration of all endeavour and action in Ireland's bitter history. Functioning in this circumscribed context these potentially revolutionising energies are squandered on trivialities, posturing and internecine bickering – word-fights. But they are there – a repository of aggressive, explosive potentials. There is nothing here of that 'dogged inarticulateness' which middle-class authors sometimes like to portray as a characteristic 'virtue' of the working class.

The scene quoted is a good example of the more general interaction and interpenetration of conflicting elements in Boyle. He launches a passionate and true attack on the historical role of the Church hierarchy, but he falters in full stride and the mood slips into maudlin self-pity. How precarious is the boundary-line! Jago-Joxer at once pounces on the weakness and fosters it. But then Boyle gets going again, and more strongly, building up to an impressive climax. Pathos–bathos–pathos. Danger for Joxer, especially as harsh reality seems to join Boyle in the sobering shout of the coal vendor. At once Joxer cunningly launches the Captain on the high seas of his favourite fantasy, making him reach for the distant stars rather than stoop to the black, hard, dirty coal blocks of reality.

Dangerous and ridiculous this reaching for the stars is, under the circumstances; empty and absurd his philosophical questions – and yet, juxtaposed to Juno's wingless pragmatism, one cannot suppress a certain admiration. There is here a refusal to acccept a life defined by coal blocks. It is childish and irresponsible, but a kind of rebellion. Hence, when the alienating-effect of the coal vendor with his question intervenes to bring Boyle down to earth with a bump, our reaction to his savage rejection is not entirely negative.

Characteristically, Boyle is first introduced singing a prayer to the spirit: 'Sweet Spirit, hear me prayer! Hear . . . oh . . . hear . . . me prayer . . . hear, oh, hear . . . Oh, he...ar . . . oh, he...ar . . . me . . . pray...er!'

Joxer (outside) comments that it is a daarlin' song, while Juno (inside) is willing to take a solemn 'affeydavey' that he's praying for anything but a job.

It is this insistence that in spite of and to spite soul-destroying conditions, man has a right to a soul, to imagination, poetry and song, this reaching, however grotesquely, for the stars, the unswerving pursuit of this need, whatever the cost – and it's a disastrous cost for him – that gives Boyle his backhanded impressiveness. He will have dignity, even if it is a ridiculous dignity. At one level O'Casey is showing his countrymen, through Boyle, that the 'stage-Irishman', that detested caricature of the Irish in the traditional English theatre, is nearer to the actual state of affairs than the romanticised heroics of Irish patriotic literature. A bitter, paradoxical piece of O'Casey irony. On another level however the stage-Irishman convention melts before our eyes, an outer shell, falling away and revealing something living, something in which potential greatness is being tragically wasted. In conventional productions aimed at an English audience the Boyle figure is used to curry laughs at the expense of this supposed stage-Irishman *par excellence*. Serious productions must avoid this pitfall, and the laughter called forth by Boyle's antics must be of a much more complex and productive kind.

In Boyle's attitude and effort there is something concealed which, when liberated from its self-alienation, is as essential to the struggle for liberation as is Juno's realism. Unite these two opposites, not in the botched and destructive 'harmony' of this Christian marriage, but in a true synthesis, and both will become fertile again. On this basis new and better heroes can arise, heroes who can master life.

In connection with all this it is time to take another look at the legacy business. We shall see that it is no mere mechanical convention used to forward the plot or something filched from melodrama to heighten the suspense. Its effect on the action is contradictory. Certain positive potentials are discovered or fostered under the conditions arising from the promise of the legacy. Alongside its negative influence it provides them with the basis for a kind of 'flowering' – limited and fleeting and deeply compromised as it is. The 'prosperity', false though it is in every real sense, functions for a time as if it were real. Juno, for instance, who has never had a breathing-space, now seems to feel solid ground under her feet for the first time and can push out her horns, extend her concern a little. In this way one catches a fleeting glimpse of what might and could be under conditions of genuine security and well-being. In its way it is a proof of their capacity to live and not merely exist.

There is nothing miserly in their behaviour on the basis of the expected money. They use the credit given in anticipation of it not as a capitalist would, to invest and make more money, but in a human way, to procure the good things of life, however tasteless they may be in form. They use it to satisfy real needs which neither the Free State nor the Republicans are satisfying for them. Joxer gets liberal hand-outs. Mrs Madigan is entitled to as much whiskey as she can drink so long as it's there.

Their behaviour and relations become, in a sense, 'socialised' under the new conditions. In true Irish style they throw a party whose culmination is a musical 'session' where each is expected to perform his or her party piece. Thus Boyle's ideal of social life, 'a quiet jar, an' a song or two', is to a certain extent realised.

As has been indicated, Boyle's worst characteristics are aggravated by the 'great expectations', but some of his better ones also seem to gather strength for a time. Fleetingly he wins an element of genuine poise and even – at one point – true dignity. His taking command of the proceedings is at once ridiculous and rather efficient. A hint of potentially real captain-talents is suggested. There is a new note in his rising tendency to ridicule their fairy godfather and potential son-in-law, Bentham, to his face. The latter's high-falutin 'Prawna' (life-spirit) is too mystical for that man-of-the-spirit, Jack Boyle – 'Prawna; yis, the Prawna. (*Blowing gently through his lips*) That's the Prawna!' His penchant for realistic social insight and generalisation seems to gain in steadiness, especially his critique of that favourite anathema of his – religion. Religion, he says, has had its day and is passing like everything else. The Dubliners of today are better acquainted with Charlie Chaplin than with Saints Peter and Paul. His pagan hedonism comes more strongly to the fore. It is something much more necessary to the people in their historic task than the traditional religious belly-crawling of Juno. Then there is that remarkable poem of his, the recital of which is the high point of the 'session':

> Shawn an' I were friends, sir, to me he was all in all.
> His work was very heavy and his wages were very small.
> None betther on th' beach as Docker, I'll go bail,
> 'Tis now I'm feelin' lonely, for to-day he lies in jail.
> He was not what some call pious – seldom at church or prayer;
> For the greatest scoundrels I know, sir, goes every Sunday there.
> Fond of his pint – well, rather, but hated the Boss by creed
> But never refused a copper to comfort a pal in need.

This is simple and dignified and devoid of bourgeois literary convention. It strongly reflects the class pride and consciousness born during the 1913 strike. It is set in a popular and working-class ballad tradition which Boyle must have been acquainted with. His cultural potential seems to have received a boost through the anticipation of a little well-being. It is new enough to surprise Juno – 'God bless us, is he startin' to write poetry!' At this point Boyle, who has revealed little or no contact with literary tradition, is suddenly able to create this poem out of nothing, it would appear, except his experience coupled with his imagination. This original creativeness puts his contribution to the session in a different category to those of the others who are content to reproduce the artistic creations of others.

Juno too, is stimulated – perhaps more than Boyle. She shows tendencies towards an inner synthesis of her own qualities with those found in Boyle. There are growing signs of interest and participation in the world beyond her nest, the beginnings of her socialisation. For the first time she ventures a comment on the state of her society – 'when we got the makin' of our own laws I thought we'd never stop to look behind us, but instead of that we never stopped to look before us!'

In contrast to the impression she has made hitherto, Juno now reveals a genuine feeling for things artistic. Standing together, she and her daughter sing 'simply' the Verdi duet 'Home to our Mountains'. The fact that this song is from another country and people is in itself a sign of her modest 'expansion'. It is as if the participation in this cultural activity stimulates the broadening of her human concern. Not long after she has sung her song she hears Mrs Tancred passing down the stairs with the other mourners to her murdered son's funeral. She stops Boyle putting a record on the gramophone. She'd forgotten they were taking the body to the church that night; now she tells Mary to open the door and give them a bit of light on the landing. She wants her light to shine out for others.

The sing-song, then, is a moment of synthesis, a high point in the expression of the positive potential of these people, their capacity for living. Only Joxer fails to come up to the mark.

But death and death-dealing reality break in on the festivities more and more massively in connection with the mourning procession for Tancred. The high moment is lost in morbid fascination with the trappings of death. Boyle's behaviour at this point is ominous. He washes his hands of all responsibility for what is happening to people: 'That's the Government's business, an' let them do what we're payin' them for doin'.' This is the money ethic victorious. The socialising effect of the anticipated legacy has not been as strong in his case as its corrupting influence. This is really the final parting of the ways between Boyle and Juno and foreshadows his rejection of his pregnant daughter because the scandal will damage his image.

Boyle fails the test because his grasp of reality and therefore his sense of responsibility are initially too undermined to provide any basis. Juno on the other hand has been able to profit from the experience of this bit of 'good living'. For her it has brought out the contrast between what might be and the way things have been. The fiasco of its quick collapse under the blows of circumstances heightens her awareness that one must not accept these circumstances but fight them. But the realist O'Casey does not simplify her progress or the difficulties which will continue to face her. Indeed, Juno finds the strength for the final break only when the tragedy has been completed with the death of her son.

Juno derives the strength to take the decisive step from her experience and what she has learnt from it. This she is able to do because all along she has had to face up to reality, and her experience has therefore been real to her. When Mrs Madigan comes to tell her that Johnny has been shot her comment is, 'I've gone through so much lately that I feel able for anything'. This great quality is indicated on a lower key in Mary and Mrs Madigan.

Juno abandons Boyle – 'he'll be hopeless till the end of his days', and goes off with Mary. This is an epoch-breaking step for Juno: *she splits the family*, the former be-all-and-end-all of her life, for the sake of deeper and wider human considerations. Together with her daughter she intends to found a new type of family unit, an unorthodox one without a male 'head of the house', one which will recognise its debt and its responsibility to the working-class community as a whole. . . .

. . . Juno learns from life but her conscious world-view is not yet as far advanced as her actual doing: there is deep unconscious irony in her plea for God to replace their hearts of stone with hearts of flesh, for this heart transplant is exactly what she has already achieved by her own efforts. She has shown that there is no need for God. Juno – that name so indicative of godlike sovereignty – now ceases to be a mockery of her who bears it.

O'Casey chose to close the play with Boyle and Joxer, incapably drunk, alone on the scene. And he gives Boyle the last word on the state of the world – 'chassis'. Why?

First, the scene shows the end of the road for Boyle. All his potentials have come to this. He subsides to the floor on a level with Joxer. The 'man of higher things' is himself the very embodiment and epitome of the 'chassis'. As soon as Juno abandons her hold on him he sinks as quickly as she rises. At the same time the scene is an alienating-effect in true O'Casey style. It provides a kind of 'comic relief' while in essence being anything but comic. With its calculated bathos it reminds us of Seumas's last line in *The Gunman*. It is a technique we shall meet again. It lowers the emotional pressure built up to a catharsis-like situation in Juno's great preceding scene, bringing us down to a more normal temperature. This enables us to appreciate that Juno and her action are still an exception and that the Irish scene remains largely defined by the Boyles and Joxers and the helpless anarchy for which they stand. They remain 'in occupation'. Juno's way is going to be no easy one.

The release-in-laughter of the final scene also allows us to sit back and take a cool look at the implications of the action as a whole, freeing us from the intense fascination with Juno's great moment alone. In making us laugh under these circumstances it forces us to ask ourselves *why* we laugh at this and why we have laughed at these characters. It raises the question – is laughter alone the adequate response? Thus the comic side of this tragedy and the laughter it evokes emerge, not as something coexistent with the tragic, but a key, a way in to a more profound understanding of the tragedy.

Lastly it places Boyle's persuasive summing up of the world in a critical perspective, encouraging us to test it and question it.

Source: extracts from *The Essential O'Casey: A Study of the Twelve Major Plays of Sean O'Casey* (East Berlin and New York, 1980), pp. 45–9, 60–70, 72–3.

NOTES

[Reorganised and renumbered from the original – Ed.]

1. Quoted by James Plunkett in *The Gems She Wore* (London, 1972), p. 193.
2. See, for instance David Krause, *Sean O'Casey, The Man and His Work* (London and New York, 1960), p. 125, and Herbert Goldstone, *In Search of Community* (Cork and Dublin, 1972), p. 42.
3. For a detailed and discerning study of O'Casey's use of speech levels, see Thomas Metscher, *Sean O'Casey dramatischer Stil* (Brunswick, West Germany, 1968).

Errol Durbach   Peacocks and Mothers: Theme and Dramatic Metaphor   (1972)

O'Casey criticism has grown weary, at last, of raking through the ashes of barren controversy – the superior excellence of the Abbey plays over the later, or (conversely) the 'expressionistic' drama over the 'realistic', or the Dublin O'Casey over O'Casey the exile. The lean years of inept and irrelevant critical judgements have been superseded in the last decade by passionate apologia,[1] full scale studies of the dramatist[2] and a reading of the plays which suggests a far closer stylistic unity between the realism of the Abbey plays and the later expressionism than had previously been acknowledged.[3] His symbolism and incipient expressionistic methods have revealed a stylistic bridge over the gulf between the two general areas of O'Casey's career; and the oversimplified view of the early O'Casey as a rude proletarian realist is yielding now to the recognition of dramatic qualities in the Abbey plays inconsistent with 'slice-of-life' drama and the 'photographic realism' with which he has frequently been (dis-) credited. It was Yeats who first insisted on regarding O'Casey as the realist of his slum milieu, rejecting *The Silver Tassie* for frustrating this conventional expectation. But to have held this view of O'Casey,

Yeats must surely have had to misread the Abbey plays with great
and unremitting determination. He was not the only critic of the
period to insist on the verisimilitude of the Dublin plays. Thus P. S.
O'Hegarty writing in 1927 of *Juno and the Paycock*:

Juno is a real tragic figure, not of ignoble but of high and ennobling import. She is true
metal, true mother and true woman, and true to actual life, from the first to the last line.
The others are true also. . . . They are recognisable and true types.[4]

It would be perverse to deny that O'Casey produced works which
looked very like the realistic character-play. But if the characters in
Juno and the Paycock live ' "slices of life" in the strictest and most literal
sense of the term,'[5] what then are we to make of someone like Mrs
Maisie Madigan?:

*. . . she has a habit of putting her head a little to one side, and nodding it rapidly several times in
succession, like a bird pecking a hard berry. Indeed, she has a good deal of the bird in her, but the bird
instinct is by no means a melodious one. . . . She is dressed in a rather soiled grey dress and a vivid
purple blouse; in her hair is a huge comb, ornamented with huge coloured beads. She enters with a
gliding step, beaming smile and nodding head.*

A form of realism, perhaps – but it is far closer to that of Dickens and
Ben Jonson than the realism of Robertson or Shaw. It distorts. It
emphasises something non-human within the recognisably 'true'
depiction of a character, so that what we observe in action is a human
being moving slowly out of the realm of the real into the surreal. Mrs
Madigan is grotesquely bird-like; and the bird encrusted upon her
humanity is, of course, the peacock – its pecking mannerism, its
purple bosom, its gliding movement, and, crowning everything, the
peacock's magnificently gaudy crest. She is merely one element in a
play that has, as one of its central themes, a flamboyant and
self-important peacockery.

The 'paycock' of the title, however, is Captain Jack Boyle himself;
and, once again, O'Casey's physical description of the man imposes
upon human movement the bizarre impersonation of the bird,
conjuring up the type of half-human-half-animal freak of Ben Jonson
and Aristophanes:

*. . . His cheeks, reddish-purple, are puffed out, as if he were always repressing an almost irrepressible
ejaculation. On his upper lip is a crisp, tightly cropped moustache; he carries himself with the upper
part of his body slightly thrown back, and his stomach slightly thrust forward. His walk is a slow
consequential strut.*

The puffed-up appearance, the backward-inclining and paunch-
protruding strut is as close as male vanity can possibly come to an
impersonation of the peacock. And with the physical appearance goes
a moral nature, a self-aggrandising pride, a constant preening of his
spurious reputation before a willing audience of parasite-birds.

Manners and morality coincide in the Captain; and O'Casey's distortion of reality is that quality of his dramatic style which makes the fusion possible.

There are others, as well, whose persons contribute towards the play's pervasive peacockery – Charlie Bentham, for instance, the 'Mickey Dazzler' whose clothes define his anomalous exoticism in the tenement room and externalize his personality:

He is dressed in a brown coat, brown knee-breeches, grey stockings, a brown sweater, with a deep blue tie; he carries gloves and a walking stick.

He is splendidly ornate in the best of overdressed taste, a peacock in moral temperament as well, sharing with the Captain 'a very high opinion of himself generally'. Bentham's affectation of manner, however, remains on this side of extreme grotesquerie – as does Mary's whose primary concerns, when we first see her, are her appearance in the mirror and the colour of the ribbon to wear in her hair. Her cosmetic frippery exists in uneasy tension with her sick brother's cry for water and her mother's lamentations on the state of her unemployed and indigent family:

> *(Mrs Boyle brings in a drink [to Johnny] and returns.)*
> MRS BOYLE: Isn't it terrible to have to be waitin' this way! You'd think he was bringin' twenty poun's a week into the house the way he's going on. He wore out the Health Insurance long ago, he's afther wearin' out the unemployment dole, an', now, he's thryin' to wear out me! An' constantly singin', no less, when he ought always to be on his knees offerin' up a Novena for a job!
> MARY *(tying a ribbon fillet-wise around her head)*: I don't like this ribbon, ma; I think I'll wear the green – it looks betther than the blue.

This is one of the first instances in the play when peacockery – by which I mean an egotistic concern with one's *self*, one's image, one's importance, one's opinions, one's appearance – comes face to face with that which consistently opposes it: the need to confront a desperate reality, the need to make provision for life's necessities – even glasses of water for thirsty boys. The title of the play crystallises the central opposition of the two dialectical principles which shape the whole: the horror of facing the reality of one's domestic crises, and the illusions which tempt one to fantasticate the horror out of all existence.

Opposing the peacocks of the play, almost single-handedly, is O'Casey's image of the indomitable mother – a dramatic metaphor which he handles with the same brilliant variety, the same extensive use as Synge's many father-images in *The Playboy of the Western World*. It is his meticulous control of the mother as myth, symbol and realistic presence that most clearly reveals O'Casey's craftsmanship and technical economy. 'Juno' – the mother as classical myth – is, of

course, the most insistent of the metaphors in the play, and like
O'Casey's other metaphors it has its basis in a solid, colloquial
reality:

BENTHAM: Juno! What an interesting name! It reminds one of Homer's glorious story of
   ancient gods and heroes.
BOYLE: Yis, doesn't it? You see, Juno was born an' christened in June; I met her in June;
   we were married in June, and Johnny was born in June, so wan day I says to her,
   'You should ha' been called Juno,' an' the name stuck to her ever since.

Human reality is juxtaposed with mythical identity, Juno gradually
assuming a mythical status in the play which ultimately transcends
reality without compromising her essential humanity. This is
O'Casey's achievement, and with remarkable aptness Juno Boyle
comes to incarnate those life-sustaining principles subsumed by her
Roman counterpart: Goddess of childbirth who, by extension,
ensures the multiplication of the race;[6] protectress of the pregnant
wife and guardian of the nation;[7] the goddess who cares for the
unborn child, who causes the mother's milk to flow; and, above all,
the Goddess of domesticity, of the family hearth, the Female Principle
of existence. Her attributes in Roman iconography are either those of
Juno Regina the sceptre, patera, and peacocks; or that of Juno Lucina
who carries a child in her arms. Such are the functions and attributes
of Juno Boyle as well, breadwinner and maid-of-all-work for a whole
family of peacocks. She is defined as soon as she enters with a parcel of
food in her hand, hurrying home from her job to cook her malingering
husband's breakfast and protect her household against his scaveng-
ing friends. Juno Regina of the Dublin slums, she performs her
mock-goddess role surrounded by her mock-symbols: her peacocks
and her plate of sausages, reality and myth coinciding in fantastic
fusion.

It is Juno's human compassion and love which ultimately make the
myth viable – this is the function of O'Casey's realism – and the
realistic presence of Mrs Tancred, mourning for her murdered son,
universalises this maternal theme. Her stark, iconographic rhetoric
speaks for all the Junos in Ireland whose domestic function has been
destroyed by a heartless and obdurate peacockery:

Ah, what's the pains I suffered bringin' him into the world to carry him to his cradle, to
the pains I'm sufferin' now, carryin' him out o' the world to bring him to his grave! . . .
An' I'm told he was the leadher of the ambush where me nex' door neighbour, Mrs
Mannin', lost her Free State son. An' now here's the two of us oul' women, standin' one
each side of a scales o' sorra, balanced be the bodies of our two dead darlin' sons.

Her ritualised expression of grief articulates the drama's central
humanistic plea – 'Take away this murdherin' hate . . . an' give us
Thine own eternal love!' – but the episode in which Mrs Tancred

appears suggests another possible variation on the metaphor. 'Still an' all, he died a noble death', says one of her neighbours, 'an' we'll bury him like a king'. To which the mother replies: 'an' I'll go on livin' like a pauper.' The spurious illusion of the heroic death is grimly balanced against the real horror of the old mother's predicament; but there is also the sentimental implication that Nationalism justifies all, that boys who die for Ireland die the death of kings. Ireland as Mother, an over-idealised abstract Nationalism, is another of the play's informing metaphors. The fervent outburst establishing Ireland's prior claim upon her sons – 'No man can do enough for Ireland'; 'Ireland only half free'll never be at peace while she has a son left to pull a trigger' – finds its most articulate expression in *The Plough and the Stars*:

CLITHEROE: You have a mother, Langon.
LANGON: Ireland is greater than a mother.
BRENNAN: You have wife, Clitheroe.
CLITHEROE: Ireland is greater than a wife.

For those indulging in the 'patriot game', Cathleen ni Houlihan is inevitably the greater lover, the greater mother. This is the offence against which Juno Boyle does constant battle – the substitution of an illusory principle for a human reality.

Ireland as reality is, of course, the living Juno – not the national symbol for which men offer up their lives. And the real saviour of her family is again Juno – not the Mother as religious icon whose presence dominates the tenement room as it dominates the whole of Ireland. The play resounds, as with a dominant motif, to the 'Hail Mary', to frequent invocations to the Mother of mercy, spiritual protectress of her children against the ills of the world. She is Johnny Boyle's only source of comfort in his horror, the constantly burning votive light reassuring him of the saving grace of the archetypal Christian mother. In his hour of need it is inevitably the Mother of God to whom the boy calls for comfort:

Mother o'God, pray for me – be with me now in the agonies o' death! . . . Hail, Mary, full o' grace . . . the Lord is . . . with Thee.
(*They drag out* Johnny Boyle, *and the curtain falls*.)

But the Mother of God is clearly a *dea abscondita* rather than a presiding deity – a mother who has seemingly deserted her children in their agonies and whose grace fails, ultimately, to supervene in the face of catastrophe. Mothers of flesh-and-blood can do little more in their sorrow than cry out against the failure of their prototype: 'Blessed Virgin, where were you when me darlin' son was riddled with bullets, when me darlin' son was riddled with bullets?' Such

constant invocations to the Mother of God begin, after a while, to
resound with a hollow irony – like the 'Hail Mary' recited by the
crowd at the Tancred funeral, wafting into the Boyle parlour while
Johnny is being terrorised by the Mobilizer. It is Juno whose comfort
and protection of her child in his emotional crises finally exposes the
ineffectuality of the Mother as religious icon:

> (*A frightened scream is heard from Johnny inside. . . . He rushes out again, his face pale, his lips
> twitching, his limbs trembling.*)
> JOHNNY: Shut the door, shut the door, quick, for God's sake! Great God, have mercy on
> me! Blessed Mother o' God, shelter me, shelter your son!
> MRS BOYLE (*catching him in her arms*): What's wrong with you? What ails you? Sit, down,
> sit down, here, on the bed . . . there now . . . there now.

The point is enacted dramatically, Juno's gesture of compassion
eloquently answering the boy's cry for the Virgin's care. It is a
compassion which grows even more insistent as the play progresses,
throwing into clear relief the steadily attenuating grace of the Mother
of God. Just as Johnny is finally dragged off to his death, the votive
light before the Virgin's picture flickers and dies leaving the stage in
darkness – save for Juno's fire burning in the hearth.

The governing idea of the play, I have been suggesting, is the ironic
(if not wholly tragic) juxtaposition of human realities in conflict with
the grandiose illusions of Irish Romanticism and the meaningless
abstractions of politics and war. It is a form of drama essentially
anti-Romantic, anti-Heroic, anti-Religious, and anti-Nationalistic –
insofar as Romance, Heroism, Religion and Nationalism constitute
those sentimental principles for which men are prepared to sacrifice
themselves. It is against such abstractions that Juno has constantly to
struggle in her attempt to hold a disintegrating world together. She
opposes her daughter's trade-unionism with commonsensical domestic fact.

> MARY: What's the use of belongin' to a Trades Union if you won't stand up for your
> principles? . . . It doesn't matter what you say, ma – a principle's a principle.
> MRS BOYLE: Yis; an' when I go into oul' Murphy's tomorrow, an' he gets to know that,
> instead o' payin' all, I'm goin' to borry more, what'll he say when I tell him a
> principle's a principle?

And she cuts through her son's nationalist idealism with the same
sober pragmatism:

> MRS BOYLE: . . . None can deny he done his bit for Irelan', if that's goin' to do him any
> good.
> JOHNNY (*boastfully*): I'd do it agen, ma, I'd do it agen; for a principle's a principle.
> MRS BOYLE: Ah, you lost your best principle, me boy, when you lost your arm; them's the
> only sort o' principles that's any good to a workin' man.

Her practicality may amount, at times, to an attitude of narrow-minded illiberalism – but one always has to bear in mind the odds against which she is fighting. It is not that she is against economic or political or moral principles *per se*. What she is opposing in her family is their refusal to acknowledge and come to terms with a desperate reality, their tendency to seek refuge from it behind 'principle', making it the excuse for their insufficiencies and relying upon the cant phrase which masquerades as sincerely held ideal. Not only do they articulate their cherished ideals in a series of clichés, but fail even to act up to their noble professions. The principle, the sentiment, is the great sham which rationalises personal failure and insulates them all against the suffering which Juno alone endures.

In all three Dublin plays it is the woman who embodies the sense of earthbound reality: Juno, Plough, and Gunman; and the man, disastrously committed to his illusions, who embodies the insubstantial contrariety: peacock, star, and shadow. Unlike Christy Mahon, O'Casey's men fail wretchedly to transform their dreams into actuality, finding it far more comfortable to luxuriate in the platitudes of Irish national sentiment. Even the noble Socialist ideal of Jerry Devine is revealed as political blather when confronted by a demand upon its professed humanity; and Joxer's parodic inversion of the humanist position makes his failure all the more morally heinous. For it is Joxer who reveals most patently the lies with which people delude themselves, a living testimony to the hypocrisy of 'principle' who consistently violates the very sentiments which he is perpetually mouthing. But he never deludes *himself* – and in this he differs from that most dangerous of all the peacocks, the self-celebrating, self-romanticising Captain Boyle. By conferring upon himself the spurious dignity of a sea-captain, with a cap to match his calling, he sets himself above the menial demands of working for a living; and by extolling his importance in bouts of fantastic bragging, he insulates himself against the shabby reality of his true identity. Like Christy Mahon, he creates himself out of the (somewhat alcoholic) poetry of the Irish imagination without, however, rising above the level of the mock-heroic. If Synge, in *The Playboy of the Western World*, celebrates the magnificence of the self-creating hero, O'Casey in *Juno and the Paycock* shows the catastrophic consequences to men who live dream lives of impossible wish-fulfilment. They present a splendid study of two contrasting Irish temperaments.

It is Juno who first confronts the captain with the reality of his pretentious claims to naval command: 'Everybody callin' you "Captain", an' you only wanst on the wather, in an oul' collier from here to Liverpool, when anybody, to listen or look at you, ud take you for a second Christo For Columbus!' But undaunted by her sarcasm, he performs his 'Captain' routine with great rhetorical gusto as soon as his audience reappears in the person of Joxer Daly. It is a piece of comic braggadocio, but even at such moments of seemingly peripheral foolery O'Casey never loses sight of his central theme. The comedy is not incidental to the play's major concerns but arises out of it and contributes towards it. This brief scene must serve as a paradigmatic example of the way in which O'Casey makes use of the comic element as thematic comment – achieved, in this instance, by a technique of dramatic contrapuntalism as the streetcries of a coal-vendor keep punctuating the Captain's performance:

> (*The voice of a coal-block vendor is heard chanting in the street.*)
> VOICE OF COAL VENDOR: Blocks . . . coal-blocks! Blocks . . . coal-blocks!
>   . . .
> BOYLE: Them was days, Joxer, them was days. Nothin' was too hot or too heavy for me then. Sailin' from the Gulf o' Mexico to the Antanartic Ocean. I seen things, I seen things, Joxer, that no mortal man should speak about that knows his Catechism. Ofen, an' ofen, when I was fixed to the wheel with a marlin-spike, an' the win's blowin' fierce an' the waves lashin' an' lashin', till you'd think every minute was goin' to be your last, an' it blowed, an' blowed – blew is the right word, Joxer, but blowed is what the sailors use. . . .

And as the rhetoric grows increasingly more preposterous, so the chanting of the vendor comes progressively nearer – an ironic descant to the major theme – until the door eventually opens and the black face of the coalman confronts the Captain: 'D'yez want any blocks?'

Chekhov is full of similar moments. Self-deluding dreamers spin their endless webs, only to find themselves caught in them like flies by the sudden and seemingly arbitrary appearance of no-one-in-particular. Sometimes, undercutting such an over-rhetorical recitation, is a secondary and quite inconsequential action, or a noise, that seems merely to corroborate the impression of an already realistic background. But the intrusion of the coal-vendor is not a further instance of verisimilitude any more than, say, Marina's cluck-cluckking after the chickens in *Uncle Vanya*. The cry of 'coal-blocks' starts just as the conversation begins turning to the 'Port-your-helm' routine; and the bombast of Christo For Columbus is punctured, every time the coal-vendor is heard, by the mocking reminder of what he was *in fact* – a two-bit collier, hauling a single load of coal over a negligible channel. Fantastic illusion and crude reality keep cutting across each other; and when the black face of the coal-vendor peers into the room, 'Captain' Boyle sees the real Jack – ugly, black, and featureless – an image of that self which his pride prevents him from acknowledging. The technique of apparent realism and the tone of farce are so skilfully transformed into a dramatic enactment of thematic idea that a superficial reading of the scene becomes the easiest thing in the world.

This form of juxtaposition in which a tragic or ironic reality keeps cutting across the comic illusion is sustained over the entire second act – the riotous gathering of peacocks, strutting about in their tinselled apartment in the expectation of a spurious bequest. It is a scene of music-hall turns and eccentric displays of character, an unleashing of maudlin Irish sentimentality and the hollow gaiety with which they veneer the horrors of their situation. Later in the act, the Captain starts the gramophone going and plays one of those sham-Irish lyrics, popular on commercial radio, giving the lie to the false national bonhomie of the peacocks indifferent, in their revelry, to the grim reality of the Tancred funeral. In the middle of Joxer's song, the parlour door opens to reveal the grieving mother in black; and the raucous din of 'If you're Irish come into the Parlour' is thrown into stark relief by the funeral hymn for the dead boy. This sense of a fool's paradise hangs ominously over the entire act. A world is collapsing, built upon the shaky foundations of false sentiment and abstraction, while those most threatened by its collapse disport themselves in complacent and nonchalant gaiety. The Boyle party has its affinities in modern drama with Madam Ranevskaia's pathetic ball in *The Cherry Orchard*.

In the third act Unpitying Consequence claims the entire family as ruination descends upon those victims of their own illusions: the bequest proves to be a delusion; the daughter is found to be 'with child'; the son is dragged off and executed; the creditors descend upon the Boyles and quite literally rip the clothes off their backs; their furniture is sequestrated; and chaos is come again. The hoary old clichés of melodrama perhaps; but O'Casey manages somehow to take the outmoded and make it strangely appropriate to the play's central theme. Take, for instance, that stock-type of melodrama – the pregnant girl, jilted by her lover and driven out of the house by an irate father. Mary may be her own victim, but she is also victim of the betrayal and hypocrisy of Irish manhood: of Charlie Bentham who dazzles her with his plumage, and then drops her; of Jerry Devine, the rhetorical idealist who turns out to be a man of straw; of her brother's contempt and her father's stony-heartedness. The Captain's independent masculine 'Republic', with its proclamation of 'the sacred rights o' man', is clearly a world without charity, compassion or moral responsibility. The two women, both victims of male peacockery, have no recourse but to leave this 'Republic' to make a better world for Mary's unborn child – the pregnant girl protected by the love and care of the Juno Lucina of the Dublin slums:

MARY: . . . there isn't a God, there isn't a God; if there was He wouldn't let these things happen.

MRS BOYLE: . . . These things have nothin' to do with the Will o' God. Ah, what can God do agen the stupidity o' men. . . . I've got a little room in me sisther's where we'll stop till your throuble is over, an' then we'll work together for the sake of the baby.

MARY: My poor little child that'll have no father!

MRS BOYLE: It'll have what's far betther – it'll have two mothers.

This last is the great Junoesque declaration that has to be made; and O'Casey can make it only by finding a traditional and well-worked situation from which to extract new meaning, new significance.

The same is true of the rather hackneyed device of the appropriating furniture men. Beyond the immediate realism of their function, they serve also to convert the stage physically into an image of chaos, pulling the room to pieces, scattering the furniture, emptying it of its pristine and gaudy splendour. The tenement parlour in the Dublin slum, so firmly rooted in reality, slowly changes into a visual metaphor not only for the condition of the Boyle family but for the chaos of the world – a room from which the heart of flesh and the eternal love have been driven, from which the Goddess of domesticity has been exiled. It resounds, now, with the shriek of drunken peacocks whose actions negate their hollow sentiments and whose slow and unsteady motion around the room, bumping into chairs, dropping their money, falling about in a welter of confusion, enact the chaos of Ireland as a world off course:

BOYLE: The counthry'll have to steady itself. . . it's goin' . . . to hell. . . . Where'r all . . . the chairs . . . gone to . . . steady itself, Joxer. . . . Chairs'll . . . have to . . . steady themselves. . . . No matther . . . what any one may . . . say . . . Irelan' sober . . . is Irelan' . . . free. . . . (*subsiding into a sitting posture on the floor*). Commandant Kelly died . . . in them . . . arms . . . Joxer . . . Tell me Volunteer Butties . . . says he . . . that . . . I died for Irelan'!

JOXER: D'jever rade Willie . . . Reilly . . . an' his own . . . Colleen . . . Bawn? It's a darlin' story, a daarlin' story!

BOYLE: I'm telling you . . . Joxer . . . th' whole worl's . . . in a terr...ible state o' . . . chassis!

The ironies are multiple. It is not only a dramatisation of chaos, but in the maudlin and sentimental rambling of Joxer and the Captain, a diagnosis of the malady in the Irish psyche which had precipitated the chaos in which they find themselves. The entire final scene calls powerfully to mind, as does the fortitude and stoicism of Juno, that splendid passage in *A Vision* where Yeats describes the tragic collapse of the tensions and control which keep civilisation from falling apart:

A civilisation [he writes] is a struggle to keep self-control, and in this it is like some great tragic person, some Niobe, who must display an almost superhuman will or the cry will not touch our sympathy. The loss of control over thought comes towards the end; first a sinking in upon the moral being, then the last surrender, the irrational cry, revelation – the scream of Juno's peacock.

SOURCE: article in *Modern Drama*, xv (1972), pp. 15–25.

NOTES

[Reorganised and renumbered from the original – Ed.]

1. See, especially, Ronald Ayling, Introduction to his edited selection, *Sean O'Casey*, in the 'Modern Judgements' series (London, 1969).

2. The finest of these are: David Krause, *Sean O'Casey: The Man and His Work* (London and New York, 1960), and Robert Hogan, *The Experiments of Sean O'Casey* (New York, 1960).

3. See Vincent C. De Braun, 'Sean O'Casey and the Road to Expressionism', and Katharine J. Worth, 'O'Casey's Dramatic Symbolism', *Modern Drama*, iv, no. 3 (Dec. 1961).

4. P. S. O'Hegarty, 'A Dramatist of New-born Ireland', in R. Ayling (ed.), *Sean O'Casey*, op. cit., p. 63.

5. A. E. Malone, 'O'Casey's Photographic Realism', in R. Ayling, op. cit., p. 71.

6. Juno Lucretia and Juno Populonia.

7. Juno Lucina and Juno Sospita. See *Larousse Encyclopaedia of Mythology* (London, 1959), 217–18.

Michael W. Kaufman   Structural Design
(1972)

For those readers and audiences who regard *Juno and the Paycock* as an amorphous play, marred by contradictory moods and incongruous actions, the concluding scenes have served only to heighten their dissatisfaction.[1] Here, after Juno sombrely exits to prepare for the funeral of her son, Boyle and Joxer stagger drunkenly on stage and the poignant action that had preceded collapses in anti-climax. Even sympathetic critics like David Krause who would defend the play treat this fantastic juxtaposition in the most general terms. According to Krause, the ultimate scene maintains the 'anti-heroic theme' and 'contrapuntal rhythm' of the whole play; O'Casey 'concludes on a tragi-comic note by contrasting Juno's heroic condition with the Captain's mock-heroic condition. For it is his play as well as Juno's; together they represent the tragi-comic cycle of O'Casey's world; together they reveal the ironic cross-purposes of life. . . . It is a final

scene of horrible humour. The Captain remains the "struttin'
paycock" in his glorious deterioration; even in his drunken raving he
remains a magnificently grotesque anti-hero.'[2] The trouble with such
a reading of the play is that it describes rather than explains these
scenes and consequently scarcely illuminates O'Casey's achievement
in *Juno*.

The primary importance of such a juxtaposition is the dramatic
emphasis that results from the sharp contrast. The symbolic opposition that O'Casey introduces through the charactonyms of the title
and maintains through his continual contrast between Juno's nature
and that of her husband, culminates in the final scenes which
effectively underscore the essential difference between Juno and the
paycock. Specifically, both characters encounter chaos – real or
imagined – and their differing responses define the polarised values
that govern the play. Most important, O'Casey achieves this
thematic contrast structurally through the scenic parallelism which
ensures that the impact of the penultimate scene will direct our
response to the conclusion. Once we have witnessed Juno's compassionate and courageous reaction to her tribulations, the paycock's
dipsomania must be understood symbolically, as his habitual intoxication, his evasion of a 'chassis' which now, ironically, seems
inescapably real. The heightened scenic contrast, then, is part of
O'Casey's structural strategy, serving to italicise the central dialectic
informing the play where the need of an unflinching acceptance of
things as they are is set against the human propensity for self-
indulgent illusions. By the play's conclusion O'Casey invites our
judgement, urging us to accept Juno's clear-sighted acceptance of life
while rejecting the paycock's self-serving fantasies and the spirit of
vanity he represents.[3]

The significance which O'Casey apparently attached to these
concluding scenes is conveyed in two ways: first, by their obvious
isolation from the rest of the play. Late in the third act, after Johnny
Boyle has been led to his execution by the avenging Republicans, the
curtain descends. It rises moments later to reveal Mary and Juno
sitting in the darkened, barren tenement where they discuss their fate
and plan their future. Now, having learned of Johnny's death, Mary
and Juno depart and the stage is emptied once again only to prepare
immediately for the entrance of Joxer and Boyle whose ludicrous
capers bring down the final curtain. These scenes, then, clearly cut off
from the preceding action, and separated in turn from each other are
meant to be viewed from a perspective that requires contrastive
judgement.

The second remarkable feature of these contiguous scenes is

O'Casey's deliberate emphasis on the characters' differing response to the events previously unfolded. Juno's moral courage exhibited in her decision to leave the tenement in order 'to face th' ordeal', and 'work for th' sake of th' baby', contrasts with the paycock's moral bankruptcy visually suggested by his inebriated retreat into the empty room and confirmed by his ironic admission that he can 'go no farther'. Juno's spiritually uplifting plea for human brotherhood emphasises the physical collapse of Joxer and Boyle, as the one tumbles into bed and the other sags in a heap onto the floor. And Juno's sober recognition of the necessity for love, kindness, and determination so desperately required to balance 'the stupidity o' men', contrasts with Boyle's drunken evasion of reality implicit in his revealing concession 'the blinds is down', an evasion O'Casey reinforces by interspersing snatches of proverb, slogan, and song whose spirit of dreamy optimism clashes so sharply with the actual conditions of living the play delineates.

The paycock's self-induced blindness, however, is merely the most apparent example of all the characters' limited vision of actuality. *Juno and the Paycock* is a play of betrayed expectations: the family's anticipation of the legacy; Mary's romantic dreams and social aspirations; Johnny's desperate hope of escaping his retribution; the paycock's vain anticipation of never having to work again; and Juno's profound wish to keep her family together. Appropriately, the anti-climactic final scenes brilliantly epitomise the entire play where the rhythm of illusion and disillusion provides the larger dramatic structure. In the overall framework O'Casey accomplishes this pattern in two general ways. First, he so structures the play that it falls into complementary halves. The first part, up to the startling intrusion of Robbie Tancred's funeral into the Boyles' celebration is devoted to the nurturing of the family's hopes; the second part, beginning with the sudden reversal of mood brings the Boyles face-to-face with disaster revealing the finality with which their hopes are dashed. The first part, as befits the theme of great expectations, is largely exuberant and expansive stretching over most of the first two acts as if to emphasise the pervasive illusions the Boyles cultivate. The second part, in harmony with the sudden deflation of those illusions, proceeds much more rapidly as reality explodes the Boyles' collective and individual dreams in the climactic scene of the last act.

Now just as the play's larger structure conveys the idea that false illusions invite catastrophes, each of the first two acts presents a completed action, a structural miniature of this rhythm. Each act is built upon the discrepancy between the characters' expectations and the very different actuality they confront. The delightfully humorous impact of the opening act derives from the paycock's profound dread of work, a fear so abiding that he repeatedly imagines approaching footsteps to be Juno's, the one actual threat to his carefree liberty. After several false alarms Juno does appear, bringing with her not the dreaded command to work but the joyous news of the forthcoming legacy.

But if the first act ends with Boyle's imagined fears harmlessly dissolving in the laughter of his apparent good fortune, the second act moves toward reversing this balance. It opens on the family's preparation to celebrate their promised legacy. O'Casey has calculated every detail to emphasise the aura of unreality about this scene. Suggestive visual details of furnishings and decorations transform the drab tenement into a setting of fantasy; cheap pictures adorn the walls and garish paper chains hang from the ceiling; 'every available spot is ornamented with huge vases filled with artificial flowers'. The final touch is achieved with Boyle's appearance 'voluptuously stretched on the sofa. . . . smoking a clay pipe.' The stage picture with its luxuriant details focuses the paycock's recently acquired majesty, but most of all this scene stresses the absurdity of human pretensions.

In the theatre these scenes assume all the exuberance and boisterousness associated with such a celebration. Accordingly, O'Casey calibrates the action along a building scale of clamorous sounds and rapid movements which reach a pitch only to have the mood ruptured suddenly: in the midst of the singing and dancing Mrs Tancred appears on the way to her son's burial. Now the solemn tolling of church bells, the muted footsteps of mourners, and the chant of somber hymns replace the sounds of the gramophone and the carousing. Nevertheless, the emphasis of these scenes is on the Boyles' festive exuberance and thus the act provides a summation of the entire play. Here, as throughout, their impulsive desire to embrace illusions simultaneously necessitates their perverse refusal to comprehend reality. In this context Robbie Tancred's funeral procession provides a sobering contrast to the Boyles' rites of celebration; but more generally the intrusion of death emphatically reminds us that the Boyles' happiness is merely transient, subject to human and natural limitations which the remainder of the play will emphasise. The synecdochical central act compresses the play's entire structure. It begins with merriment born of the Boyles' wishful expectations, rises to a climax that suggests the *hybris* of their expectations, and ends with the clear anticipation of their nemesis.

The second general way in which O'Casey underlines his contrast between human self-deceptions and actuality is implicit in the play's three plots.[4] Each presents a variation on the theme of how reality defeats human illusions. The ironic difference between dream and actual outcome is most clearly established by the loss of the promised legacy which as the main plot line stands at the structural and symbolic center of the play. This significant defeat of the family's hopes is revealed during the crucial interlude just after the scene of the Boyles' jubilant rejoicing. Their fortunes which up to this point have been in the ascendent are now suddenly reversed by a chance misfortune, the result of Bentham's legal blunder. But if the loss of the inheritance suggests the capricious way life conspires to dash human expectations, the subsidiary plots involving the Boyle children present parallel ways in which man's self-delusions encourage disaster. Both Johnny and Mary, present during the opening scene, reveal their own particular confusion between wish and actuality. Not far from the votive light whose flickering flame suggests his own insecure faith, sits Johnny 'crouched beside the fire', the external manifestation of his hellish fears. Here the illusions a character entertains are most dangerous, therefore the consequences are most grave. Johnny whose patriotic fervor has already cost him the use of his hip and arm, now vainly hopes that his wounds constitute full payment of his debt to Ireland's cause. His delusion of disentangling himself from the patriotic ideals he once espoused is made painfully clear by the brutal retribution that finally overtakes him, an end that only affirms what he has already been told: 'No man can do enough for Ireland!' And as the Civil War raging outside becomes in O'Casey's hands the symbolic correlative of the several betrayals the play enacts – a universal treachery violating sacred precepts of brotherhood and nation – so is Johnny's callous betrayal of his boyhood friend a dramatic expression of the fragility of his high-minded principles.

Introduced preening her hair, insensitive to her brother's anguish, Mary, on the other hand, forms part of a richly evocative stage picture; the cluttered, shabby tenement clashes sharply with her youthful vitality and freshness. But essentially what O'Casey stresses is Mary's preoccupation with appearances, a preoccupation which reveals the serious distortion of human values she entertains. Early in the play O'Casey makes clear Mary's vanity and cultural pretensions. Her flaunted displays of refinement, her embarrassment regarding her family, and her obsession with fashions reveal her childish concern with appearances; and this vanity anticipates her blindness in rejecting the devoted Jerry Devine for a 'Micky Dazzler' with a walkin' stick an' gloves'. But most significantly, Mary's absolute allegiance to the Trades Union, her unthinking endorsement of Jennie Claffey, her insistent reduction of life's complexities to the phrase 'a principle's a principle', and her infatuated attachment to the shallow Bentham demonstrate her naive elevation of romance over reality.

All three plots, then, present variations on the common theme of the vanity of human wishes variously related to wealth and status, love and honor. But O'Casey also strengthens this theme through his masterful use of the setting. The play's three acts unfold within the unchanging set of the Boyle home which itself seems a secured haven from the Civil War outside. But the tenement is not only a family dwelling; its physical separation into two rooms becomes a visual metaphor for the way men attempt to escape their sordid reality. Most of the action takes place in the living room where the family learns of its rising and falling fortunes. To the left of the set, however, is a door leading to an interior room which is rapidly associated with the secure sanctuary to which the Boyle men frequently retreat to avoid their responsibilities. On the other side of the stage a window and door provide access to the street, the outside world where war, death, and love are powerful elements in human experience.

Within this scenic arrangement the characters acquire significance as they move between the two rooms – and in and out of the tenement itself. Early in the play O'Casey establishes such a pattern when Johnny quickly runs to the room on the left while Mary and Juno discuss Robbie Tancred's murder. For Johnny, who has ample reason to fear life's actualities, the inner room becomes his vain refuge from his ghastly fate, and he fittingly spends most of his time secluded within. While Johnny provides O'Casey's deliberate indication of the significance of the setting, both Juno and the paycock are measured within this pattern as they stand at opposite extremes; and their contrastive movements in the final scenes make the point better than any dialogue of their willingness to confront life's actualities.

Captain Boyle, his self-styled title derived from a single voyage on a coal barge, embodies the strutting vanities his name implies, a cankered pride that results from his overweening, self-indulgent nature. Whether by overt falsehood or covert deceit, Boyle's overmastering obsession is to evade life's demands either by improvising ailments or by escaping into drunken reveries. Significantly, he moves between the two rooms, appearing in the living quarters only when actual affairs conform with his private fantasies. During the second act when the Boyle fortunes are at their zenith, he is securely ensconced in the living room, reigning over the festivities, directing the celebration. At the beginning of the third act, however, after all the family's hopes have been defeated, he is as firmly entrenched in the inner room from which he emerges only to abandon the tenement altogether. It is perhaps O'Casey's most forceful reminder of Boyle's unwillingness to face reality that the paycock is on stage both at the beginning and the end of the third act, but conspicuously absent when the full catastrophe comes upon his family.

At the other extreme is Juno who is furthest removed from the fantasies and escapism her family practices. She rejects the abstract principles her children espouse and exposes the deceits her husband perpetuates. Fittingly, she enters the inner room only to minister to the needs of her family, and her dramatic departure from the barren tenement in the last act implies her final and complete rejection of the sentimental and selfish illusions her family has cultivated.

It is, however, one of the clearest proofs of O'Casey's artistry that even Juno who understands life's realities best must gradually achieve a still deeper consciousness of the ways of the world. Significantly, the play opens with Mary's calm rehearsal of a neighbor's death. Neither she nor Juno, who enters immediately, is aware of the implications of the event they here treat so cavalierly. Now Juno can only comprehend the political significance of Robbie Tancred's death, insisting that 'everybody's sayin'' that he was a Die-hard' and thanking God 'that Johnny had nothin' to do with him this long time'. Juno's disdain for political affiliations and her insensitivity to Mrs Tancred's suffering is emphasised during the second act where Juno callously asserts that her neighbor's grief is justified: 'In wan way, she deserves all she got; for lately, she let th' Die-hards make an open house of th' place; an' for th' last couple of months, either when the sun was risin' or when th' sun was settin', you had CID men burstin' into your room, assin' you where were you born, where were you christened, where were you married, an' where would you be buried!' If Juno reproves the celebrating company and reproaches herself for 'forgettin' about him bein' brought to the church to-night, an' we singin' an' all', she is still not sensitive enough to apprehend fully the solemnity and significance of Robbie Tancred's funeral. Thus with barely restrained excitement she exhorts her husband to 'put on a record', and joins her friends first at the window and then in the street to watch the spectacle of the procession.

It is, therefore, of utmost significance for Juno's developing awareness that the *memento mori* assumes an increasingly heightened function in the play's design. From the initial dispassionate mention of a neighbor's death, to the immediacy of Robbie Tancred's funeral, up to the death of Johnny Boyle in the final act, the reminder of the actual world of Time and Death presses more closely in on Juno's consciousness. Late in the second act in response to her husband's peremptory dismissal of the death and destruction as beyond their

concern, Juno recognises the pervasive implications of such events:
'I'd like to know how a body's not to mind these things; look at the
way they're afther leavin' the people in this very house. Hasn't the
whole house, nearly, been massacreed? . . . Sure, if it's not our
business, I don't know whose business it is.'

But while there is an essential sanity to Juno's expression of
concern here, the dramatic evidence for her deepening compassion
occurs during the last act where her former callous attitude toward
the Tancreds is qualified immensely by her own son's murder.
'Maybe I didn't feel sorry enough for Mrs Tancred', Juno reflects as
she confronts and accepts the fragility of the human condition in its
ultimate symbol: the death of her own child. The scene is important
not merely because Juno recognises the limits of mortality, but
because that acceptance elicits her deeper compassion for human
suffering and her renewed commitment to living.

If O'Casey dwells for most of the three acts on the comic and cruel
discrepancies between man's illusions and the actualities of life they
ignore, the play's closing moments move toward an acceptance of
human limitations. O'Casey carefully shapes a testament to human
resilience and life's continuity, a testament profoundly left simply
because Juno affirms it in the face of impending doom. As she
confronts Mary, who has just renounced her faith in God and in life
because of the ordeal she faces, Juno rejects the course of self-pity,
insisting that man must accept responsibility for life's vicissitudes:
'These things have nothin' to do with the Will o' God. Ah, what can
God do agen the stupidity o' men!' Appropriately, Juno urges on
Mary the imperative need to go on living, to make a new life; the need
not only to face disillusionment, but to create anew in spite of it.

And the fitting symbol of this ability to affirm hope out of despair,
to wrestle meaning out of misery is Mary's pregnancy, at once the
product of life's betrayal and the testimony to life's continuity that
Juno recognises as the source of man's faith: 'We'll go. Come, Mary,
an' we'll never come back here agen. Let your father furrage for
himself now; I've done all I could an' it was all no use – he'll be
hopeless till the end of his days. I've got a little room in me sisther's
where we'll stop till your throuble is over, an' then we'll work together
for the sake of the baby.' Before Juno can lead Mary out of the past
and with her literally create new life, she must momentarily pause to
bury the old; she must attend to the painful task of burying her son. It
is this effort that elicits her poignant prayer, which, as has been
frequently noted, repeats Mrs Tancred's benediction of Act II. But
O'Casey's dramatic language is more subtle than mere repetition
would suggest. The parallel phrasing and balanced repetition of Mrs

Tancred's prayer create a sense of poetic harmony which contrasts emphatically with her personal sorrow and the chaos in the world. Moreover, the rhythm of Mrs Tancred's prayer suggests her exalted sensibility which enables her to achieve an understanding of personal suffering that transcends political allegiances and social divisions and forges a moral bond between men. Thus, Mrs Manning whose son was a Free Stater and herself whose child fought for the Republicans are no longer adversaries but mourning mothers whose personal losses balance the 'scales o' sorra'.

When in the final act Juno is forced to a consciousness of a world subjected to change and death, of men victimised by their own betrayed illusions, O'Casey carefully underscores her deepening perception of what it is that gives meaning and significance to human life. Born of an awareness of Mary's anguish and her own intense grief, Juno remembers her former reaction to Robbie Tancred's death, and chides herself now to recognise what she didn't then – that 'he wasn't a Diehard or a Stater, but only a poor dead son'. Like Mrs Tancred, Juno learns her symbolic equality with her neighbors. But that experience, which had established for Mrs Tancred the bond between two grieving neighbors, becomes for Juno the more embracing community of suffering, and now Mrs Tancred's benediction for 'the pair of us' no longer suffices. Juno's recognition of universal human frailty receives its full and climactic expression when she begins her prayer for compassion with the plea that 'Mother o' God, have pity on us all!'

After O'Casey strips away the illusions and self-deceptions of which men are guilty what remains is the sense of life in its harsh actuality and the need for acceptance and sympathy despite, or rather because of, the betrayals and human limitations the play has enacted. Consequently, the paycock's drunken evasion of consciousness provides the important contrast to Juno's unequivocal acceptance of life's realities. David Krause is surely correct when he suggests that in Boyle, O'Casey portrays a type of comic resilience – the ingenious sense of self-indulgence and self-preservation.[5]

But the crucial effect of O'Casey's dramatic contrast is to accentuate the difference between Juno's creative endurance within the world of human affairs and the paycock's sterile self-preservation within the realm of drunken fantasy. If 'Irelan' sober is Irelan' free', this concluding scene dramatises concretely Juno's liberation and the paycock's imprisonment within his own deluded self-importance.

The paycock is not so much witty in himself as he is the cause of wit in other men and herein lies his primary function in O'Casey's dramatic design. The play's expressed judgement, everyone agrees, is in favor of Juno's capacity to endure which in a very significant sense is bound up with her capacity to suffer. But the corollary valuation the play enforces is the complete rejection of the paycock's willful retreat from actuality, his perversion of the creative energy of which human nature is capable. His ability to absorb reality into the life of the imagination which we have found so amusing up to now, here becomes a dangerous hallucination which works to transform the very real ruin his family faces into an imaginative and therefore harmless 'chassis'. The concluding scenes then are meant to create a structural pattern that is itself a dramatic image of O'Casey's thematic dialectic between reality and illusion. The shifting point-of-view forces us first to face life with Juno deprived of the palliating fantasies and then to laugh critically *at* the paycock, representative of the foolish illusions and pompous selfishness that genuinely threaten chaos in our world.

SOURCE: article in *Quarterly Journal of Speech*, LVIII (1972), pp. 191–8.

NOTES

[Reorganised and renumbered from the original – Ed.]

1. For the earlier critical hostility to the concluding scenes of *Juno*, see Saros Cowasjee, *Sean O'Casey: The Man Behind the Plays* (London, 1963), pp. 48–9. A more recent condemnation of the play's ending appears in J. L. Styan, *The Dark Comedy: The Development of Modern Comic Tragedy* (Cambridge, 1968), pp. 174–5, 263. Styan suggests that O'Casey made a 'fatal miscalculation' at the end of *Juno* since the final scene brutally contradicts the emotional impact of Juno's pathetic prayer.

2. David Krause, *Sean O'Casey: The Man and His Work* (London and New York, 1960), p. 79.

3. O'Casey certainly intended Boyle's strutting vainglory to be symbolic of his dangerous self-aggrandisement. In a letter written to Ronald G. Rollins reprinted in part in 'Form and Content in Sean O'Casey's Dublin Trilogy', *Modern Drama*, VIII (Feb. 1966), p. 424, O'Casey wrote: '*Juno* is a tragedy of vanity and of relinquishment to vanity. There are many Captain Boyles in this world – in love with their own images. Most of us have many minor vanities but they do not cripple our ability to act sensibly. But the Captain and his parasitical companion have let their selfish, petty interests ruin their lives – and the lives of others.'

4. Criticism of *Juno* has dwelled persistently on the apparent lack of connection among the play's major plot lines. Cf. Cowasjee, pp. 48ff. Cowasjee cites the hostility of early reviewers who could discover no clear relation among the play's three plot lines. Cowasjee himself weakly argues that the connection is not necessary since 'O'Casey is giving us a realistic picture of tenement life, and he often sees in each life a rounded plot in itself'. Even Robert Hogan, one of O'Casey's most perceptive critics, in *The Experiments of Sean O'Casey* (New York, 1960), p. 37, understands the major fault of the play to be 'that the exterior action of the gain and loss of the legacy has little connection with some of the interior action'.

5. Krause, op. cit., p. 71.

PART FOUR

The Plough and the Stars

The Plough and the Stars

Première: 8 February 1926, Abbey Theatre, Dublin.

First London production: 12 May 1926, Fortune Theatre.

First New York production: 27 November 1927, Hudson Theatre.

A film version was made by RKO Radio Pictures in 1936, with its first screening in New York in January 1937. Directed by John Ford, it starred Barry Fitzgerald, Barbara Stanwyck and Eileen Crowe.

1. COMMENT AND REVIEWS

Gabriel Fallon   (1961)

. . . Yes, he was working on a longer play. He was thinking of calling it *The Plough and the Stars* after the name of the flag of the Citizen Army, the design for which had been suggested by the poet George Russell. He didn't like work. (Who did?) He had to drive himself to it. In fact he had to write on a piece of paste-board which he displayed on his mantel-piece: GET ON WITH THE BLOODY PLAY! He *was* getting on with it. Would I like to hear some which he had written that day? It was a scene in which a Catholic priest tried to cajole two male characters into attending the Mission which was being held at a neighbouring church. It never appeared in the play; it had to go in the general cutting from a script that in its final form was much too long for presentation. So far as I remember, it was a very funny scene and mainly concerned the Covey. . . .

Lennox Robinson came to '422' [North Circular Road, O'Casey's lodgings] on one occasion, a most unfortunate one, as it so happened. For a rising jealousy of the new playwright had impelled him to upset completely O'Casey's casting of *The Plough and the Stars*. Availing himself of his privilege as producer of the play and his position as Director of the Abbey Theatre, he insisted on putting most of the players in parts for which they were never intended. This, added to the political machinations of one Director [W. B. Yeats], and the moral objections raised by another Director [George O'Brien], led to a situation in which the play that O'Casey wrote failed to reach an Irish audience until many years after the riot-bedevilled first production. But that is another story.[1]

However, it was clear that the author himself – apart from the miscasting confusion brought about by Lennox Robinson – had a few preproduction misgivings. One was that he had written the part of Bessie Burgess for the great Sara Allgood. Sara was not available for the first production, and he doubted Maureen Delany's ability to give the part its full tragic quality, particularly in the death scene. As it happened Delany played the part surprisingly well for Delany, a fact which the dramatist generously admitted.

He told me that he had had some difficulty in writing this particular death scene. 'Now, had Bessie been a Catholic', he said, 'she would say an "Act of Contrition" knowing she was at death's door. What would a Protestant do? That was my problem. And then this hymn – a rather nice hymn, by the same token – occurred to me.'

> *I do believe, I will believe*
> *That Jesus died for me*
> *That on th' cross He shed His blood,*
> *From sin to set me free . . .*

And he sang it for me. 'I feel it's just possible', he said, 'that the words of this hymn might return to the semi-consciousness of the dying Bessie.'

He appeared to be somewhat worried about 'The Voice of the Man' outside the public house in Act II. Feeling that the scene was considerably heightened in drama by the Voice – indeed, that the Voice was the dramatic backbone of the scene – I assured him that he had nothing to be worried about. But his worries were not of the dramatic kind. 'You see, Gaby', he said, 'that speech is made up of extracts from speeches delivered by Padraic Pearse and there are people who knew Pearse who might object.' I tried to assure him that, objections or not, it would be ruinous dramatically to tamper with or remove the speech. As it happened, there were others, including William Butler Yeats, who saw the possibility of objectors feeling that the dramatist was deliberately mocking one of the revered leaders of the Easter Rising. But that, as I said, is another story.

SOURCE: extract from 'The House on the North Circular Road – Fragments from a Biography', in *Modern Drama*, IV (1961), pp. 231–2.

NOTE

1. [Ed.] The story is retold in Gabriel Fallon's book, *Sean O'Casey: The Man I Knew* (London, 1965).

Lady Gregory   (1925–26)

March 11, 1925: [staying with W. B. Yeats] O'Casey came last night [for] Yeats' 'Monday' [literary evening 'at home'], also A.E. and Mr Jewell and Alan Duncan and Gogarty dropped in late. . . . O'Casey, sheltering by me, interested me most. .... When the others were talking of hashish, Casey told me he had been all but shot in the Rising. He had taken no part in it, but a shot had been fired from some house he was in or near, and the soldiers had dragged him out and were actually raising their rifles to fire at him – 'I felt in a daze, just from instinct I said a prayer, was certain death was there. But someone fired a shot that just missed their captain, and they ran to see where it came from, and I ran for my life through the fields and escaped.' He thinks the Rising was 'a terrible mistake and we lost such fine men. We should have won freedom by degrees with them.' . . .

August 23, 1925: [at Coole Park] Casey arrived yesterday. His play, *The Plough and the Stars*, had come in the morning with a letter from Lennox Robinson saying he and W. B. Yeats liked it. I slipped away after dinner and read the first act to myself, and finding it so good I took it to the library and read it to Jack [B. Yeats] and his wife (and the author), and they liked it, a fine opening but tragic. He has been working on it for thirteen months and is tired and glad of a rest, his delight in the country as great as ever, for he still lives in his tenement room.

Sept. 2: Dolan [actor and director, then manager at the Abbey] writes objecting to *The Plough and the Stars*. 'At any time I would think twice before having anything to do with it. The language is – to use an Abbey phrase – "beyond the beyonds". The song at the end of the second act, sung by the "girl-of-the-streets", is impossible.'

Sept. 20: Yeats came on Friday evening, 'important Abbey business', his telegram had said, and it is important. 'Trouble with George O'Brien, the new Director' [then recently appointed by the Irish government, upon the granting of an annual subsidy to the Abbey – Ed.], he said, and showed me the letters. He objects to *The Plough and the Stars*. I said at once: 'Our position is clear. If we have to choose between the subsidy and our freedom, it is our freedom we choose. And we must tell him there was no condition attached to the subsidy, and though in connection with it another Director was suggested, I cannot be sure whether by me or Blythe [then Minister of Finance and responsible for the subsidy – Ed.], there was no word at all of his being censor, but only to strengthen us on the financial side, none of us being good at money-matters or accounts.' . . .

Yeats says Casey said about the song that must be removed from his play. 'Yes, It's a pity. It would offend thousands. But it ought to be there.'. . .

[The *Journal* then quotes] a letter from George O'Brien: 'Mr Yeats and I have read O'Casey's new play and are convinced that it would be quite as successful as any of his others if produced. There are, however, certain particulars in which I think the play in its present form would seriously offend the audience, and I think it must be amended in certain respects before it can be staged.' . . .

Yeats answered: 'We agree with you about Clitheroe and his wife. That love scene in the first act is most objectionable and, as you said, does not ring true. What is wrong is that O'Casey is there writing about people whom he does not know, whom he has only read about. We had both decided when we first read the play that he should be asked to try and modify these characters, bringing them within the range of his knowledge. When that is done the objectionable elements will lose their sentimentality and thereby their artistic offence. We decided that if he cannot do this the dialogue would have to be greatly modified in rehearsal.

'Now we come to the prostitute in Act II. She is certainly as necessary to the general action and idea as are the drunkards and wastrels. O'Casey is contrasting the ideal dream with the normal grossness of life and of that she is an essential part. It is no use putting her in if she does not express herself vividly and in character, if her "professional" side is not emphasised. Almost certainly a phrase here and there must be altered in rehearsal but the scene as a whole is admirable, one of the finest O'Casey has written. To eliminate any parts of it on grounds that have nothing to do with dramatic literature would be to deny all our traditions.

'The other passages you mention are the kind of things which are dealt with in rehearsal by the producer (in almost every one of O'Casey's plays the dialogue has been here and there a little modified and he has never objected to our modification), but we are inclined to think that the use of the word "bitch" in Act IV is necessary. It occurs when Bessie, receiving her mortal wound, turns furiously on the woman whose delirium has brought it on her. The scene is magnificent and we are loth to alter a word of it. If you do not feel that this letter entirely satisfies you we can have a Directors' meeting on the subject. WBY.'

Sept. 24: The Directors' meeting. Dr O'Brien making his objections to the play: I, chiefly spokesman (by request), telling him Blythe had made no condition whatever in giving the subsidy and certainly no hint of appointing a censor. I told him of our old fights about *Countess*

Cathleen (with the Catholic Church), *Blanco Posnet* (with the Government), Lord Aberdeen's efforts to get passages left out of the play (as now played in England), and my refusal (though there was a real threat of closing the Theatre). Yeats also spoke in the same sense. O'Brien sat up in his chair reiterating at intervals, 'That song is objectionable.' (We had already decided that it must go, but left it as a bone for him to gnaw at.) 'And that word bitch', etc. We told him cuts are usually made in rehearsal, by producers and players, but that we had at the beginning told Casey the Clitheroe parts must be rewritten, etc., and at last got O'Brien to confess, 'I had mistaken my position' (of censor). But he wants to see a rehearsal a little later. . . . It was a long meeting: I wished some artist could have looked in, Yeats and I so animated, Lennox Robinson so amused, George O'Brien sitting upright repeating, 'That song must be left out!'

Sept. 25: Directors' meeting easy. O'Brien like a lamb, though after it he held back Perrin to say, 'I think Mr Robinson has now given up that song.' . . .

Jan. 10, 1926: Yesterday to the Abbey, and saw part of a rehearsal of the *Plough and the Stars* – the public-house scene, it will go well, I think, a good deal of variety in different points of view. . . .

Feb. 14 1926 Sunday: On Friday I left for Dublin to see *The Plough and the Stars*. I got the post and papers in Gort and when the train had started opened the *Independent* and saw a heading right across the page, 'Riotous Scenes at the Abbey. Attempt to stop O'Casey's play', and an account of wild women, especially, having raised a disturbance, blown whistles, etc., prevented second act from being heard and had then clambered on to the stage – a young man had struck Miss Delany [actress playing the part of Bessie Burgess] on the face, etc., etc. Then the police had been sent for, and quiet apparently restored for the rest of the play to be given. . . .

At Athenry I got the *Irish Times*, which gave a fuller account. Yeats had spoken from the stage but the clamour had drowned his speech, but the reporters had got some of it. . . .

Yeats met me at the station and gave his account of the row; thought of inviting the disturbers to a debate as we had done in the *Playboy* riots, but I was against that. . . .

We found the Abbey crowded, many being turned away. Yeats said that last night he had been there by accident, for he does not often go to more than one performance. Robinson had not come that evening and when the disturbance began and he wanted to call for police he found it was Perrin's night off and the telephone had been closed up. But at last the Civic Guards came and carried the women off the stage and the play went on without interruption to the end. . . .

I thought the play very fine indeed. And the next day [Saturday, 13 Feb.] at the matinée, when, though the house was full and overflowing, there was no danger of riot and I could listen without distraction, it seemed to me a very wonderful play – 'the forgiveness of sins', as real literature is supposed to be. These quarrelling, drinking women have tenderness and courage, showing all through, as have the men. At intervals in the public-house scene one hears from the meeting being held outside fragments of a speech of Pearse (spoken in Stephenson's fine voice with extraordinary effect). One feels those who heard it were forced to obey its call, not to be afraid to fight even in the face of defeat. One honours and understands their emotion. Lionel Johnson's lines to Ireland came into my mind:

> For thy dead is grief on thee?
> Can it be thou dost repent
> That they went, thy chivalry
> Those sad ways magnificent?

And then comes what all nations have seen, the suffering that falls through war, and especially civil war, on the women, the poor, the wretched homes and families of the slums. An overpowering play. I felt at the end of it as if I should never care to look at another; all others would seem so shadowy to the mind after this.

SOURCE: extracts from *Lady Gregory's Journals*, edited by Lennox Robinson (London, 1946), pp. 86–92, 94–8, 259–60.

Sean O'Casey

I A Retrospect   (1960)

It is strange how simple things and simple incidents weave a way into a life and often shape its ends; or is it the Destiny that Shakespeare says 'shapes our ends, rough hew them how we will'? Well, I suppose that things and incidents are parts of that Destiny that raises us up or knocks us down. An odder thing is that Destiny's knockout may, after all, happen to have been a good thing, whereas Destiny's uplift may, in the end, prove to have been the sorriest thing that ever happened to us. So in Destiny's knockout – courage; within Destiny's uplift – an occasional remembrance that what happens to every golden lassie and every golden lad happens to us; and that after Destiny's everlasting knockout we shall be where our brightest success doesn't mean a damned thing.

Well, the play called *The Plough and the Stars* came into existence in an odd way; and the effects of its living presentation on the stage gave Destiny an opportunity to shunt me from the way I went on to another and stranger road altogether. I, of course, lived in the midst of all the events described in the play. There I was part of them, yet subconsciously commenting on all that was said, much that was done, to be coloured afterward (though I had no inkling of this at the time) through my imagination, seeing at the same time, the sad humour and vigorous tragedy of this historic time to Ireland.

I had been one, with Jim Larkin, to welcome the flag [which gives the play its title]; to unfold it and fix it to the staff; to expose it, like a sacrament to the Citizen Army members, who gave it a great cheer, and from every point of view the flag deserved one. It was this flag that fired in my mind the title for the play; and the events that swirled around the banner and that of the Irish Volunteers, the tricolor of green, white and orange – now fading to an incoherent yellow – that gave me all the humour, pathos and dialogue that fill the play.

Another odd incident gave me an urge to the writing of it: after *Juno and the Paycock* I wrote two one-act plays, *Kathleen Listens In* and *The Cooing of Doves*, which I sent in to the Abbey Theatre for consideration. I doubted any acceptance of the first play, but was quite confident about the second one. A few weeks later a letter came when stars were failing, to say that *Kathleen Listens In* had been welcomed, but the other play, *The Cooing of Doves*, wasn't considered to be a sparkler and was herewith returned with thanks. A shock! Two shocks! One for the rejection itself; the other for the bad judgement of the directors in thinking the accepted play better than the one rejected. Hints before in letters and conversation, now a definite realization that Abbey Theatre judgements were hooped with fallibility, like all other opinions of error-garlanded man.

. . . Meanwhile, I remembered that I had written a play about the Black and Tan period; about the period of the Civil War; but no play yet around the period of the actual Easter Rising, which was the beginning of all that happened afterward. So I set about illumining and ravaging my mind for a new play about the Easter Rising, setting down scene and dialogue, taking notes on any piece of paper that was handy when an idea or word struck me.

I never make a scenario, depending on the natural growth of a play
rather than on any method of joinery. Things I saw, things I heard,
flooded my mind, and the germ became the gist, with a title vaguely
selected of *The Easter Lily Aflame*; but the Banner and its design came
too often before my mind to be set aside, so the title eventually became
The Plough and the Stars. Then it was that I began to know more about
the artistic, middle-class and intelligentsia face of Dublin, and it
wasn't so delightful as I had assumed it would be; brimstone and
sulphur fumed out from the white flame. A most unhappy time at
rehearsals; Lennox Robinson irritable, at times abusive; some of the
Roman Catholic members of the company in revolt against the play,
one of them declaring she wouldn't say that she never had a kid born
outside the borders of the Ten Commandments – as if it were a sin, an
occasion, even, of sin to be born within their borders; another aflame
with fear and dismay at the song sung by Fluther in the pub scene; still
another declaring in dressing room and in the wings that he would
never, never say 'snotty,' though it is an Anglo-Saxon word, meaning,
according to Skeat's etymological dictionary, 'mucus from the nose'.

I was a little bewildered by the apparent agitation on the stage, not
knowing yet all that was happening there, and troubled at the time
with a painful bout of eye inflammation, I had too much on my mind
to bother. Then came the performance and the great roar – a roar that
shook the homes of Dublin and the corn waving in Ireland's four
beautiful fields! Scholars, saints, hurlers and bards shouted down
O'Casey; and in spite of the herculean defiance of the indomitable
poet, Yeats, I felt as Ruth felt among the alien corn; I was an alien in
my own land. The next day, angry and abusive letters against the play
shone darkly from the Dublin papers, and O'Casey was told by many
symbols in speech and letter that the shamrock wasn't for him to
pluck. It was time to go.

All the time, there was hovering in my mind that *The Cooing of
Doves*, the play rejected by the Abbey Theatre, now formed the
much-praised second act of the play: the stone the builders rejected,
though not a cornerstone, was an essential part of the building; the
Abbey was fallible. (Lady Gregory, alone of the others, remembered,
and when I went to visit her she mentioned how happily *The Cooing of
Doves* welded into the heart of another play. It went in with but a few
minor changes.) . . .

SOURCE: extracts from '*The Plough and the Stars* in Retrospect', *New
York Times* (4 Dec. 1960).

ii The Political Background   (1964)

The Plough and the Stars was the banner of the Irish Citizen Army, a body of men formed from the Irish Labour Union to protect members from police strikes in 1914. The Plough on the banner symbolised labour; the Stars, the aspirations of the Labour Movement.

The Irish Volunteers, built up on the plan of Lord Carson's Volunteers, were formed to 'protect the liberties common to all Irish', but, inspired by members of the secret society called 'The Fenians', really worked to overthrow British rule in Ireland. These two organisations united together in 1916 and fought against England in the rebellion, known in Ireland as 'Easter Week'.

The first scene of the play shows Captain Clitheroe called to an assembly of both organisations, held to inspire the members for the fight that was soon to come. He leaves his wife to join the meeting and procession. The second act shows the meeting in progress outside a public-house, the Volunteer Leader speaking to his men, and the effect of his words on the civilians present. The third act shows the rebellion in full swing, with three Irish soldiers – including Captain Clitheroe – falling back on their Headquarters – one of them wounded. It shows, too, the civilians – who were hostile to the fighting – taking advantage of the confusion, to loot all they can lay their hands on. The fourth act shows the city of Dublin – a lot of it in flames – in the hands of the British troops, who are closing in on the Volunteers, making their last stand together in the Headquarters of the Irish Army, and the happenings in the tenement home during the fighting.

SOURCE: Programme Note written for the Abbey Theatre production which opened on 27 April 1964 at the London International Festival of Drama.

Brigid O'Higgins   (1926)

Sean O'Casey's powerful drama, *The Plough and the Stars*, is in the tradition of the great French and Russian realists, though it is nothing of a slavish imitation, for the dramatist is his own master. In this play he gives a critical, cynical and impassioned picture of existence in the

Dublin slums during the historic years of 1915–16. He does not shrink
from portraying tenement life as he himself knew it, and if at very rare
intervals the tragedy verges on melodrama – for O'Casey still lacks
restraint – the man is honestly striving for the truth and is seldom very
far from it.

Despite some palpable exaggerations which, when they appear,
mar the artistry of the drama, and a certain looseness in construction,
there is strength, sincerity and genius behind the work. It does not
reach the same heights of dramatic intensity as its predecessor, *Juno
and the Paycock*, nor does it touch the emotions so keenly – perhaps it is
not so great a play – but there is a more terrible force, a more
turbulent passion, a more ghastly Nemesis, which make it more
robust than the earlier tragedy.

In his delineation of character, O'Casey is most convincing. He
attains less success in the kneading of incident into a dramatic whole.
The characters in *The Plough and the Stars* are real men and women,
and, while the dramatist is merciless in his depiction of these tenement
dwellers, making no excuses for their shiftlessness, their inefficiency,
there is nothing condescending in his treatment of them – rather is
there a delicacy of touch, for too well O'Casey knows the pride of the
poor. Throughout the drama the strength of the blood-tie is there.
These people of the slums are his own kith and kin: he understands
them, and, while castigating them, he loves them. It is his very love for
his kind which causes his terrible cynicism and which gives the
passion to his theme. Urged on by it, he must ease his heart and cry
aloud of the starved, monotonous, wretched lives of these people – his
cry reaches all of us who pass by the way!

What the result of this impassioned though cynical analysis of slum
conditions in our city is like to be is a debatable point. This at least the
dramatist has achieved: by forcing us to face the facts of life as they
are, the true, unpleasant things, Sean O'Casey has shaken our
smugness; he has ruthlessly dispelled that convenient smoke-screen
which would shut out from our comfortable drawing-rooms the awful
reality of a side of Dublin life that men and women, our fellow-
citizens, are daily up against. The dramatist has shown a remarkable
courage in facing facts and a broad sympathy in his treatment of
them. Perhaps he asks us to do the same?

So much for the artist's message! Sometimes an over-emphasis
hampers O'Casey in the artistry of its delivery. The lengthy,
well-polished speeches do not always sit quite easily on the lips of the
men and the women one meets in *The Plough and the Stars*. The form of
the drama suffers somewhat from a lack of restraint. With regard to
the handling of the matter, it might be remarked that it lacks

cohesion, the incidents are isolated and need a linking up. Perhaps O'Casey overcrowds the canvas somewhat? But, realist before artist, he feels that if he is to present any full and faithful picture of the wretched lives of slum dwellers, he must work in incidents which are dramatically unconvincing, but without which no comprehensive account of existence in the tenements would be complete. For this reason he crowds in Rosie Redmond, the street girl, and little Mollser, the consumptive child. These characters are in no wise essential to the dramatic unity of the play – rather do they stand aloof, for neither knits herself into the heart of the tragedy. Ruthless in the presentation of facts, O'Casey philosophically accepts the first as an unpleasant reality and introduces the youthful victim of the white scourge so that her death may lend a deeper tone to the general gloom of the picture. Her frail body adds another corpse to the pitiful pile. Both these unfortunate girls find it is not 'the things that are beautiful, but the things that are' which are mirrored in *The Plough and the Stars*. . . .

For Sean O'Casey, the champion of the civilians, 1916 only meant war. He rages against all war, because of its terrible reaction on the lives of the people, more especially of the awful tragedies in its wake for women. Influenced by this view, he only sees one side of the 1916 rising, and he is out of sympathy with the higher one. O'Casey has missed the soul of the insurrection – a simple people's sublime act of faith in themselves and in their right to nationhood. There was a courage and a quality about it, which left him untouched. He probably viewed it as an ill-planned, ineffective military coup, which brought still more hardships to an already heart-broken people, still more wretchedness into the starkness and horror of life in the slums. To the dramatist who was socialist before nationalist, it was war, and war meant death and madness and terrible futility. . . .

. . . Those of us who are not fashioned in heroic mould are deeply indebted to the author of *The Plough and the Stars*, for he is the defender of the rights of the poor, the weak and the unheroic. . . . To speak of these people and for them, to be the singer of the underworld – that is Mr O'Casey's mission.

SOURCE: extracts from '*The Plough and the Stars* as a Woman Saw It' (1926), in the *Irish Statesman* (27 Feb. 1926).

2. CRITICAL STUDIES

Robert G. Lowery   Prelude to Year One: Sean
O'Casey before 1916   (1976)

The Plough and the Stars is a play about revolution. It dramatises a part
of Easter Week 1916: a week which, depénding upon your interpretation, was either the culmination of a seven hundred year struggle
against British oppression or the first of the twentieth-century
national liberation movements. Nationalists often refer to it religi-
ously as 'The Rising' and it was also, according to Lenin, a situation
which presented socialists with an opportunity to test their revolutionary theories. Between and beyond these interpretations is a
continuum of opinion; somewhere in the midst of these was Sean
O'Casey's interpretation.

O'Casey's attitude toward 1916 is generally believed to have been
that expressed in *The Plough and the Stars*. But the interpretations of the
play have been as varied and confusing as the interpretations of the
event it portrayed. Gabriel Fallon, one of the actors in the first Dublin
performance and later director of the Abbey Theatre, called the play
'pacifist'; the *Daily Worker* panned the first us performances and, a
quarter century later, still spoke of 'O'Casey's dubious 25-year-ago
conception of a young Marxist worker [Covey]'; the nationalists' riot
at the Dublin production speaks for itself. Nationalist and Communist, socialist and religionist all came to the same conclusion: it
was not their kind of play. There is, in addition, another, perhaps
broader, audience which Jacques Barzun spoke for:

Try to find out from the body of his work whether he is for or against the church, for or
against the working man, for or against poets, for or against social revolution – you
cannot.[1]

Yet the play flourished and its admirers grew in number, so much so
that by 1965, it was reported that its 457 performances made it the
most performed play in Abbey Theatre history.[2] It has been
translated into at least seven languages and is a guaranteed gate
attraction wherever it is performed.

Still, the question of O'Casey's views on 1916 remain a relatively
unexplored subject. This is so because it has little to do with drama
and perhaps because it has everything to do with a situation still alive

in the Irish national consciousness. The 'troubles' today in the north of Ireland are a vivid testimony that the ideals of 1916 are still a burning issue; it is also evident that the pain and suffering of which O'Casey wrote continues.

O'Casey's views on the Easter rebellion can best be examined in his writings during the years leading to the rebellion and by his antagonism toward James Connolly, the martyred leader of the Irish Citizen Army (ica), a workers' defense force formed during the 1913 Dublin strike. To O'Casey, it was Connolly who betrayed the labor movement, who instigated a premature uprising, and who abandoned the socialist ideal for the nationalist cause. To O'Casey, Connolly's sin was greater than that of Pearse. One could not have expected Pearse and the others who called for a blood sacrifice to act otherwise; their heroic stand at the gpo dictated their dramatic martyrdom and was the logical outcome of a collective Gaelic mysticism infused with republicanism. But Connolly was a Marxist, a man who had founded the first socialist party in Ireland, a leader who spent the best part of his life on two continents in the trade union and socialist movements. Like O'Casey, Connolly played an important role in the struggles of 1913, when the Dublin employers tried to starve the workers into submission. Like O'Casey, Connolly was in favor of a militant socialist army to protect the workers' rights and lives. Like O'Casey, Connolly organised and fought for the day when the working class would take power and rule Ireland in the interests of that class. However, unlike O'Casey, Connolly gave his life in a rising that left the world socialist community aghast. It seemed incredible that a man who lived the kind of life Connolly did would die this way. O'Casey shared that incredulity, but being closer to the scene and able to analyze and describe the situation, he knew it was coming.

O'Casey's role as a radical and militant agitator and organiser should not be underestimated. From 1906 to 1914, he was in the mainstream of Irish nationalist, then socialist, activity. He was recruiting for the secret Irish Republican Brotherhood (irb) and was a member of the Gaelic League. He worked as a laborer on the Great Northern Railway of Ireland for nine years and was fired for his membership in Jim Larkin's Irish Transport and General Workers' Union. He began writing articles for the union's newspaper, the *Irish Worker*, in June 1912 and became Secretary of the Wolfe Tone Memorial Committee a year later. It was no surprise, then, that O'Casey took an active part in the 1913 strike, which, at its height in August, saw 25,000 Dublin workers on the streets. During the strike, the need for a workers' force became evident. Police and employers combined to attack and intimidate all legitimate attempts to organise

the workers. O'Casey became secretary of the new organisation – the
Irish Citizen Army. In addition, O'Casey was asked to be the
secretary of the Women and Children's Relief Fund for the duration
of the strike. He wrote that he

borrowed a stick, and hobbled down to be from ten in the morning till twelve at night in
and out of Liberty Hall, helping with the Army, and, in his spare time, writing letters
appealing for funds to help the women and children of locked-out workers.[3]

It was his experiences both during the strike and after which solidified
his political opinions into a militant socialism, a position he was to
maintain for the rest of his life. It was also a time of rubbing elbows
with the names who, in 1916, would burn their way into Irish history.

One of these was Countess Constance Markiewicz née Gore-Booth,
the Jane Fonda of the Irish struggles, of whom O'Casey wrote: 'She
never reached the rank of failure, for she hadn't the constitution to
keep long enough at anything in which, at the end, she could see a
success or a failure facing her.' The photographs of her in a soup
kitchen, ladling out broth to the strikers irritated O'Casey, for he
never saw her do 'anything anyone could call a spot of work'. She only
appeared when reporters from English and Irish journals were
around taking photographs. Her problem, said O'Casey, was from
having too much of the 'Ay, ay Madame, you're right of the Sligo
peasants.' To O'Casey, she was a sham. 'No part of her melted into
the cause of Ireland, nor did she ever set foot on the threshold of
Socialism.' He noted that she met Connolly, who was down from
Belfast, and 'dazzled his eyes with her flashy enthusiasm'.[4] . . .

After nine months, the strike began to fail. Defeated and dejected,
the workers returned to work, their lives in shambles, to try to pick up
the pieces. The Irish Citizen Army was equally depleted and
unorganised. Sean O'Faolain wrote that by early 1914, 'the little
"army" of working men had dwindled, like the strike, to nothing'. In
March, O'Casey took the leading part in reorganising the ICA. Ralph
Fox, the official biographer of the Army, wrote:

Sean O'Casey suggested to Captain White, who was beginning to lose hope, that the
army should be given a more definite place in the labour movement; a constitution
should be drafted and submitted for approval; a council should be selected to arrange
for systematic drills, to open a fund for equipment, to arrange for public meetings and
to form companies of the Irish Citizen Army where possible.[5]

O'Casey was more modest, writing that 'he was called upon to take
the Irish Citizen Army in hand, now moving vaguely from this place
to that, and to put an orderly and adoptable shape to it'. Again
O'Casey threw himself into the work. By April, he had written and
designed the ICA's manifesto, the membership card, the original draft

of the constitution as well as handbills and posters. In May, he began a regular column for the *Irish Worker*.

O'Casey's newspaper articles were full of appeals for workers not to forget that the future of Ireland rested with them, and not with the capitalists. The National Volunteers came under special attack. A bourgeois nationalist group, formed only a month after the ICA, it contained within its ranks the very employers who broke the strike. O'Casey was adamant that there should be no union with the Volunteers as they were then organised. The ICA should be maintained, said O'Casey, as a separate labor force, and workers should 'yield allegiance to no movement that does not avow the ultimate destiny of the workers'. The capitalist 'has always opposed . . . national aspirations that may be opposite to their monetary and commercial interests'. O'Casey called for 'the utter alteration of the present social system', and for workers to separate themselves from 'every movement that does not tend towards the development of the faith that all power springs from and is invested in the people'. O'Casey ripped into the Volunteers time and again, maintaining that there was a distinct difference between the ICA and them. These fundamental differences were too great to speak of union. 'Irishmen differ very widely as to the end to be attained and the means to be used, and that on these points, there can be no apparent or actual union . . . there can be no Union of Light and Darkness.'[6]

Although O'Casey criticised and berated the 'deluded wage slaves of the Volunteers', it should not be deduced that he harbored ill-feeling toward them. Many were former members of the ICA and as proletarian as O'Casey. O'Casey's criticisms were directed at those who allowed themselves to be led by capitalists and by the Irish Parliamentary Party of John Redmond. The ICA had often made overtures of friendship toward the Volunteers, but were rebuffed each time by the leadership.[7] And as long as the rank and file of the Volunteers tolerated their own leadership, O'Casey's attacks continued.[8]

In October 1914, the Provisional Committee of the Volunteers became infiltrated and undermined by the inclusion of 25 nominees from the Parliamentary Party. The ICA's distrust grew. O'Casey wrote that 'the Volunteers made the cleavage of principle between themselves and the Citizen Army deeper than ever'. Ralph Fox wrote that 'O'Casey desired to intensify this cleavage'. Noting that Countess Markiewicz was an officer of both the ICA and the Volunteers, O'Casey called for her resignation, saying that the two had contradictory class interests. A vote was taken and O'Casey lost. Markiewicz demanded an apology; O'Casey refused and resigned.

Perhaps it was fate, for within weeks of O'Casey's resignation, the
Volunteers reversed their position and a breakaway group formed the
Irish Volunteers. More important though, Jim Larkin, O'Casey's
friend and mentor, left for the United States and James Connolly
assumed control of the ICA.

In 1969, Michael O hAodha wrote of O'Casey: 'He could not . . .
praise his lifelong hero Larkin, without seeming to disparage
Connolly, the most vital social thinker of that generation.'[9] One can
agree with both of O hAodha's conclusions. O'Casey has been one of
Connolly's most persistent critics, and Connolly was certainly one of
the most dynamic thinkers of any generation. Beginning in 1896, he
formed the Irish Socialist Republican Party, and a year later,
prophetically wrote: 'We are resolved upon national independence as
the indispensable ground work of industrial emancipation.'[10] An
organiser and author, Connolly worked with socialist and syndicalist
groups in his native Scotland, Ireland and, for seven years, in the
United States. He wrote some of the most perceptive essays that have
ever been published in Ireland. As a student of Marx, Connolly was
the precursor of advanced socialist theory. As a historian, his *Labour in
Irish History* was the first serious attempt to examine the role of the
Irish working class through the centuries of resistance to British and
capitalist rule. As a revolutionary, he died, strapped to a stretcher
propped against a wall, before a firing squad. As a tribute, every
revolutionary group in Ireland since 1916 has claimed his blessing.
Yet O'Casey attacked him; to some, unnecessarily.

In 1919, O'Casey wrote a short 72-page pamphlet describing bits
and pieces of the ICA's development. It was not so much a history as
what the title described: *The Story of the Irish Citizen Army*. O'Casey
wrote as both a participant and as an observer, using notes he had
made during his membership. Towards the end of the pamphlet,
O'Casey wrote that the immediate effect of Connolly's role as
commandant on the ICA was 'an appreciable change . . . in the
attitude of the Citizen Army Council toward the Volunteers'. This
was possible because Connolly had never attacked the Volunteers as
vociferously as had Larkin and O'Casey. Connolly had, in fact,
played a moderate role in the controversy. It was easier for him to
build a bridge of cordiality to the Volunteers. I have noted earlier that
O'Casey was never opposed to a union with the rank-and-file
Volunteers, but he was apparently angered by the manner in which
Connolly was proceeding. If there was to be a union, it should be the
Volunteers who made common cause with the ICA and not the other
way around. The nationalists were co-opting the socialists and it was
clear, said O'Casey, that 'the Citizen Army was . . . becoming the

militant Left wing of the Irish Volunteers'. O'Casey recognised that it was not all Connolly's fault. After the split in the National Volunteers, the ica and the Irish Volunteers found themselves combined in opposition to the Irish Parliamentary Party. However, as the two bodies began to participate more in joint activities, they coalesced to the extent that 'it became obvious . . . to all that the Irish Volunteers and the Citizen Army was essentially one in ideal and would eventually be one in action'.[11]

It was not merely the manner of union of the two organisations that alarmed O'Casey. It was 'the almost revolutionary change that was manifesting itself in Connolly's nature'.[12] Ralph Fox also sees a change in Connolly during this period. He wrote that by the end of 1914, Connolly was 'prepared to accept the aid and co-operation of any section going his way'.[13] In his excellent biography of Connolly, C. Desmond Greaves wrote that Connolly was deeply grieved by the outbreak of World War One in August 1914. It represented the total failure of the Second International (a loose collection of the world's socialists) to halt the carnage. Worse, the very socialists who spent their lives calling for peace and the abolition of standing armies were now voting war credits and for larger armies and navies to protect their nations from 'the aggressor'. Connolly may have felt that an example for the international socialist community must be set. If so, this example could only have been in the form of rebellion.[14]

It could not have been a secret that Connolly was moving toward insurrection. After May 1915 Connolly's articles in the *Irish Worker* took on increasing militancy. He began publishing his own articles about the 1905 Revolution in Russia, the Paris revolts of 1830 and 1848, Lexington, and the Tyrol insurgents. On July 24, in an article on 'street fighting', Connolly wrote that 'defence is of overwhelming importance in such warfare as a popular force like the Citizen Army might be called upon to participate in'.[15] O'Casey wrote that Connolly had become the virtual embodiment of the ica. 'He banished the [ruling] Committee and now ruled alone.' Connolly was a man possessed; he saw an opportunity and was determined not to let it pass. He cajoled, prodded, argued, and persuaded others to follow him. According to O'Casey, he 'was shoving the Volunteers forward, quicker than they wanted to go'. If they would not follow him, he would go out alone.[16]

This change had other manifestations. Always the pragmatist, always in favor of 'less theorising and more fighting', Connolly's actions wedded the ica to the blood sacrifice cult of Pearse, Thomas MacDonagh, Sean MacDermott and Joseph Plunkett. Desmond Ryan wrote that 'Connolly's influence upon Pearse was profound and marked'.[17] Ryan was referring to the social questions to which Pearse addressed himself in his last published pamphlet, *The Sovereign People*. However, one must wonder just who influenced who. The change in Connolly was more radical after 1914 (when he and Pearse became more than just acquaintances) than was the change in Pearse. O'Casey gives us an example of the 'pre-Connolly' Pearse in *The Plough and the Stars*, when 'The Voice of the Man', speaking, incidentally, to a combined rally of the ICA and the Volunteers, says:

Bloodshed is a cleansing and sanctifying thing, and the nation that regards it as the final horror has lost its manhood.[18]

The dialogue comes from Pearse's speech 'The Coming Revolution' delivered in November 1913. The second appearance by O'Casey's orator includes lines from the 'post-Connolly' Pearse of December 1915, this time factually addressed to the combined forces of the Volunteers and the ICA.

The old heart of the earth needed to be warmed with the red wine of the battlefield . . . such homage was never offered to God as this: the homage of millions of lives given gladly for love of country.[19]

Connolly is reported to have gagged at this last statement of Pearse's, saying: 'No! We do not think that the heart of the earth needs to be warmed with the red wine of millions of lives. We think anyone who does is a blithering idiot.' And yet, Connolly himself, only two weeks before, had written:

Should the day ever come when revolutionary leaders are prepared to sacrifice the lives of those under them as recklessly as the ruling class do in every war, there will not be a throne or despotic government left in the world.[20]

And two months later, at a time when he was supposed to be influencing Pearse, Connolly wrote:

Without the slightest trace of irreverence but in all due humility and awe, we recognise that of us, as of Mankind before Calvary, it may truly be said 'without the shedding of Blood there is no redemption.'[21]

O'Casey is reported to have gagged.

Though O'Casey was formally out of the movement, he tried to counter Connolly's drift and sought to dissuade others from what he thought to be the wrong path. He could see the revolt coming and he knew that both organisations – now virtually one since January 1916 when Connolly joined the Military Council of the Volunteers – would fight. He argued that 'their methods were those of the days of the red-coats, busby, and plume, salute your superior officers, fix bayonets, and charge boys'.[22] It was insane, said O'Casey, that they should pit their small force against the British Empire; it was worse than insane to give them the target of a uniform to aim at. O'Casey's methods were those of the very people Connolly wrote about: the guerrillas who hit and ran at Lexington or the mass movement of class conscious workers in Russia. 'Take off your uniforms', said O'Casey, 'and keep them for the wedding, the wake, the pattern, and the fair. Put on your old duds that make you indistinguishable from your neighbours.'[23] O'Casey became enraged when Pearse and Connolly asserted that the British would never use artillery on capitalist property. Connolly, the historian, the socialist, had forgotten that, at the Paris Commune, 'the French soldiers battered their way over the Communard barricades with canon-fire, careless of what property the bursting shells destroyed'. O'Casey tried in vain to reason with Connolly and Pearse. He suggested a debate on the subject; they did not reply. He sent an article to *The Volunteer*; it was not published. O'Casey, dejected, waited.

After the rebellion, Ireland was stunned. A great historical moment has risen and passed and all there was to show for it were graves and gutted buildings. Though 'Easter Week became the Year One in Irish history', it was not until 1918 that the struggle would attract a mass following. The international socialist community, for whom Connolly was so eager to set an example, almost to a man condemned his part in it. A 'putsch' said Karl Radek, soon to become a prominent figure in another struggle in Russia; 'dazed' was the reaction from James Larkin in America, who tried desperately to get back to Ireland. Only Lenin saw that the rebellion was an objective attack upon capital and the British Empire, and anything which hindered either or both heightened the revolutionary situation in Europe. Contrary to traditional Left thinking though, Lenin's endorsement did not constitute an approval of Connolly's part in the rebellion anymore than it signified an acceptance of the blood sacrifice crowd. Lenin would have found the same objective conditions in the rebellion even if Connolly and the ICA had not taken part in it. On the other hand, if Connolly had started the rebellion alone with only the small ICA, as he was ready to do in December 1915, there can be little doubt that Lenin would have added his voice to the condemnations of adventurism.

Although O'Casey wrote that 'the Easter Rebellion had pulled down a dark curtain of eternal separation between him and his friends', he continued as before. He joined the fledgeling Socialist Party of Ireland and continued to write. *The Story of Thomas Ashe*, a lament for his friend and comrade, was published in 1918; *The Story of the Irish Citizen Army*, a year later. In the next few years, O'Casey found a newer and redder star on which to hang his hat, but the

promising months of 1913 and the shattering week of 1916 would
never be more than a memory away.

In this essay, I have tried to illustrate O'Casey's political state of
mind in the days and months prior to the Easter Rising. Using his
political writings as a barometer, I have suggested how O'Casey
could have been expected to react to the rebellion. It is clear that he
had a decided socialist preference, but it is also clear that he was
neither a reformist Labourite in the mold of the world socialist
community of that time, nor was he a wild-eyed romantic committed
to revolutionary martyrdom. A legitimate question, then, is: do
O'Casey's early writings find adequate expression in *The Plough and
the Stars*? And the answer would have to be yes, but in a different
manner. There are, of course, the well-known themes that manifest
themselves throughout the play – the uniform issue, the blood
sacrifice idea, the destruction of capitalist property: all issues which
O'Casey argued pro and con prior to the Rising – but they are subtly
woven into the action rather than being blatantly ridiculed, as
O'Casey did before the Rising. One may argue that there is a
qualitative difference between journalism and playwriting, yet this
does not negate the fact that both genres are compatible with all sorts
of uses. O'Casey's wit and powers of analysis sharpened as the years
passed, but he retained separate and distinctive styles for his essays
and for his plays. His political essays at the age of 80 are very close in
style to those essays written before 1916. They are still passionate
clarion calls for class struggle or they are discursive and analytical
stream of consciousness visions of the progress of Mankind. Only
rarely did O'Casey allow himself to combine the essayist's style with
that of the dramatist's (*The Star Turns Red* is the best example). In
addition, the earlier O'Casey is writing with a sense of immediacy
whereas the O'Casey of the mid-1920s is writing from a perspective of
reflection. Ten years passed between the Rising and its staged
portrayal, and, in that interval, there were various influences that,
while not altering his views on 1916, did contribute to a different
appraisal of the rebellion. There was, for instance, his enthusiastic
support of the 1917 Russian Revolution which enabled him to place
the Irish rebellion in a wider context. There was also the shabby
treatment accorded Larkin and himself by a defunct and non-
revolutionary labor movement. This latter influence may have
contributed in no small way to the caricaturisation of a socialist (the
Covey) who was not necessarily representative of socialist thought in
1916. In general, the ICA and the small socialist movement supported
the rebellion whereas the Covey refuses to have anything to do with it.
The Covey is a composite of several people O'Casey knew and does

not represent O'Casey's feelings about socialism or his attitude towards Connolly. The Covey's pronouncements are more representative of a sick, mechanical and sterile labor movement that was prevalent after the rebellion.

Had O'Casey chosen to write a more didactic political play, we may have been treated to an early *The Star Turns Red*. Having said that, though, it should be noted that it would not have been possible for O'Casey to write such a play about 1916 unless he engaged in fantasy or divorced himself totally from his role in the early years. The Easter Week certainly contained all the elements necessary for a heroic drama, but only if one conceived of it as heroic and worthy of such treatment. To most of Ireland, the Easter Rising came to represent the single greatest event in their modern history, but to O'Casey, who in 1926 was cognisant of the Rising Red Star over Moscow which to him heralded a new wave of the future, the Easter Rising could only have been a tragic and premature lost opportunity.

Source: article in *Sean O'Casey Review*, ii (1976), pp. 92–102.

NOTES

1. Jacques Barzun, 'O'Casey at Your Bedside', in R. Ayling (ed.), *Sean O'Casey*, 'Modern Judgements' series (London, 1969), p. 122.
2. Ernest Blythe, *The Abbey Theatre*, National Literary Society (Dublin n.d.). Incidentally, second place was *Juno and the Paycock*, 373 performances, and fourth place was *The Shadow of a Gunman*, 308 performances.
3. *Drums Under the Windows*, p. 312.
4. Ibid., pp. 314–16.
5. R. M. Fox, *The History of the Irish Citizen Army* (Dublin, 1943), p. 63.
6. See O'Casey's letters and articles for early 1914 in *Feathers from a Green Crow*, pp. 101–15.
7. See the chapter 'Pilgrimage to Bodenstown, 1914' in O'Casey's *The Story of the Irish Citizen Army*, for the feelings of fraternity between the Volunteers and the ica; reprinted in *Feathers*, pp. 209–14.
8. How effective O'Casey was is a matter of judgement, but Tom Clarke felt the need to mention it in his now well-known letter to John Devoy; O'Casey was called 'disgruntled' and accused of stirring up trouble between the two organisations.
9. Michael O hAodha, *The Abbey – Then and Now* (Dublin, 1969), p. 60.
10. *Shan Van Vocht*, August 1897.
11. *Story of the Irish Citizen Army*, reprinted in *Feathers*, p. 228.
12. Ibid., p. 226.
13. R. M. Fox, *James Connolly: The Forerunner* (Tralee, 1946), p. 172.
14. C. Desmond Greaves, *The Life and Times of James Connolly* (London, 1961), p. 283. O'Casey deals with the desertion of the European socialists during World War i in *The Plough and the Stars*. See the conversation between Covey and the British soldiers, one of whom is a socialist, Act iv.
15. Fox, *Connolly*, p. 180.

16. Various theories abound about the possibility of Connolly going out alone. Some feel that this was the reason he was 'kidnapped' in late December 1915 by the IRB.

17. Desmond Ryan, *The Man Called Pearse* (Dublin, 1919), p. 108.

18. *The Plough and the Stars*, Act II, *Collected Plays*, v. 1, p. 193.

19. Ibid., p. 196.

20. *Workers' Republic*, November 27, 1915.

21. Ibid., February 5, 1916.

22. *Drums*, pp. 402–4.

23. Ibid.

William Irwin Thompson   Easter 1916: O'Casey's Naturalistic Image   (1967)

Unfortunately for his life in Ireland, O'Casey used Ireland for material, and in his ungentle hands, Ireland became a most resisting medium. All those who had not participated in Easter Week (and, probably, those who had never taken Irish nationalism seriously) loudly praised those who had, and gave the returning warriors a hero's welcome upon their release at Christmas of 1916. When O'Casey, certainly no conspicuous patriot, took the Rising as material for a naturalistic play, he was only asking for trouble, and no doubt he knew it. It could only seem to the Catholic middle classes that the Abbey, already notorious for its apparent Protestant slander on peasant Catholic Ireland, was intentionally trying to bait them. Swearing allegiance to no one party, O'Casey stood outside the crowd and watched. The picture he saw infuriated saloon and salon alike, for the mob rioted, and 'the new school' of Irish writers, F. R. Higgins, Liam O'Flaherty and Austin Clarke, attacked the play in the columns of A.E.'s journal.[1]

The first scene of *The Plough and the Stars* is set neither in the General Post Office of history nor the humble thatched cottage of Irish dramatic tradition. It is set in a tenement, and from the beginning we sense a confinement, a closing-in in which life does not have quite enough room to behave in a proper manner. Mrs Gogan is receiving someone else's package and opening it up for inspection and comment; Peter is wandering around in various stages of dress. Fluther is fixing a door, and when the Covey enters, an argument breaks out between them, while Peter curses in trying to fix his collar. O'Casey thus keeps up three independent lines of action within the single room, and this independence of simultaneous action contributes to a comic stylisation of the characters' behavior. In the first act, O'Casey dwells upon the comic possibilities of slum life, upon the manner in which the socially expected thing is not quite possible in so cramped a space. For the moment, suffering is kept off stage.

But as soon as the audience has accepted the tenement for what it is, then the affectations of the characters appear, and the appearance increases the ridiculousness of their behavior. The Covey, who is modeled upon Shakespeare's Fluellen, has pretensions of intellectualism and quotes continually from his favorite book on the evolutionary idea of the proletariat. Peter, in his Forester's uniform, is the comedy natural to this Irish version of a Shriner; his aspirations are toward the middle class. Jack wants to cut a hussar-like figure in the uniform of the Citizen Army. When Jack's wife Nora enters, with her broken grammar and proud attention to refinements, the genteel scene is complete. Each of the characters is lost in a private dream of self-importance, but each lacks a definite, effective, relationship with his world. Since they are lower class, they lack power; since they lack power, they have atrophied wills; since they have atrophied wills, they dream themselves into the places where they matter. The vice is natural to the situation; the satirical bite of the comedy is, however, that the vice applies to the nation, and not merely its lower class.

The tenement now begins to take on an existence of its own, a prismatic one, for things that we know about, the history that is happening outside the window, take on a different color and quality as they pass through the windows and doors of the room in front of us. The characters talk about the great torchlight procession and parade on Sunday, October 25, 1915 that effected the reconciliation between the working-class Citizen Army under Connolly and the middle-class radical Volunteers under Pearse. We are viewing a historical event through the windows of a tenement. We are also viewing the tenement's participant in that event, Jack Clitheroe, through the eyes of the less exalted members of the proletariat, Fluther and Mrs Gogan. The technique is, of course, as old as Greek drama, but here the incommensurate relation between the on-stage world and the beyond-stage world is not because of a physical inadequacy of the stage to accommodate a large action; it is a suggestive use of dramatic space that is one of the central symbols in the play.

A quarrelsome scene has been set by the interlopers in the room of the Clitheroes, but when Jack and Nora finally come on stage, the quarrel is intensified and defined: Jack and Nora are suffering from a post-honeymoon disappointment. As Mrs Gogan says: 'after a month or two, th' wonder of a woman wears off'. Fluther's opinion, on the man's side of things, is: 'when a man finds th' wonder of one woman beginnin' to die, it's usually beginnin' to live in another'. The other woman for Jack, however, is Cathleen ní Houlihan. Disappointed that marriage isn't everything, Jack longs for the glory of an officer's role in the Citizen Army. Nora, of course, wants no part of trouble. A real woman, and not a mythic one, she wants her man alive, not bleeding into a dirt made sacred because of its nationality. Unfortunately, Nora, the real woman, does not really confront the mythic Cathleen to fight for Life; she cries and whines, and is a tender frail thing who cannot understand a man's desire for glory. In short, Nora is a cliché taken untransformed from the melodramas upon which O'Casey's apprentice years were fed. Nevertheless, though the conflict between Nora and the daughter of Houlihan is not as fully realised as it could be, the opposition is no mere subterranean movement in the play. Jack is presented as a man losing interest in his young wife after only a few months of marriage; were he an ordinary Irishman of the working class, he would be slipping out to spend his nights in the pub while his wife was occupied with pregnancy. But Jack is no ordinary man; his gaze is directed beyond the pub to Liberty Hall. Jack does leave his home and his wife's side, but only because she deliberately failed to pass on the news that he had been made a commandant in the Citizen Army. Nora, in attempting to hold Jack, loses him. Disturbed by the problem of a woman of flesh and emotion, Jack leaves in anger and offers his services to the abstract woman of black. As the warrior leaves, the female characters take over the stage: little Mollser, the consumptive child who seeks company to protect her from a lonely death; Bessie Burgess, the Protestant whose son has enlisted in the English army and is fighting in the trenches; and Nora. The women are left, not yet to keen, but to keep a kind of deathwatch. The curtain for Act One comes down on this grim chorus of women.

At the end of the first act we have both a comedy based upon the traditional device of social affectation and a melodrama that threatens to become a tragedy. The comedy itself is one that creates instantaneous laughter, but the afterimage of the laugh is a formless and dark uneasiness. The comedy darkens as one abandons the necessary comic distance and approaches the characters for a closer look. Each of the characters suffers from some delusion or futile dream, and even the two men who are trying to assert their wills in a definite action do not really seem capable of changing their situation. O'Casey tells us that Jack has 'a face in which is the desire for authority, without the power to attain it'. And The Covey, the intellectual Marxist, is such a caricature that he cannot be taken seriously at all; his pretensions and his one book, Jenersky's *Thesis on th' Origin, Development, an' Consolidation, of th' Evolutionary Idea of th' Proletariat*, are mere farce. Interestingly enough (and most uncharacteristically for O'Casey, who in the *Autobiographies* sentimentalised himself and his opinions) all of O'Casey's personal opinions about Irish nationalism, communism, and the Citizen Army are placed in the mouth of The Covey. The Plough and the Stars, the flag of the Citizen Army, is a labor flag, and The Covey regards Connolly's nationalism as a sell-out of the proletariat. Though communist, The Covey's dream of power and glory differs little from the dreams of the others. Nora has dreams of respectability, but her actual efforts to achieve respectability and gentility only incur the scorn and resentment of Mrs Gogan and Bessie Burgess, and her own husband is too busy with his dream to bother about respectability. Mrs Gogan is a Catholic busybody, and Mrs Burgess is a Protestant drunk. Though all the tenement-dwellers share a common Georgian home, they cannot agree upon a common dream. In fact, even beyond disagreement, all the characters fail in their relationships with one another. The failure of the marital relationship between Jack and Nora highlights the human failure of all the characters. In the first act we see nothing but bickerings and quarrels; the characters do not have enough room to move about in freedom and peace. However comic the first act may be, the image of Irish life that O'Casey presents, with all its futile dreams, broken wills, and alienation of the sexes, is not a pleasant one. Though not giving the audience cause to riot, he places them in the proper mood.

The curtain in Act One falls upon three sorrowful women, but the curtain for Act Two rises upon an entirely different kind of woman: Rosie Redmond, the prostitute. The scene has shifted from the tenement-hearth where the women live, to the pub where the men live. The night is not a profitable one for a prostitute, for the men are 'all thinkin' of higher things than a girl's garters'. The openness of Rosie's talk and the actual presentation of a prostitute upon a public stage was a piece of naturalism that was bound to offend an Irish audience, but the casual manner in which her existence is taken for granted would seem intentionally insulting. Rosie describes how hard it is for her to make a living, not because men are sinless, but because her landlord raises the rent when she brings a man home. This involvement of the middle classes in the vices of the working classes would not please a theater-going audience. The most maddening feature of this riot-inciting second act is that the whore's speech is followed by the words of Pearse, whose speech to the crowd outside can be heard within the pub. The juxtaposition of prostitute and patriot is unkind, and O'Casey does not weaken the force of his irony, for he chooses to use the most absurd, the most banally saber-rattling, the most ignorantly heroic speech in all of Pearse's four volumes. '. . . bloodshed is a cleansing and sanctifying thing', says the Catholic patriot, but what the rioters didn't realise was that O'Casey's three dots did a service to Pearse. What O'Casey neglects to quote are the preceding words: 'We may make mistakes in the beginning and shoot the wrong people; but bloodshed is a cleansing and sanctifying thing, and the nation which regards it as the final horror has lost its manhood. There are many things more horrible than bloodshed; and slavery is one of them.'[2] Lieutenant-Colonel Ferguson-Smith once gave similar counsel to the Royal Irish Constabulary in June 1920: 'Sinn Fein has had all the sport up to the present, and we are going to have the sport now. . . . You may make mistakes occasionally and innocent persons may be shot, but that cannot be helped, and you are bound to get the right parties sometime.'[3] A few days later the Colonel was shot dead while sipping his whiskey in his club in Cork, but his remarks made marvelous propaganda. The Collins-Childers organisation made the most of it, thus winning Ireland's freedom by converting America, the English Church, the Labour Party, and King George v to the side of Ireland against Lloyd George's government. O'Casey could have attacked Pearse more fiercely, had he wished to do so, for it is obvious that the Irish patriots were trying to claim that the murder of innocents by Irishmen was an act of heroism, but the murder of innocents by the English was a world-shocking atrocity. But for once in his life, O'Casey had the prudence to restrain himself. The 'twenties in Ireland was a time of mutual assassination, not critical retrospection.

Pearse's speech is heartily endorsed by the prostitute; perhaps as a white slave to an economic system, Rosie agrees that slavery is worse than bloodshed, but Pearse would have been embarrassed to receive her endorsement. Again the juxtaposition of prostitution and patriotism is provoking, but simple justaposition is not O'Casey's only technique. Peter and Fluther come rushing into the pub, flushed with the excitement that Pearse's speech has inspired in them, and as the speech is repeated and handled by these comic characters, the sacred becomes profane and the speech contagiously becomes infected with the comedy of the absurd buffoons who have been lifted to such heights of enthusiasm. Here again the relation between the on-stage and off-stage actions allows a symbolic use of space. In the first act we felt confinement; society was seen from the inside of a tenement; now we observe the revolution from the inside of a pub, and whatever ideological purity and sincerity are present in Pearse's thought cannot pass through the dark window of the pub. In the play we cannot see the noble face of Pearse; we can only perceive a disembodied voice, and we watch that voice take on, tragically but believably, the bodies of the characters before our eyes. The speech presented is not Pearse at his noblest, but Pearse in his very worst attempt at stirring oratory. Whatever ideals the man had cannot be exchanged with the listening mob; his language fails him. The mob hears what it wants to hear and goes about its business with new slogans to rationalise private desires. Necessarily, the revolution breaks away from the revolutionary. Fluther and Peter gulp their drinks and hurry out for the headier wine of patriotism.

Dropping the green thread of action, O'Casey now picks up the red. In rushes The Covey, who is sickened at the sight of the proletariat cheering on the bourgeoisie. The Covey's denouncements, however, do not add up to a serious alternative, for The Covey is as simple-minded a zealot as his nationalistic comrades. Rosie Redmond slides over to him and begins her solicitation, and here, perhaps, O'Casey is having a little fun. The whore's name suggest the rose of England and the leader of Ireland's pro-England Parliamentary party. At this moment of history, Redmond was busy trying to win recruits for England. Keating once described Ireland as the harlot of England, so perhaps one can infer a joke into the text: the English seduction of the Irish working classes. O'Casey makes fun of both sides, but he does not allow such abstractions to blur the comedy, for in the particular case of The Covey, the attempted seduction is futile. The Covey is so taken up by the doctrines of his system of thought that he can no longer perceive the reality of his situation: namely, that he is getting a come-all-ye from a whore. The Covey's response is to offer to lend Rosie his copy of Jenersky's thesis. Rosie has little left to do but throw off her shawl to expose the top of her bosom in open proclamation of her calling. Ironically, this Marxist is more a prude than an advocate of free love; the concrete is more than he can handle, so The Covey retreats back quickly into the abstract. The Covey waves a different banner and chants different slogans, but he does not add up to a free thinker or a free lover. Having achieved a minor resolution of one line of action, O'Casey sends The Covey hurrying off stage and returns to the green thread.

Peter and Fluther return to the pub, but this time they are accompanied by Mrs Gogan. Mrs Gogan has been visibly awed by the parade and the speeches, especially by the beautiful green uniform of the Irish Foresters, and her womanly comments return to the theme of sacrificial death for Ireland and Cathleen ní Houlihan.

. . . The loveliest part of the dress, I think, is th' osthriches plume. . . . When yous are goin' along, an' I see them wavin' an' an' noddin' an' an' waggin', I seem to be lookin' at each of yous hangin' at th' and of a rope, your eyes bulgin' an' your legs twistin' an' jerkin', gaspin' an' gaspin' for breath while yous are thryin' to die for Ireland!

Here sacrifice for Ireland is seen to be comic because of a shift in point of view. From the human point of view, life is what counts, and living for Ireland is the supreme value. From the supra-human point of view, dying for Ireland is salvation, but the pretentiousness of the appeal, this affection of being beyond humanity, is as much a source of comedy as Fielding's peasant playing the lord. Fluther, as well as Mrs Gogan, is willing to puncture the Forester's bladder of hot air, for he comments that he doubts patriotism would be the actual crime for which a Forester would be hanged. The bickering begins again. O'Casey's skill in this act is singularly fine, for he handles his dramatic action with considerable energy and variation by quickly introducing a vigorous action, arresting it, then introducing another line of action. No sooner are Fluther and Peter at it again, than in walk Mrs Burgess and The Covey, and Peter and Fluther's quarrel subsides while Mrs Burgess and Mrs Gogan have a go at it. The women, however, are a little more fierce. Bessie Burgess accuses the Catholics of bad faith since the Irish Catholics have not enlisted in the war that is to help poor little Belgium. A row is on, but before the fight can progress, the figure of Pearse reappears in the window, and, appropriately, he is speaking of the current war in Europe with all its magnificent spilling of blood: 'When the war comes to Ireland she must welcome it as she would welcome the Angel of God.' As Pearse disappears, the women resume their fight. The sight of two old hags brawling with one another about their virtue – and this after the lofty words of Pearse – is a fierce image, an image, perhaps, of Civil-War Ireland when many thought that the Treaty was the fate worse than death. Bessie and Mrs Gogan almost come to blows, but the barman throws them out. New combatants quickly fill the vacuum, and The Covey begins arguing with Rosie and Fluther. Fluther, in his inimitable grand manner, now plays the rescuing knight to Rosie's damsel in distress. Again a fight threatens, but again the barman intervenes to throw The Covey out. In the ensuing peace and quiet, Fluther effects his pick-up of Rosie, and as he leads the whore off-stage, the Irish Tri-Color comes on.

And that was it. The sight of exit-whore, enter-flag, and flag in a pub at that, was too much. With a good deal more provocation than they had had with *The Playboy*, the Irish began to rip the seats from the floor.

After the police had thrown out the more vigorous protesters, the play continued. Fluther and Rosie move out of sight and into the snug to exchange words, and the soldiers come on stage to recite the litany of the patriot.

LIEUT. LANGOON: Th' time is rotten ripe for revolution.
CLITHEROE: You have a mother, Langoon.
LIEUT. LANGOON: Ireland is greater than a mother.
CAPT. BRENNAN: You have a wife, Clitheroe.
CLITHEROE: Ireland is greater than a wife.

The figure of Pearse returns to the window, and in a final burst of exultation, the men conclude their litany.

CAPT. BRENNAN (*catching up The Plough and the Stars*): Imprisonment for th' Independence of Ireland!
LIEUT. LANGOON (*catching up the Tri-Colour*): Wounds for th' Independence of Ireland!
CLITHEROE: Death for th' Independence of Ireland!
THE THREE (*together*): So help us God!

As the soldiers hurry off stage summoned by a bugle call, Fluther and Rosie come out of the snug on their way to Rosie's.

O'Casey's irony is ferocious, but, artistically, it is an irony that works by suggestive juxtapositions, and the manner in which these juxtapositions are placed in a context of comedy darkens the comedy in an almost expressionistic manner. The caricatured faces of the traditional stage-Irishmen become grotesque in the act's total configuration of meaning. The slapstick, burly, blustering, stage-Irishmen undergo a sea-change in the depths of our thoughts; their smiles become leers, and their seemingly innocuous patter becomes threatening. As tragicomedy Act Two is a masterpiece, and its greatness as a one-act play is not helped by its association with the melodramatic triteness of the other acts. Only an absolute master and genius knows when to stop, knows just how much is needed and has the courage to present a great one-act tragicomedy rather than a marred four-act tragedy with epic pretensions. Act Two stands by itself; its climax and resolution of action do not depend on the other acts; its allusions do not require the first act. It is a shame O'Casey felt it necessary to go on, but the fault is shared, for the common prejudice is that a one-act play is not 'a major work'. O'Casey went on to attempt a major work, a 'Tragedy in Four Acts'.

In Act Three the thematic use of dramatic space is less exciting than in Act Two, for in order to place an insurrection on stage, O'Casey had little choice but to use the traditional horizontal flow across the stage. As in Roman drama, the action takes place in a public street just outside a great house, but here, significantly, the great house, an old Georgian mansion, is a tenement with not a single pane of glass remaining in the once elegant tracery of the fanlight. Against this background of the past (and, one infers, of a past social order) gone to ruin, the slum dwellers come and go as the insurrection blazes and thunders off stage. The time of crisis has come, and, of course, in drama, crisis is the moment which reveals character entirely.

The time of crisis does not inspire any heroism for Ireland, but it does inspire the heroic behavior of one human being for another human being. Fluther, having played the clown, now plays the man. Nora has foolishly gone out to wrest her man from the clutches of the daughter of Houlihan, and it is Fluther who goes out to save her from death in the streets. And even Peter and The Covey have become friends in the frightening situation. But O'Casey is not moving toward any affirmation of Irish heroism, for the poor do not rally round the green flag but pour out of the slums to loot and pillage while the police and the army are distracted by the rebels. To the naturalistic imagery of prostitutes and brawling hags, O'Casey now adds the looters, and those who do not steal but stay home do so out of cowardice, not morality. O'Casey is remorselessly true to fact, but he is not a bleak naturalist, for having reached a nadir and sounded a bottom to humanity, he begins to reascend. O'Casey's ascent, however, is on his own terms: for him only the breath of life is worth carrying up; all the heavy abstractions of God and country are cut from the body and left to sink. The ascent involves a growth of character: Fluther attempts to become the hero he has always taken himself to be, and Nora, more unhappily, is pushed toward womanhood by the force of her suffering. Nora attempts to meet her crisis; she goes out to do battle with the mythic woman of black, but, unfortunately, Nora is armed with little more than tears and imploring tugs at the sleeve. Taunted by the slum women who have no husbands out in the Rising, Nora learns the futile emptiness of the abstractions and slogans with which Jack and his men have been distracted.

NORA (*wearily*): I could find him nowhere, Mrs Gogan. None o' them would tell me where he was. They told me I shamed my husband an' th' women of Ireland be carryin' on as I was. . . . They said th' women must learn to be brave an' cease to be cowardly. . . . Me who risked more for love than they would risk for hate. . . . [*Raising her voice in hysterical protest.*] My Jack will be killed, my Jack will be killed! He is to be butchered as a sacrifice to th' dead.

Unfortunately, little that Nora has accomplished on stage convinces us that she has risked more for love than the others have for hate. She has risked death to find Jack, but the gesture is a futile one of guilt and frustration; she is not saving Jack, she is imitating him. O'Casey is trying to lift Nora's laments into the realm of tragedy, but Nora is incapable of understanding her situation, and therefore she is incapable, as a dramatic figure, of generalising her situation into anything resembling a tragic predicament. . . . Her personal cry of suffering cannot echo with the anguished cry of mankind, and since she cannot lift her predicament into the dimension of tragedy, it falls into pathos. It is difficult to make a tragic heroine out of a pretty girl, and many respectable dramatists before O'Casey have encountered the same difficulty. The Ophelias, Cordelias and Desdemonas are always the *means* of bringing suffering to others, but the tragedy takes place in Hamlet, Lear and Othello. It is only when woman exults in destruction, when the womb of life becomes the organ of death, that we have the inversion of natural order that creates the terror necessary for tragedy. Medea, Clytemnestra, Lady Macbeth: these are tragic heroines, but poor Nora is only an object of pity. Nora has her moment of insight; she sees that all the men are afraid, that they are out, not because they are brave, but because they are cowards who wish to prove themselves brave in the eyes of others. Mrs Gogan denies Nora's insight, and thinks that the men are brave, but this sort of denial opens the way to comedy, and, perhaps, the horrors of comedy are most suited to O'Casey's view. Unfortunately, failing to achieve the terror necessary for tragedy or the grotesque ironies necessary for tragicomedy, O'Casey relies upon Boucicault melodrama.

Nora is led off stage in one direction; the looters go out in the other direction. It only remains for Jack and Nora to confront one another, and the confrontation is a predictable one. The Rising fails; Jack, in retreat, stops momentarily at the tenement. Nora pleads and pulls at Jack; Jack casts her to the floor. Nora sobs. The scene is only too complete when we learn, at the curtain of Act Three, that Nora was with child when her husband cast her to the floor.

In the final act the three women of sorrow from Act One return to the stage: little Mollser has died, in the midst of the gunfire, from the consumption she feared, and Nora's baby has died under the broken heart of her mother. The only energy remaining in the play is that created by the reversal in character of Bessie Burgess, a reversal that began at the end of Act Three when Bessie went out to find a doctor in the midst of the bullets. O'Casey's indictment of the Rising is seen clearly in his creation of pro-British Bessie as heroine, but, artistically, this inversion of villain into heroine in a time of suffering is a revelation of humanity and compassion, and it is this humanity that becomes the central value of the play. . . .

. . . Of the three women of Act One, only Bessie remains. Mrs Grogan appears for the funeral of her little Mollser and tries to console Nora by telling her that if she had only been married a little longer, the death of her husband wouldn't bother her so much. The manner in which O'Casey portrays the alienation of the sexes in Catholic family life is, without a doubt, an indication of his religious bias; it is also a dominant theme in the play and it achieves its final realisation in Mrs Gogan's consoling remarks. Bessie feels sorry for Mrs Gogan because she has lost a daughter, but Fluther, more Irish than Mrs Burgess, is quick to rid her of that delusion.

BESSIE: Oh th' poor woman, o' course. God help her, it's a terrible blow to her.
FLUTHER: A terrible blow? Sure, she's in her element now, woman, mixin' earth to earth, an' ashes t' ashes an' dust to dust, an' revellin' in plumes an' hearses, last days an' judgements.

O'Casey's enraged indictment of the Irish cult of death in the *Autobiographies* is well known, but one is in no danger of reading the play in terms of his other work, for the indictment could not be plainer within the text: the funeral is the central celebration of Irish life.

The drama now moves to its close, and O'Casey resolves his work with some skill. The symbolic use of space continues to the end, and in a return to the confinement of the first act, O'Casey crams all the characters into one room, and to intensify the pressure, the conquering soldiers enter to escort the coffin of little Mollser out into the bullet-filled streets. There is no room to live in the tenement; finally, the soldiers come in to evacuate it. At the close of the play the tension of space is relaxed, and there is room to take a few last breaths; but the momentary quiet exists only to highlight and silhouette the death of Bessie. Nora in her distraction runs to the window while the soldiers are busy trying to root out whatever snipers remain in the block. Bessie pulls her out of danger, and is shot herself. Her Christian act kills her. Bessie's end, however, is no act of forgiveness, for she screams out in full, human anger at the indignity of death.

. . . (*to Nora*) I've got this through . . . through you, you bitch, you! O God, have mercy on me! (*to Nora*) You wouldn't stop quiet, no, you wouldn't, blast you!

Bessie's humanity is seen in her crudity and vulgarity; compassionate as she is, she is no embodiment of abstract goodness. A drunkard and a foul-mouthed brawler, she is a celebration of basic humanity, without pretension, without abstract virtues, without lies. Bessie struggles to die with faith, but O'Casey breaks the hymn upon her dying words; it is almost as if she were trying to remember something but can't because it is so distant and irrelevant to her situation. Bessie dies, and Nora whimpers in the corner. The inversion is complete; the sweet heroine of genteel pretensions has become a useless object; the brawling, porter-swilling hag has become, in death, a proletarian redeemer. As in the case of another Marxist playwright, Brecht and his *Mother Courage*, the celebration of humanity takes place at the bottom, not the top.

SOURCE: extracts from *The Imagination of an Insurrection, Dublin Easter 1916: A Study of an Ideological Movement* (New York and London, 1967; paperback edition, New York, 1972), pp. 203–23.

NOTES

[Reorganised and renumbered from the original – Ed.]

1. See the *Irish Statesman*, v (20 Feb. 1926), pp. 739–40; also (6 March 1926), p. 798.
2. See Padraic Pearse, *Collected Works: Political Writings and Speeches*, p. 99.
3. See Brigadier-General Crozier, *Ireland For Ever* (London, 1932), p. 286.

Vincent C. De Baun   O'Casey and the Road to Expressionism   (1961)

Students of Sean O'Casey generally agree that his plays describe a course of technical development from naturalism to expressionism. The point of definite change of genre is usually established as the second act of *The Silver Tassie* (1928). Shortly after the first performance of the play, Curtis Canfield wrote: 'In *The Silver Tassie* [O'Casey] gives evidence of relinquishing a medium and a method in which he was most effective for the sake of a different subject matter and a different technique. . . . *The Silver Tassie* opens in the familiar Dublin tenement but the last acts move away from realism into the realm of philosophic expressionism.' A decade later, the same interpretation persisted. For example, Walter Starkie commented that in *The Silver Tassie* O'Casey 'left behind the plays of his former manner, and he began to grope towards new dramatic values. . . . The first act is written in true O'Casey manner – there is movement, there is life: the characters are real beings. . . . The second act, which is set in the trenches "somewhere in France", is a queer, fantastic scene that recalls slightly the dream play in *Masses and Man* by Toller.' After still another decade, S. Marion Tucker and Alan S. Downer were indicating that in *The Silver Tassie* O'Casey 'began experimenting with form and trying his hand at expressionism'.[1] And so on. Numerous other examples could be offered.

The point of this paper is that O'Casey's application of expressionistic techniques actually began not with *The Silver Tassie*, but
with *The Plough and the Stars* (1926). The expressionistic techniques
are, to be sure, not dominant – the earlier play is almost universally
recognised as realistic or naturalistic – but still they appear strongly
enough to warrant interested study.

Exactly what 'naturalism' or 'expressionism' may be, of course, is
open to debate.[2] There are probably as many analyses as there are
commentators. However, it should be made clear that for the
purposes of this study, naturalism is conceived as being basically a
picture of life in which people, places, and events appear as they really
are, without any coloring of idealism, romanticism or sentimentality.
Insofar as is possible, the naturalist observes the scene scientifically
and coolly and describes it objectively. 'These are', he says, 'the facts.
I have merely presented them. I have not interpreted them.' In
expressionism, conversely, the playwright takes 'the facts' and uses
them – most often in intentionally non-realistic ways – to give image
to some inner vision, some personal view of experience. He may use
colors, speech patterns, sound levels, or dozens of other devices, most
of them freighted with symbolic values, to create his effects. 'These
are', he says, 'facts which I have *interpreted* by shaping them in a way
beyond their customary literal dimensions.' (Obviously these defini-
tions ignore the academic distinctions often made regarding the
sordidness of naturalism, its deterministic essence, and so on, or the
intuitional and associative aspects of expressionism, with other
related qualities. Such distinctions, though valid, do not directly
apply to this essay.)

With these highly limited fields of reference in mind, we may turn
to *The Plough and the Stars*. To begin with, a study of the characters in
the play suggests that none is a truly dominating personality, except,
perhaps, Bessie Burgess. This evenness and solidity of characterisation is one of several indications that O'Casey was moving toward a
less naturalistic form. Whereas naturalistic plays most often feature
one or two characters who stand out beyond the others and who carry
a great part of the burden of the drama (e.g., O'Casey's own Juno),
the characters in an expressionistic play are apt to exist on the same
phantasmal 'dream-level', and have none of the clear-cut traits that
distinguish the real from the unreal.

Now, it certainly could not be said that any of the characters in *The
Plough and the Stars* is 'unreal'. The points being made here are that
although each character is an individual, he is still made subservient
to the author's purpose in the creation of a total effect – i.e., the
author's interpreted and shaped 'facts' – so that we must therefore

view the play as a total work of art where no single character can legitimately draw our attention from the playwright's tragic purpose. To be sure, O'Casey has not created a tragedy in the classical sense; he has simply created an ordinary group of people whom we see trapped by circumstance. But he has been careful not to distract our attention from the group by the presence of a single dominating individual. It is this 'levelness' of characterisation which indicates a part of his first leaning toward expressionism.

The Plough and the Stars shows other (and more positive) indications of O'Casey's drift away from naturalism. Toward the end of Act I, for example, Bessie makes a drunken entrance. In the distance is the fading sound of marching feet, a brass band, and soldiers singing 'It's a Long Way to Tipperary'. Her intoxication has inspired one of her occasional surges of religious fervor, and she is speaking in taglines from Scripture. Her speech is weirdly prophetic: 'Yous'll not escape from th' arrow that flieth be night, or th' sickness that wasteth be day. . . . An' ladyship an' all, as some o' them may be, they'll be scatthered abroad, like th' dust o' th' darkness!' This strange whirl of metaphors, spoken in a half-light by a dishevelled harridan, is an unusual device in a naturalistic play.

Other passages of burgeoning expressionism can be found in Act II. Throughout the episodes in which Rosie Redmond tries to seduce The Covey and Fluther while the men argue about nationalism and patriotism, a shadow is cast against the window and we hear the stirring rhetoric of a young revolutionary inciting a crowd. The words are actually those of Padraic Pearse,[3] an Irish rebel who was executed by the British in 1916. This strange juxtaposition of beer and lust in the pub, with doomed patriotism on the street outside, symbolised by the shadow on the window, is another step toward expressionism. First the young revolutionary is heard saying: 'Bloodshed is a cleansing and sanctifying thing, and the nation that regards it as the final horror has lost its manhood. . . . There are many things more horrible than bloodshed, and slavery is one of them!' The speaker departs for a moment, but he returns to deliver three more fragments of his speech. (Questions: Why does he come and go? Why does he not deliver the speech in one fixed location, in a continuous oration? Can his seemingly unmotivated arrivals and departures be called 'natural'?)

On his second appearance he provides a climax to an absurd blather of patriotic multiloquence from Peter and Fluther. This fragment ends: 'Such august homage was never offered to God as this: the homage of millions of lives gladly given for love of country. And we must be ready to pour out the same red wine in the same glorious sacrifice, for without shedding of blood there is no redemption!' The passage has, of course, its particular symbological effects, especially for a predominantly Catholic Dublin audience – the allusions to the Catholic doctrines of Transubstantiation (changing of the wine in the Mass to the Blood of Christ); sacrifice (the essence of action in the Mass, as Christ's Body is offered to feed His people); and redemption through blood (the drama of the Crucifixion).

The third time the speaker appears, he orates ringingly of the 'exhilaration of war' and cries out that Ireland 'must welcome it as she would welcome the Angel of God!' This grandiose sentiment soars over a scene of vulgar quarreling and bickering involving Bessie, Mrs Gogan, The Covey and Peter.

At his last appearance, his fragment of speech comes in the center of an exchange among Brennan, Langon and Clitheroe, three rebel officers. They are tremendously excited, and their unconsciously metric speeches have a rhythmic, chanted quality. The author's stage direction makes this clear: 'They speak rapidly, as if unaware of the meaning of what they say. They have been mesmerised by the fervency of the speeches.' They speak in antiphonal succession:

We won't have long to wait now.
Th' time is rotten ripe for revolution.
You have a mother, Langon.
Ireland is greater than a mother.
You have a wife, Clitheroe.
Ireland is greater than a wife.
Th' time for Ireland's battle is now – th' place for Ireland's battle is here.

Here, the ghostly speaker breaks in again:

Our foes are strong, but strong as they are, they cannot undo the miracles of God, who ripens in the hearts of young men the seeds sown by the young men of former generations. They think that they have pacified Ireland; think they have foreseen everything; but the fools, the fools, the fools! – they have left us our Fenian dead, and, while Ireland holds those graves, Ireland, unfree, shall never be at peace!

The three young men shout:

Imprisonment for th' Independence of Ireland!
Wounds for th' Independence of Ireland!
Death for th' Independence of Ireland!
So help us God!

The curtain comes down, then, on the passionate fervor of their determination to fight and die – but only after Fluther and Rosie make it clear that they, at least, are interested in matters other than martial.

As usually performed, Act III is naturalistic, but there is further incipient expressionism in Act IV. Its effect is felt almost at once. Within the first minute, the cry 'Red Cr...oss, Red Cr...oss! . . .

Ambu...lance, Ambu...lance!' is heard in the distance.[4] First, it has a weird, song-like quality that is definitely unreal; the author's stage direction specifically calls for a 'lilting chant'. Second, it punctuates and reinforces, obligato-like, points of special dramatic tension. Third, it interweaves, as a chant, with songs and hymns that create a pattern, through the closing action.

The first time we hear the cry, we have just realised that Fluther, Peter and The Covey are casually playing cards in a room where Mollser's body lies in a coffin: that Nora, whose baby has died, is moaning madly next door; and that outside, the revolution-torn city is aflame. Then there follows an episode in which Nora, babbling in delirium, enters the room and is led away by Bessie, who sings to her the opening stanza of 'Lead, Kindly Light'. Then a soldier comes into the room from the street. He has just spoken with unintentional brutality about 'closing in on the blighters. It was only a bit of a dog fight', when there is a sudden 'sharp ping of a sniper's rifle, followed by a squeal of pain'. Immediately the chant rises once more: 'Red Cr...oss, Red Cr...oss! Ambu...lance, Ambu...lance!'

The soldier thereupon orders the card-players to prepare to be taken into custody until the fighting is over. Cheerfully advising them to bring along some food, he begins to sing in a 'lilting' voice, 'Oh, I do like a snice mince pie, / Oh, I do like a snice mince pie', when suddenly 'again the snap of a sniper's rifle rings out, followed by a scream of pain'. At once comes the growingly familiar chant, 'Red Cr...oss . . . Red Cr...oss! Ambu...lance . . . Ambu...lance!'

When the men leave, Nora enters the room. Bessie, who has been nursing her, has fallen into an exhausted sleep. Demented, Nora 'lilts gently, as she arranges the table', setting out tea. The song is a sentimental ballad about violets scenting the woods, chestnut blooms in a glade, robins singing, and the charms of love. She stops then to murmur vacantly, 'I can't help feelin' this room very strange. . . . What is it? What is it? . . . I must think. . . . I must thry to remember. . . .' Her words are cut by the 'chanting' of voices, now heard for the fourth time: 'Ambu...lance, Ambu...lance! Red Cr...oss, Red Cr...oss!' Uncaring, Nora goes back to her song, which is interrupted by 'a burst of rifle fire . . . followed by the rapid tok-tok-tok of a machine gun'.

Bessie wakes at this, and in trying to pull Nora away from the window, is hit by British gunfire when she is mistaken for a sniper. In her death throes she sings:

> I do believe . . . I will believe
> That . . . Jesus . . . died . . . for . . . me,

> That . . . on . . . the . . . cross He . . .
> shed . . . His . . . blood
> From . . . sin . . . to . . . set . . . free.

Two soldiers rush in, but it is too late to save Bessie. A neighbor leads Nora away, whimpering and screaming. The Tommies see the tea things and sit down casually. 'In the distance is heard a bitter burst of rifle and machine-gun fire, interspersed with the boom, boom of artillery.' As the act builds to its close, the cry comes for a final time: 'Ambu...lance, Ambu...lance! Red Cro...ss, Red Cro...ss!' The curtain falls while the soldiers, sipping tea, join in a chorus of their comrades, whose voices rise from the streets below in a rendition of 'Keep the Home Fires Burning'.

This summary of Act IV has of course placed a strong emphasis on aural effects that would probably not make themselves particularly obvious to an audience watching the play on stage. However, it should be clear to one who is studying the play as a technical exercise, that the whole pattern of sound has been designed in a fashion that is hardly naturalistic. The cry for the ambulance is in chilling contrast, in varying degrees, to Bessie's hymns, Nora's ballad, and the soldiers' songs. Furthermore, it may be observed that the gunfire from outside builds its own pattern – from the single 'ping' of a sniper's rifle, to rifle plus machine-gun, to rifle plus machine-gun plus 'boom, boom' of artillery.

These expressionistic effects, considered with those previously noted – Bessie's witch-like appearance in Act I after the chorus of 'Tipperary'; the silhouette of the speaker, with his passionate rhetoric, flashing intermittently through Act II; and the hypnotised rhythm of the speeches of the three young rebels at the end of Act II – all suggest strongly that O'Casey's technical experimentation began some while before his definite break with naturalism in Act II of *The Silver Tassie*.

Curiously enough, this incipient expressionism seems to have gone virtually unnoticed. Most critics of the early O'Casey have agreed with Andrew E. Malone, who wrote (presumably before he saw *The Silver Tassie*, but in a book not published until 1929) that the playwright was 'a realist of the most uncompromising kind, and a traditionalist' who had 'accepted the realist tradition of the Abbey Theatre.'[5] Of all contemporary commentators on the subject, only Denis Johnston seems to have detected the development of new tendencies in *The Plough and the Stars*:

As for a new prophet, it is becoming increasingly clear that as a realist, he [O'Casey] is an impostor. He will tell you the name and address of the person who made each individual speech, in any of his plays, but we are not deceived. . . . His dialogue is becoming a series of word-poems in dialect, his plots are disappearing and giving place to a form of undisguised Expressionism under the stress of a genius that is much too insistent and far too pregnant with meaning to be bound by the four dismal walls of orthodox realism. It will be interesting to see how long he will try to keep up so outrageous a pretence.[6]

It is worth noting that in the works of O'Casey, as in scores of other literary and dramatic works, seemingly sudden changes often cast long shadows before them.

SOURCE: article in *Modern Drama*, IV (1961), pp. 254–9.

NOTES

1. C. Canfield, *Plays of the Irish Renaissance* (New York, 1929), p. 296; W. Starkie, 'Sean O'Casey', in *The Irish Theatre* (London, 1939), pp. 166–7; S. M. Tucker and A. S. Downer, *Twenty-Five Modern Plays* (New York, 1948), p. 723.
2. Probably one of the people least interested in a definition is O'Casey himself. In 1949 I exchanged several letters with him on this subject. He wrote me on 17 April: 'I've often heard of, & read about, "naturalism" & "expressionism", but, God's truth, I don't know rightly what either means.'
3. Starkie, op. cit., p. 160.
4. This effect was especially pointed out to me by O'Casey in his letter of 17 April 1949: 'You are right in your idea of what you call expressionism appearing in The Plough; where you say, and in the outside calls for Ambulance, Ambulance, Red Cross, Red Cross.'
5. A. E. Malone, *The Irish Drama* (New York, 1929), p. 218.
6. D. Johnston, 'Sean O'Casey: An Appreciation', *Living Age*, CXXIX (1926), p. 163.

Ronald Ayling   Character Control and 'Distancing' Effects in *The Plough and the Stars* (1970)

. . . Too little critical attention has been paid to practical aspects of Sean O'Casey's stagecraft.[1] Though this essay deals with only one facet of the subject, it involves a detailed analysis of one of the most significant and effective dramatic devices used in *The Plough and the Stars* and *The Silver Tassie*: this is the means whereby certain characters and their actions are 'distanced', when it looks as though they might become too well liked by the audience, or if there is the likelihood of spectators identifying themselves uncritically with the feelings or values of the stage creations. The effect is obtained in various ways. For the sake of convenience, we use the word coined by Bertolt Brecht to describe the phenomenon. John Willett writes that Brecht's *Verfremdung* means 'estrangement, alienation or disillusion in English; *dépaysement*, *étrangement* or *distanciation* in French: a wide choice of equivalents, none of which is exactly right',[2] but if none of them precisely describes O'Casey's method, either, they still offer useful shorthand guides to what he is attempting.

From the late 1920s, Brecht became increasingly opposed to naturalist character-creation and acting. He was hostile to heroes and heroines as such, preferring an objective stage presentation of men and women as social beings and as individuals. Similarly, at the time that *The Plough and the Stars* was first performed in Dublin, O'Casey said in a debate on the play that he 'was not trying, and never would try, to write about heroes'.[3] Brecht, moreover, distrusted empathy. He thought that the essential message of a writer was sometimes destroyed because people identified themselves with, or felt sorry for, morally undesirable characters, and that social criticism was blunted by individual compassion. Instead of emotional identification Brecht wanted intellectual distancing: characters in plays were to be regarded solely as stage figures created for a particular purpose by a playwright and imitated for an audience's entertainment by actors who were not to appear on the stage as other than imitators. However heroic or admirable a personality might appear to be, the onlookers must never relax their vigilance and accept that character at his or her face value or identify his joy or suffering too completely with their own experience.

In his dramatic writings Brecht used many distancing devices to prevent empathy and to make spectators aware, throughout the play, that they were witnessing a stage performance. There were very few attempts to use lighting for illusion or to simulate realistic stage settings, though essential stage properties (like Mother Courage's cart) were faithfully reproduced; the plot or narrative outline of the drama was often divulged in advance of the action by means of placards or film projection. Songs and spoken narration interrupted acted sequences, and broke any illusion temporarily created by the actors. These *Verfremdung* techniques were designed to combat unthinking emotional responses on the part of audiences and to encourage spectators to criticise and judge the dramatic action as it proceeded. Brecht was not, of course, completely hostile to emotion on the stage or to leading characters who dominate the action in a play – we find both in his work – but he believed that both the emotion and the characters should be strictly controlled and subservient to the theme or message of the play as a whole.

The objective presentation of dramatic events is to be found, in various forms, throughout the history of drama – the use of the chorus in Greek Tragedy is an obvious example. Brecht's innovation was his deliberate use of a wide range of objective methods to serve his own didactic purposes. In this essay, however, we are primarily concerned with those aspects of alienation that involve characterisation. Some degree of estrangement of stage characters from the sympathy of audiences has been practised by playwrights in all ages, and writers far less didactic in intention than Brecht have found it necessary, consciously or unconsciously, to employ one or other of the devices that he used quite deliberately. Because dramatic figures are represented on the stage by flesh and blood people, it is possible for them to take on what is almost an independent life of their own and, accordingly, for them to unbalance the dramatic as well as moral basis of the play in which they appear. There is always the danger, too, that the audience will fall in love with stage characters even against the wishes of the author.

Shakespeare's Falstaff and O'Casey's Captain Boyle are both characters who seem so much larger than life, and so full of humour and vitality, that undesirable and anti-social traits in their characters, that would be attacked were they living people, have been overlooked and even excused on the stage. How else can one explain the fact that critics, from Maurice Morgann in the eighteenth century to A. C. Bradley and John Palmer in the twentieth, have spoken so indignantly of Hal's cold-blooded inhumanity when he behaves as any socially responsible man would do in his circumstances, and, on becoming monarch, banishes Falstaff from his company? The newly crowned king's speech of rejection – 'I know thee not, old man: fall to thy prayers' – merely makes explicit what was inevitable in the dramatic pattern of *Henry IV* from the beginning of the first part, and what the subtle distancing effects have implied throughout the whole play, especially in the second part. As examples of character alienation, for example, one might instance the increased stress on the age, disease and lechery of Falstaff and also the coarsening of his wit in Part 2. Moreover, unfavourable aspects of his character which – in Part 1 – had been criticised verbally are *seen* in action in the second part, and this is more damaging: in particular, his callous treatment of the conscripted soldiers and his exploitation of Mistress Quickly and Justice Shallow. In Act II, scene iv of Part 2 we witness Falstaff making love to Doll Tearsheet, and the grossness of the episode is pointed in a Brechtian manner by the critical commentary of Hal and

Poins. Thus we may find the *Verfremdungseffekt* in traditional forms of drama, and when Brecht's terminology is used to describe O'Casey's techniques it is not because he deliberately followed the German playwright's theories – on the contrary, he was totally unaware of Brecht's plays and theoretical writings when he wrote *The Plough and the Stars* and *The Silver Tassie* – but because today we can see that his aims and approach in these plays were in some ways similar to those of Brecht in his work.

O'Casey's methods were chosen for his own purposes. It is no accident that any detailed analysis of plays like *The Shadow of a Gunman* and *Juno and the Paycock* must be largely taken up with matters relating to characterisation. Yet, though this is an important element in both plays, O'Casey still showed something akin to Brechtian detachment in his character drawing. Even in his portrayal of 'Juno' and Mary Boyle there is considerable criticism of their failings as well as genuine warmth and understanding; indeed, the sympathy is impressive precisely because it is so open-eyed.[4] Throughout his works, including his most experimental writings, there are varying admixtures of emotional involvement and critical detachment; and even in the works most influenced by expressionist techniques there is a deliberate attempt to reconcile two-dimensional stereotype figures with more rounded human characters. . . .

When O'Casey wishes spectators to view the dramatic action and its social implications with critical insight, he does not necessarily demand detachment at the same time – as Brecht did, in theory if not always in practice. Instead, as in the final act curtain scenes of *The Shadow of a Gunman* and *Juno and the Paycock*, he seeks to arouse feelings of disgust and, sometimes, anger as well. Even the use of stylisation and ritual, as in the second act of *The Silver Tassie*, does not preclude emotion in favour of abstract or dispassionate criticism. The ironic and sometimes moving effects created by familiar liturgical language and rhythms, for one thing, invoke an archetypal response on the part of the audience at a level other than the rational. O'Casey never scorned emotional involvement by the audience; indeed, he actively encouraged it by using (among other things) sentimental hymns, music-hall songs and full-blooded infusions of melodrama – elements which some critics have apparently found too obvious or superficial for serious dramatic purposes.[5] The intrusion of blatant farcical material at moments of tragic intensity is another method used to forestall any possibly complacent or stereotyped reaction on the part of an audience.

O'Casey's playwriting allows for a considerable degree of *rapport* between spectators and certain of his *dramatis personae*, yet the empathy thus engendered does not impede distancing or criticism. On the contrary, the distancing that O'Casey achieves for critical purposes is reinforced, and not undermined, by the creation of empathy for particular individuals, from whom the audience's sympathies are subsequently estranged by shock tactics of one kind or another. The depth and quality of the spectator's emotional attachment to a particular stage creation necessarily conditions the impact of the eventual alienation. If the character is initially well liked the disillusionment will be the more unexpected and painful. For one thing, the *volte-face* is a blow to the spectator's self-esteem and belief in his or her own judgement. The shock may thus produce a more critical scrutiny of the spectator's values and judgements, fresh recognition of the unpredictability of human nature, and of the uncertain conditions of life.

O'Casey was never as theoretically minded as was Bertolt Brecht and the extent of his conscious awareness of the implications of his technical experimentation in *The Plough and the Stars*, and even *The Silver Tassie*, must remain uncertain. All that one can be quite sure about is the strength of his reaction against surface realism and his deeper commitment to group experience in the late 1920s and the 1930s. Writing in defence of *Within the Gates* at the time of that play's New York première (1934), he argued that there is

a deeper life than the life we see and hear with the open ear and the open eye, and this is the life important and the life everlasting. And this life can be caught from the group rather than from the individual. . . . Know a man all your life and you do not know him wholly, and how then can we expect to picture the nature of a man in the space of a couple of hours?[6]

Moreover, his well-known letter to W. B. Yeats on the subject of *The Silver Tassie* stressed the deliberate control of characterisation in that drama. One thinks of that passage where he spoke of the (obviously conscious) diminution of character in each of the plays that followed *Juno and the Paycock*:

I'm afraid I can't make my mind mix with the sense of importance you give to 'a dominating character'. God forgive me, but it does sound as if you peeked and pined for a hero in the play. Now is a dominating character more important than a play, or a play more important than a dominating character? In *The Silver Tassie* you have a unique work that dominates all the characters in the play. I remember talking to Lady Gregory about *The Plough* before it was produced, and I remember her saying that *The Plough* mightn't be so successful as *Juno*, because there wasn't in the play a character so dominating and all-pervading as 'Juno', yet *The Plough* is a better work than *Juno*, and, in my opinion, . . . *The Tassie*, because of, or in spite of, the lack of a dominating character, is a greater work than *The Plough*.[7]

I do not think there is any doubt that, after *Juno*, O'Casey consciously toned down his characters in order to avoid creating personalities so dominant as Seumas Shields or Jack Boyle. There were probably various reasons for him to do this, one of the most important being that Dublin audiences and critics had so much revelled in the personal idiosyncracies of these figures that they had often ignored the social and moral criticism implicit in the plays: criticism that was primarily directed at the irresponsible fantasies and hypocritical values of such characters. Even in *Juno*, indeed, there is an attempt in the last act to tone down the more attractive qualities that undoubtedly are to be found in 'Captain' Boyle in the first two acts and to expose quite unambiguously the selfish and vicious traits in his nature. As with Falstaff, critics have been only too willing to take Jack Boyle at his own estimate and to regard the character as first encountered in the play to be the only reality. Actors in both roles, moreover, often play up the genial humour and mitigate savage characteristics in them. Saros Cowasjee writes in *Sean O'Casey: The Man Behind the Plays* that 'Captain Boyle remains so irresistibly comic that we often forget to pity Juno and Mary'.[8] This is certainly not true by the third act, though it may have been so earlier. Even a critic as well-balanced as David Krause can say, somewhat sentimentally: 'The Captain remains the "struttin' paycock" in his glorious deterioration; even in his drunken raving he remains a magnificently grotesque anti-hero. Juno must reject him, yet we can forgive him, for he maintains his falstaffian spirit to the end.'[9]

He remains a 'grotesque anti-hero', to be sure, but there is nothing glorious or magnificent or falstaffian about him at the end. On the contrary, he is in turn maudlin and vicious, self-pitying and vindictive. The really savage attack on his pregnant daughter is meant to sicken us; the scene should be performed with no redeeming features whatsoever. Moreover, earlier, more attractive, qualities in his character appear in a debased form in the final act. His humour lacks its former bite and exuberance, deadened as it is by the whining self-pity that increasingly engrosses him. What's more, his earlier resourcefulness appears to desert him and 'friends' and neighbours like Joxer, Mrs Madigan and Nugent – formerly dominated and exploited by him – take advantage of its decline. The rich idiomatic language that characterised his speech in the first two acts disintegrates until it becomes broken and largely incoherent phrases, while the imaginative fantasy of 'the deep sea sailor' of Act 1 becomes drunken babble about the Easter Rising at the end of the play. As Boyle's personality wilts in the face of the misfortunes that strike the family, his wife's character progressively gains in stature: the contrast naturally emphasises Boyle's deterioration even more markedly. Though the technique of gradual self-exposure is subtly practised in *Juno and the Paycock*, the process is taken further in later dramas where the malignancy of the villains and the dangerous effects of anti-social behaviour by the wastrels are presented in more overtly critical ways.

It is noticeable, too, that in the plays that immediately follow *Juno* no one character is allowed to disturb or disrupt the overall dramatic balance. In *The Plough* both Bessie Burgess and Fluther Good, and in *The Tassie* Harry Heegan, are potentially dominating characters, but they are carefully controlled and their personalities either subdued or subsumed within the larger dramatic patterns of the action whenever it looks as though their undue prominence might undermine the drama as a whole. In other words, characterisation is subordinate to theme – though individual and even idiosyncratic portraits are still memorable in *The Tassie* and *Within the Gates*, while *The Plough* presents a diverse group of dramatic figures. 'Group' is the operative word, of course, in each of these works. Increasingly, we see in them the individual forced to conform to a set pattern of behaviour, or occupied in a group or mass activity which drastically reduces his or her individuality. Huge forces in contemporary society, in peace as in war, dwarf the individual; increasing mechanisation in social organisation and greater political conformity are other aspects of modern life reflected in O'Casey's drama. In each case, the process is realised theatrically by various devices of stylisation and distancing. O'Casey's earlier method of characterisation was thus modified in response to a drastic enlargement of theme: the change accompanied an increasing emphasis on formal arrangement in settings and other theatrical devices aimed at presenting his vision of society in a more objective manner.

This conclusion may appear self-evident, yet, though several critics have recognised some such process at work, few have tried to come to terms with the playwright's intentions and practice in this respect. To my knowledge, only Mr Vincent De Baun has attempted to describe this facet of the author's stagecraft, though he does not trace the technique in action in any detail, and his definition has, in any case, been strongly criticised by Saros Cowasjee.[10] Mr De Baun's main contention (which is italicised in the following quotation) seems valid from any point of view, however, and may be abundantly illustrated from a close analysis of the text.

A study of the characters in the play suggests that none is a truly dominating personality, except, perhaps, Bessie Burgess. . . . It certainly could not be said that any of the characters in *The Plough and the Stars* is 'unreal'. The points being made here are that *although each character is an individual, he is still made subservient to the author's purpose in the creation of a total effect* – i.e., the author's interpreted and shaped 'facts' – so that *we must therefore view the play as a total work of art where no single character can legitimately draw our attention from the playwright's tragic purpose.* To be sure, O'Casey has not created an ordinary group of people whom we see trapped by circumstance. But he has been careful not to distract our attention from the group by the presence of a single dominating individual. It is this 'levelness' of characterization which indicates a part of his first leaning toward expressionism.[11]

Unfortunately, in the article itself Mr De Baun goes only halfway towards an understanding of the playwright's new methods. To me, one of the most impressive formal achievements in *The Plough* is to be found, not so much in the subordination of characterisation to thematic design – though this is the final effect of the technique, of course – as in the superb control that is exercised in modulating the rise and fall, attraction and alienation of character in the course of the drama. Despite the deliberate diminution of character and the author's concern to see that no single figure is allowed to distract attention from the total effect, it is not true to say that there is no 'truly dominating character' or that there is a uniformity of portrayal. De Baun's 'levelness of characterization' gives the impression that dramatic tension is drained from the play, leaving it colourless, restrained, even (perhaps) monotonous. Instead, individual figures come to the fore in the course of the narrative, appear to be about to monopolise the action, but are then firmly distanced before they can disrupt the balance of the whole. As we shall see, this method is particularly marked in the case of Fluther Good and Bessie Burgess. Far from creating uniformity, the technique makes for a fluctuating and unpredictable portrait-gallery which maintains the intrinsic psychological interest and individual energy afforded by good naturalist 'character drama', yet subjects the spectators to the shocks and surprises of unexpected developments in plot and in character, while keeping individual characterisation strictly subordinate to the overall dramatic design.

At certain moments in the action different individuals are outstanding. In the first act, for instance, Nora is in complete command of the short tea-scene; she dictates the speed and progress of the action and 'bosses' all the men on stage. Fluther Good is dominant for much of Act II. In the fourth act, Bessie is conspicuous for much of the time, and may be said to command most attention, though it is clear that the overall impression by this stage in the drama is of the communal rather than the individual disaster. At other points in the action one or more figures – it might be two, or groups of pairs, as in the superb quarrel scenes in the second and third acts – temporarily take the initiative or dominate the scene and the other people on the stage. In every case, such ascendancy is short-lived. The important aspect, technically, is O'Casey's success in engaging the audience's interest in, and (where necessary) sympathy for, individual characters at particular moments in the action, and his ability afterwards in changing or distancing these feelings, in response to the requirements of the theme. Conversely, his operation of what one might call the reverse-alienation technique is equally effective, in making us see – at unexpected moments of revelation – creative and positive human qualities in people who had earlier been dismissed as seemingly worthless or good-for-nothing characters. Our expectations are turned upside down and we are consequently forced to reconsider our values and judgements.

O'Casey is sceptical of the personal and political values of the Easter Week 'insurgents' in *The Plough and the Stars*. But it is not only the Platform Orator, Clitheroe, and those characters who participate actively in the political struggle who are distanced critically in the course of the action. We are deliberately restrained from complete empathy with *any* of the characters in the drama. Important characters are omitted for entire acts. Nora Clitheroe, for instance, does not appear at all in Act II, although the preceding act revolved about her and built up the story of her personal dilemma. Jack Clitheroe, who seemed to be the potential hero of the play in the first act, only appears for a few seconds in Act II (and then without individuality and for only four lines of dialogue); he has one short though important scene in Act III, but is absent altogether from the last act. We are not allowed, moreover, to dwell overlong on any one of the personal tragedies, being moved rapidly from one situation to another in the last two acts: from Mollser to Nora; from her to Langon and back to Nora; we return to Mollser with news of her death, followed by Nora's madness, the report of Jack's death in action, the shooting of Bessie, and, finally, the torment of a whole city in flames.

In *The Plough and the Stars*, as in *The Silver Tassie*, it is the crushing and dehumanising experience of war that, however temporarily, compels people into group attitudes and group responses, dominated by the conformity bred of fear or military discipline or both. In *Within the Gates*, the economic depression of the 1930s is responsible for the involuntary mobilisation of an army of the Down-and-Out, whose individuality has been completely destroyed in the struggle for physical survival. The mass subjugation of personality is realised most comprehensively, of course, in the second act of *The Silver Tassie*, where hitherto lively and free-wheeling characters like Harry and Teddy are absorbed into the automaton ranks of fatigued soldiers in the rest camp near the front line. The same process is seen in *The Plough and the Stars*, though in a minor key. Jack Clitheroe, who was depicted as a distinct if weak individual in the first act of the play, has altogether lost any sign of a separate identity when he makes a brief appearance in Act II. He and the other two freedom-fighters, Brennan and Langon, have been deeply influenced by the mass emotions of the meeting. They move and speak as though in a trance, conversing in antiphonal-like responses: 'You have a mother, Langon' – 'Ireland is greater than a mother' – 'You have a wife, Clitheroe' – 'Ireland is greater than a wife'. In striking contrast to the unpredictable, boisterous and passionately contentious characterisation realised in Act I and in the pub scene throughout Act II, the language and actions of the three men are stylised and rigidly controlled – 'they have been mesmerised by the fervency of the speeches', as a stage direction indicates. The complete unanimity of their aims and ideals also stands out in sharp and mechanical relief against the clamorous dissensions (on every subject) of all the other characters in the action. Like the British soldiers in *The Silver Tassie*, the three men are represented, temporarily, as an unthinking part of a mass-movement, subsumed in a corporate experience. Thus, in stylisation and incantatory language alike, the short scene with the three 'rebel' soldiers in the public house looks forward to the large-scale expressionism of the second act of *The Silver Tassie*.

A further diminution of personality, as the result of adverse circumstances, is realised in the last act of *The Plough* without using stylisation. Although the ebullient nature of Fluther is never wholly suppressed, nor the bickerings of the Covey and Uncle Peter altogether stopped, they are nonetheless much subdued by, first of all, the presence of the sick Nora sleeping in the next room, and, later, by the armed invasion of the Tommies, who herd the men together as prisoners and lead them away. By subduing the hitherto irrepressible non-conformity of the tenement menfolk in this way, O'Casey is enabled to convey the overall tragic situation without irrelevant distractions; or, to put it another way, the particular historical situation itself creates a subdued scene of collective suffering. It is not without significance that the playwright, who had allowed leading characters the last words in each of his earlier plays (Davoren and Shields in *The Shadow of a Gunman*, and Joxer and Boyle in *Juno and the Paycock*), is careful to remove all the important characters from the concluding scenes of *The Plough* and *The Tassie*. The menfolk having been forcibly removed in the former play, the death of Bessie and the departure of Nora and Jinnie Gogan leave the final curtain scene to two minor figures. In like manner, Harry and Teddy in *The Silver*

Tassie leave the dance hall, accompanied by their relatives, just before the end of the play, and it is left to two relatively insignificant characters, Simon Norton and Mrs Foran, to bring the drama to a similarly ironic close. O'Casey's change of technique may have been motivated by ignorant critical interpretations of the first two plays. Attracted by the wayward eccentricities of Shields and Boyle, the final effect of each work on Dublin audiences and reviewers was uncritical laughter rather than horror. Accordingly, the playwright may have resolved to make the tragic irony chillingly unmistakable in his subsequent curtain-scenes.

The distancing of characters performs another important function in addition to broadening the social criticism and realising something in the nature of group drama; it is also able to show more than one side to a given situation, and more than an individual perception of reality. In *The Plough* and *The Tassie*, for instance, the effects of poverty and warfare are depicted in both a personal, subjective manner and an external, objective one, too. Such shifts of viewpoint are achieved by using expressionist and symbolic as well as naturalist techniques, of course, but character estrangement contributes a significant part of the effect. In practice, it means that the dramatic figure concerned is placed in a full social context, so that the audience's relationship with the character is accordingly modified. This entails seeing that one's natural predisposition to favour (that is, to pity or even identify oneself with) a human being in adversity or distress is not exploited at the expense of other characters in the play.

The audience's fluctuating attitude towards Harry Heegan in the course of *The Silver Tassie* is a case in point; Nora Clitheroe's position in *The Plough and the Stars* is somewhat similar. We are never wholly unsympathetic to either person, and, at times, we are very close to both Harry and Nora in their mental and physical anguish. Yet at certain significant moments the playwright deliberately prevents us from coming emotionally too near either figure, so that we are forced to recognise the priority of other people's needs over theirs. Nora's appalling situation towards the end of Act IV, for instance, is suddenly overshadowed by the death of Mrs Burgess, which takes place in Nora's presence. The fact that the terrified Nora makes no move to help Bessie in her death agonies inevitably (if temporarily) affects the audience's response. Insane as she is, Nora can no longer be held morally responsible for her actions – or inactivity; but the spectators, deeply moved by Bessie's sufferings, which follow hard upon her devoted nursing of Nora, can hardly ignore Nora's presence at such a moment, nor be indifferent to the dying woman's denunciation of her, however unjust that attack may be. One's response must be

compounded of conflicting feelings at this point, and – whichever
emotion is dominant – the interplay of human relationships and
feelings is projected in a complex and challenging manner. Similarly,
while never wholly estranging our sympathies from Harry Heegan,
O'Casey makes us view him as self-absorbed and impossibly
possessive – an understandable result of his physical incapacity, of
course – at significant moments during the last two acts of *The Tassie*,
when his selfishness threatens the future welfare or happiness of other
people like Jessie, Barney, and even Susie. On such occasions, we are
distanced from his personal dilemma by seeing it in a broader
perspective: that is, in relation to the situation of the other characters
in the action.

It is in his handling of Fluther Good and Bessie Burgess, however,
that the playwright shows most clearly his consummate command of
stagecraft in *The Plough and the Stars*. It has been intimated already that
they are both potentially dominant figures. At certain moments, each
one is heroic in the conventional sense. In Act III Fluther risks his life
to find Nora at the barricades. Bessie faces death in the same act to
bring a doctor to the sick woman. In Act IV we see Bessie's great care
of and devotion to the mad woman, with whom she had fought earlier
in the drama, and we hear of Fluther's courage in making arrangements for Mollser's funeral while heavy fighting continues in the
neighbourhood. But at other crucial moments in the action, our
sympathies are alienated from both characters. After his heroism
early in the third act, for instance, Fluther joins in the looting of the
shops; he returns dead drunk and is incapable of helping Nora when
she most needs it. Bessie, who, until this moment in the play – and we
are almost three-quarters of the way through it – has been consistently estranged from the audience's sympathies by her coarse and
unpleasant brawling, is the only one in the tenement who will bring a
doctor to Nora.

　　This episode in Act III is a powerful scene of fluctuating moods and
moral judgments. When Fluther enters he is a conquering hero, for all
the visual comedy of his appearance. We saw his heroism earlier in
the act, and we enjoy his racy language and exuberance:

> (*Bessie looks at Nora lying on the street, for a few moments, then, leaving the window, she comes
> out, runs over to Nora, lifts her up in her arms, and carries her swiftly into the house. A short pause,
> then down the street is heard a wild, drunken yell; it comes nearer, and Fluther enters, frenzied,
> wild-eyed, mad, roaring drunk. In his arms is an earthen half-gallon jar of whiskey; streaming
> from one of the pockets of his coat is the arm of a new tunic shirt; on his head is a woman's vivid blue
> hat with gold lacing, all of which he has looted.*)
> FLUTHER (*singing in a frenzy*): Fluther's a jolly good fella! . . . Fluther's a jolly good fella!

Up the rebels!... That nobody can deny! (*He beats on the door.*) Get us a mug or a jug, or somethin', some o' yous, one o' yous, will yous, before I lay one o' yous out!... (*Looking down the street.*) Bang an' fire away for all Fluther cares ... (*Banging at door.*) Come down an' open th' door, some o' yous, one o' yous, will yous, before I lay some o' yous out![12]

But we soon become aware of the essential selfishness of his attitude, and his irresponsibility when his subsequent yell, 'Th' whole city can topple home to hell, for Fluther!', is immediately followed by 'a scream from Nora, followed by a moan'. Oblivious to all about him, however, he continues to sing 'furiously' and to kick at the hall-door:

(*His frantic movements cause him to spill some of the whiskey out of the jar.*)
FLUTHER: Blast you, Fluther, don't be spillin' the precious liquor! (*He kicks at the door.*) Ay, give us a mug or a jug, or somethin', one o' yous, some o' yous, will yous, before I lay one o' yous out!
(*The door suddenly opens, and Bessie, coming out, grips him by the collar.*)
BESSIE (*indignantly*): You bowsey, come in ower o' that ... I'll thrim your thricks o' dhrunken dancin' for you, an' none of us knowin' how soon we'll bump into a world we were never in before!
FLUTHER (*as she is pulling him in*): Ay, th' jar, th' jar, th' jar!
(*A short pause, then again is heard a scream of pain from Nora. The door opens and Mrs Gogan and Bessie are seen standing at it.*)
BESSIE: Fluther would go, only he's too dhrunk.... Oh, God, isn't it a pity he's so dhrunk! We'll have to thry to get a docthor somewhere.
MRS GOGAN: I'd be afraid to go ... Besides, Mollser's terrible bad. I don't think you'll get a docthor to come. It's hardly any use goin'.
BESSIE (*determinedly*): I'll risk it.... Give her a little of Fluther's whiskey.... It's th' fright that's brought it on so soon.... Go on back to her, you.
(*Mrs Gogan goes in, and Bessie softly closes the door. She is moving forward, when the sound of some rifle shots, and the tok, tok, tok of a distant machine-gun bring her to a sudden halt. She hesitates for a moment, then she tightens her shawl round her, as if it were a shield, then she firmly and swiftly goes out.*)
BESSIE (*as she goes out*): Oh God, be Thou my help in time o' throuble. An: shelter me safely in th' shadow of Thy wings!
                          Curtain

Fluther has been diminished before our eyes, while Bessie's strength of purpose and courage rise to the occasion magnificently, being thrown into sharp relief by the comic helplessness of Fluther and the cowardly evasions of Jinnie Gogan. Bessie is contemptuous of them both, yanks Fluther inside the house and orders the woman indoors with scarcely concealed disregard: 'Go on back to her, you.' She doesn't think of trying to find excuses, but fixes her mind on what has to be done. Her prayer acts as a fine curtain to the act, coming as it does as a striking reversal of her usual use of biblical language, which has earlier served exclusively either for malevolent prophecy (at the end of Act I) or maledictory abuse.[13]

After this episode at the end of Act III Fluther never regains dominance (though it should be noted that he is not at all prominent in a large part of the first act, either, and he is carefully kept out of much of the action in Act III itself), despite his spirited verbal resistance to the English soldiers in the final act. By the end of the play Fluther is only one of a group herded into captivity, unable to alter or influence the course of events in any way. Though livelier in spirit than the others, he has become part of the mass of helpless, if not entirely passive, human beings affected by the war situation, and he is soon forgotten, when led off-stage by the troops, because the action on-stage is immediately intensified with the entrance of Nora and the subsequent killing of Bessie. Like the other tenement characters of Act IV, Fluther is overshadowed by the masterful personality of Bessie Burgess, toned down though this is by O'Casey's deliberate stress on her fatigue throughout the act, and the subdued speech and actions necessitated by the close presence of the sleeping Nora. A striking example of Bessie's domination is demonstrated when the card game among Fluther, the Covey and Peter Flynn looks as though it is getting out of control. The men quarrel noisily, but Bessie's terse threat, 'If I hear a whisper out o' one o' yous again, I'll . . . gut yours', rapidly subdues them. Once Bessie has gained ascendancy, at the end of the third act, she maintains it until her death; but her mastery is achieved without sacrificing theme or diverting attention from the situation of the tenement folk as a group.

Bessie is herself alienated from the audience's sympathy, though never from its interest, for the major part of the play. There appears to be nothing worthwhile about her character and actions in the first half of the drama. She is merely a drunken, brawling virago with a gift for invective. The other inhabitants of the tenement know Bessie well and seem to have little or no respect for her, though we later discover that this is an erroneous impression. Mrs Burgess maintains her pugnacity throughout the first three quarters of the play, and though Nora is her opponent in the first act, the street vendor is particularly antagonistic towards Mrs Gogan in the following two acts. The incessant hostility between the pair of slum women parallels the constant bickering of Peter and the Covey. As the action gathers momentum, Bessie is further alienated from the spectator's sympathies: the 'choke th' chicken' sequence in Act III shows her at her most selfish if dynamic. Taunting the insurgents and their civilian supporters among the tenement people from her attic window, from time to time through the act – her interjections are carefully selected by the playwright, so that she can act as a critical irritant and (occasionally) counteract any possible sentimentality evoked by Nora's sufferings – Bessie is increasingly disliked by the audience as well as by the *dramatis personae* involved in the action. This increase in hostility is occasioned by the worsening position of the 'rebels' and the civilians. As the war comes closer, Bessie's provocative actions become more intolerable. When all that is known of the fighting is based on gossip and rumours, many of doubtful validity, Bessie's chanting of 'Rule, Britannia' has genuinely comic connotations. But her vindictive intervention as the anxious and hysterical Nora is brought in by Fluther, evokes a strong reaction from him which almost certainly represents the audience's attitude also:

NORA: My Jack will be killed! . . . He is to be butchered as a sacrifice to th' dead!

BESSIE (*from upper window*): Yous are all nicely shanghaied now! Sorra mend th' lassies that have been kissin' an' cuddlin' their boys into th' sheddin' of blood! . . . Fillin' their minds with fairy tales that had no beginnin' but, please God, 'll have a bloody quick endin'! . . . Rule, Britannia, Britannia rules th' waves, Britons never, never, never shall be slaves!

FLUTHER (*with a roar up at the window*): Y' ignorant oul' throllop, you!

We are most strongly estranged from Bessie during the episode a little later, when Clitheroe and Brennan enter, helping the wounded Langon to retreat from the firing line. Her jibes at them show both her courage – for they are armed and have already threatened to fire upon a street crowd barring their way – and her insensitivity also, for the men are in trouble, facing heavy odds, while Langon is evidently badly injured. Her shouts and jeers – 'Runnin' from th' Tommies . . . choke th' chicken! Runnin' from th' Tommies . . . choke th' chicken!'[14] – act as an effectively jarring counterpoint to the poignant struggle taking place in the street below, with Clitheroe torn between comforting his wife and helping his dying comrade. Bessie's role here, in fact, contributes a further method of alienation, preventing the scene from becoming either too sentimental or heroic. Whatever Clitheroe's decision, wife or duty – and the one chosen is that which could have been depicted in melodramatically chauvinist terms – Bessie's critical commentary ('General Clitheroe'd rather be unlacin' his wife's bodice than standin' at a barricade') will allow romanticising of neither love nor patriotism. And Bessie herself seems least humane *immediately* before she enters to pick up Nora – thrown to the ground by Clitheroe – and carry her indoors, to nurse her devotedly. We are flung straight from disliking her, into admiring her.

Yet there have been indications earlier, in occasional deft touches, that Bessie is a more complex personality than appears at first sight. Even while slanging the Republicans, at the beginning of the act, a hint of her innate kindness is revealed to the audience, though not to her neighbours on stage. She emerges in the doorway of the tenement house (near which the sick Mollser sits sunning herself), hiding something beneath her shawl; few spectators will notice Bessie's furtive movement as the attention on stage at the moment is directed towards the exhausted Nora, who is being attended to by Mrs Gogan:

She is led in by Mrs Gogan as Bessie comes out with a shawl around her shoulders. She passes by them with her head in the air. When they have gone in, she gives a mug of milk to Mollser silently.

Significantly, Bessie *says* nothing kind or gentle – though she must have made a special point of remembering Mollser, for Bessie's flat is at the top of the tall building – contenting herself with a scornful outburst directed at Fluther and the Covey as she passes by them on her way off stage. No doubt Mrs Burgess would hate anyone seeing her give the milk to the poor consumptive child; she deliberately cultivates a rough and belligerent manner, and the girl is the child of her arch-enemy, Mrs Gogan. But Mollser is undoubtedly neglected, and Bessie obviously has a soft spot for her; it is clear from Mrs Gogan's revelations in Act IV, after Mollser's death, that Bessie's act was not an isolated one.

Once Bessie becomes an acknowledged heroine in her own right at the end of Act III, the audience remains favourably disposed towards her for the duration of the play. There is the real danger, however, that her forceful personality might overshadow the other figures in the final act, and care is taken to see that she does not disrupt its delicate tragic-comic balance. She is worn out, physically, in Act IV, as a result of her care for Nora; and is forced to sit and doze through a large part of the action on-stage. Her speech and actions are consequently unusually restrained throughout. This is an effective and credible way of subduing her while retaining the audience's new-found sympathy. Her muted behaviour in Act IV – in itself a striking reversal of her role in the first three acts – is skilfully accomplished by the playwright, and is perfectly attuned to the prevailing mood and atmosphere of the scene.

The street fruit-vendor's death brilliantly realises the two conflicting sides of her nature. Generosity and kindness are responsible for her receiving the fatal gunshot wound; she dies cursing Nora and singing a sentimental hymn:

BESSIE (*with an arrested scream of fear and pain*): Merciful God, I'm shot, I'm shot, I'm shot! . . . Th' life's pourin' out o' me! (*To Nora.*) I've got this through . . . through you . . . through you, you bitch, you! . . . O God, have mercy on me! . . . (*To Nora.*) You wouldn't stop quiet, no, you wouldn't, you wouldn't, blast you! Look at what I'm afther gettin', look at what I'm afther gettin' . . . I'm bleedin' to death, an' no one's here to stop th' flowin' blood!

She is a fine woman, epitomising some of the major faults and virtues of her class. We neither admire nor despise her indiscriminately, for her heroic stature is enhanced, though never exaggerated, by seeing her character in perspective. In subtle particulars of stagecraft her role in the play is thus subordinated to the total thematic pattern: like *The Silver Tassie*, indeed, *The Plough and the Stars* is 'a unique work that dominates all the characters in the play'. The tragedy is that of the tenement society as a whole, not simply that of two or more individuals in that society, and the dramatist has taken care to emphasise the general suffering as well as the individual anguish. . . .

In this essay we have examined distancing or estranging effects in *The Plough and the Stars* with reference only to characterisation. The present line of enquiry could profitably be extended to other aspects, and, preferably, should go on to include a detailed analysis of the superb stagecraft of *The Plough and the Stars* and *The Silver Tassie*. Such lines of enquiry are of value in coming to terms with critical problems of general significance for contemporary drama, as well as in evaluating O'Casey's pioneering contributions to the search for new dramatic forms in which to express the duality of modern life, its individual complexity and its mass conformity. Brecht's *Verfremdung-seffekt* and various forms of Expressionism were techniques developed in order to realise theatrically – with some degree of critical detachment – the essential antinomy in contemporary history. O'Casey's wish to communicate the universal significance of poverty and of modern warfare, and his awareness of man being (as Ernst Toller wrote) both 'an individual and a mass-man at one and the same time', led to his own creative experiments in a parallel direction.

SOURCE: essay in *James Joyce Quarterly*, VIII (1970); abbreviated and revised by its author for this casebook.

NOTES

[Reorganised and renumbered from the original – Ed.]

1. The present essay was written in the late 1960s; recently criticism has begun to recognise and evaluate O'Casey's sense of stagecraft – notably in Carol Kleiman's monograph, *Sean O'Casey's Bridge of Vision: Four Essays on Structure and Perspective* (Toronto, 1982).

2. John Willett, *The Theatre of Bertolt Brecht* (London, 1959), p. 179.

3. Quoted in news report in *Irish Times* (2 March 1926). The debate was held under the auspices of the University College of Dublin Republican Club on 1 March 1926. O'Casey was replying to Mrs Sheehy Skeffington's remarks on *The Plough*, as reported in the press, among which she said: 'There was not a single gleam of heroism throughout the play, and its theme was the folly of it [heroism]. That was why it [*The Plough*] cut to the bone, because they looked to see some of the heroism that produced Easter Week.' In reply, O'Casey is reported to have said that 'he was not trying, and

never would try, to write about heroes. He could write only about the life and the people that he knew. These people formed the bone and the sinew, and ultimately he believed they would be the brain of the country as well.'

4. For a more detailed discussion of this aspect, see my essay ' "Two Words for Women": A Reassessment of O'Casey's Heroines', in *Woman in Irish Legend, Life and Literature*, ed. S. F. Gallagher (Gerrards Cross, 1983), pp. 91–114.

5. Raymond Williams's early views on O'Casey reflected this attitude: see his *Drama from Ibsen to Eliot* (London, 1952; rev. edn 1964). Subsequently, Professor Williams has radically revised his evaluation; see his *Drama from Ibsen to Brecht* (London, 1968), reproduced in part in Part One of this Casebook.

6. 'From Within the Gates', *New York Times* (21 Oct. 1934); reprinted in O'Casey's *Blasts and Benedictions*, ed. R. Ayling (London, 1967), pp. 113–14.

7. Undated letter, written in April 1928, first published in the *Irish Statesman* (9 June 1928); reprinted in *Blasts and Benedictions*, p. 101. What O'Casey regarded as a strength Yeats had condemned as a weakness in the play. In his letter to O'Casey dated 20 April 1928 the poet had complained: '[In *The Tassie*] there is no dominating character, no dominating action, neither psychological unity nor unity of action; and your great power of the past has been the creation of some unique character who dominated all about him and was himself a main impulse in action that filled the play from beginning to end.' – *Letters of W. B. Yeats*, ed. A. Wade (London, 1954), p. 741.

8. Saros Cowasjee, *Sean O'Casey: The Man Behind the Plays* (London, 1963; rev. edn 1965), p. 49.

9. David Krause, *Sean O'Casey: The Man and His Work* (London, 1960), p. 79.

10. Saros Cowasjee, *O'Casey* (London, 1966), pp. 47–48.

11. V. C. De Baun, 'Sean O'Casey and the Road to Expressionism', *Modern Drama*, IV (1961), p. 255 (my italics).

12. *The Plough and the Stars*, Act III, in *Three Plays* (London, 1966), pp. 197–8; all further citations are from this edition.

13. The use of Biblical imagery here to realise a significant reversal of values (from Old Testament to New Testament ethics, as it were) and growth in a character's moral stature may be compared with Raymond Williams's judgement that O'Casey uses 'the undiscriminated rhythms of the scriptures' merely to heighten the emotional impact of his work. The critic specifically mentions Bessie Burgess as an example, but it is possible to do this only by taking individual speeches of hers out of their context.

14. *Three Plays*, p. 106. The taunts are explained, of course, by the fact that one of the three men, Captain Brennan, is a chicken butcher by trade.

Bobby L. Smith   'The Game of Chance'
(1978)

... Nora Clitheroe is rather obviously an Irish version of Nora Helmer in Ibsen's *A Doll's House*; she too is called by pet names. She is Jack's 'little red-lipped Nora'; she tries heroically to save her husband, who is as insensitive and as vain as Torvald; she, too is blamed by her husband for her deception; she tries to improve the world around her, and early in the play, as quoted by Mrs Gogan, describes the tenements as 'Vaults . . . that are hidin' th' dead, instead of homes that are sheltherin' th' livin' '. O'Casey's Nora, unlike Ibsen's, is ineffectual and is destroyed by that which she combats. It is she rather than the door that is slammed; it is she rather than her husband's hollow pride that is destroyed. As the play ends, she has gone with Mrs Gogan to sleep in the dead Mollser's bed.

The card game played by the Covey and Fluther in Bessie's room with Mollser's coffin symbolises for O'Casey the methods which shape the destinies of human beings; the players continue to shuffle, wager, and argue as the card game is interrupted by Bessie's commands that they be quieter, by Brennan's entrance in civilian clothes, by Nora's entrance and her eerie comments to her husband. They stop the game long enough to carry out the coffin as requested by Corporal Stoddart and would resume the game except for Stoddart's assurance that they are to be locked up – all the men are. They take the cards with them, for as Fluther notes, 'I don't think we'd be doin' anything derogatory by playin' cards in a Protestan' Church.' The card game goes on and on as does the violence outside, though the players have some difficulty keeping track of who played what card.

The game of chance and the abandoned cards – like the looting scenes themselves – reflect the total lack of order, the madness of society at war. It is a chaos to which Fluther Good is particularly suited, as is revealed by his many vows of temperance and by his answer to the Covey's urging that he 'thry to keep a sup for tomorrow'. Fluther responds,

Spread it out? Keep a sup for to-morrow? How th' hell does a fella know there'll be any tomorrow? If I'm goin' to be whipped away, let me be whipped away when it's empty, an' not when it's half full!

The card game, the drinking, and the making of tea are rituals which give the only semblance of order to the chaotic world at war. This fact emphasises the terror and the irony of the situation when the two British soldiers, both routinely performing their tasks, invade the apartment of the slain Bessie and drink the tea so recently prepared by Nora. Their professional and impersonal attitude is revealed in their matter of fact comments, 'Oh Gawd, we've plugged one of the women of the 'ouse', and 'Whoy the 'ell did she gow to the window?' Then they drink the tea and join their comrades in song as the play ends. Life and the rituals of life do go on even in the midst of mayhem.

Though *The Plough and the Stars* was ill received by many of those about whom and for whom it was written, Lady Gregory discovered it to be

A wonderful play . . . [about] the forgiveness of sins, as real literature is supposed to be. These quarreling, drinking women have tenderness and courage showing all through, as have the men . . . and then comes what all nations have seen, the suffering that falls through war, and especially Civil War, on the women, the poor, the wretched homes and families of the slums. An overpowering play. I felt at the end of it as if I should never care to look at another; all others would seem so shadowy to the mind after this.[1]

This is the last of O'Casey's Irish plays, and it serves as a fitting finale, as O'Casey includes the rawness of the slums, the reality of war, and the true tragedy of discarded lives – lives discarded even as Fluther and the Covey throw down their cards. *The Plough and the Stars*, it seems to me, is the best of the Irish plays, combining the humor, pathos, and tragedy of the other four. The satire is further reaching and more bitter as O'Casey seeks to identify to the world's eye the factionalism and the adolescent grandeurs that caused and co-existed with the bloodshed and madness of Easter Week. For him, the Easter Rising was not a holy war, and those who fought during Easter Week were no more heroic than those who participated in the 'murdhering hate' of the Irish Civil War six years later. . . .

SOURCE: extract from *O'Casey's Satiric Vision* (Kent, Ohio, 1978), pp. 53–5.

NOTE

1. Quoted in Elizabeth Coxhead, *Lady Gregory* (London, 1961), pp. 203–4.

Jack Lindsay   *The Plough and the Stars*
Reconsidered   (1976)

The fact that there is still much controversy as to just what Sean O'Casey was saying in his early plays, and what is their fundamental content, is no argument for any confusion, uncertainty, or obscurity of artistic intention and achievement. The deepest and most prolonged discussions that go on about works of art concern their content. Even now could we say that we have finally settled what *Hamlet* and *Lear* are about? It has been the penetration into new aspects of their meaning that has given us a fuller and clearer notion of their form. Meditation on this sort of problem led me many years ago to put out a formulation that no one has discussed: the form of a work of art is the resolution of the inner conflict in the material (which is also an inner conflict in the artist). In *Hamlet*, for example, the content is not the obvious issue of what one does if one finds that one's father has been murdered and one's mother has married the murderer. The question of one's reaction to a discovery of the world's evil, how one deepens one's understanding of the situation and what one does about it, is bound up with one's total human sensibility. The fuller the grasp of the content, then, the more enriched and complex will be the form in which one seeks to define the inner conflict (ultimately one with the outer issues) and to bring it to a point of finality, to the resolving form of the work of art.

I am not suggesting that *The Plough and the Stars* is a tragic expression on the level of *Hamlet*; but it is a true work of art that has engaged the whole of its author's being, his grasp of the world and his sensibilities at all levels. Any analysis we make of it is not likely to exhaust all its qualities and meanings; and any simplified interpretation is not going to enter into its real nature as a work of art at all.

The historical and directly personal factors involved in the creation of the play are well known, and need only to be briefly recapitulated. O'Casey in his early years, vigorously reacting to the multiple injustices and cruelties of his world, was drawn into many activities of protest: the Gaelic League and the Irish Republican Brotherhood, then the Labour and Trade Union Movements, through which his republicanism was merged with a devoted adherence to the cause of socialism. As the first Secretary to the Irish Citizen Army, who drew up its rules, principles and constitution, and who wrote its first history (published in 1919), he could not but have remained devoted to the ideals of Irish Freedom; but that does not mean he would be ready to accept wholeheartedly any and every strategy or tactic put forward in its name. While still in the republican ranks he had sought to make his fellows grow aware of wider horizons and to see the national struggle in the perspective of the international socialist movement. However much he might disagree with the methods or idiom of the republicans, there could be no question at any time of opposition to their aims. So, during Easter 1916, we could not expect him to take a simple attitude to the uprising. He naturally sympathised with any Irish effort to throw off the English yoke, but he might well think the procedures of the revolt to be ill-timed and badly prepared as well as far too limited in their ideology and too narrowly based. Luckily he was prevented from having to make a personal choice in the midst of the violent event through being shut up for the night in a church and then detained in a granary.

We must in particular stress his growing sense that if the national movement was not linked with the struggle of the workers for emancipation, it would inevitably stay tethered to middle class romantic illusions and ultimately to middle class ideals and applications. It is important then to cite here the familiar passage from *Drums Under the Windows* in which he depicts the Irish Republican Brotherhood (IRB) leadership.

They were immersed in the sweet illusion of fluttering banners, of natty uniforms, bugle-blow marches . . . All guns and drums, but no wounds. Not a thought, seemingly, about the toil, the rotten sweat, the craving for sleep, the sagging belly asking silently for food; the face disfigured, one eye wondering where the other had gone; arm twisted into a circle or a figure of eight; the surprised lung, bullet-holed, gasping for breath; or the dangling leg, never to feel firm on the earth again. All these thoughts he [O'Casey] forced before them, asking them to think of ways now by which they might be made less terrible . . . Our methods won't be dashing cavalry charges, or daring and irresistible charges by massed infantry. It will be a modified example of the Boer way of fighting . . . Sean had always had a bent for criticism, now it had been sharpened by Shaw, and those who heard it resented the disturbance of their dreams. (pp. 190–1)

But when all is said about such matters, we must turn to the play itself. The historical details may help to clarify certain points and to provide lines of approach, but what matters in the last resort is solely the artistic and human definition of the play itself.

There are critics who see in it essentially a pacifist sort of exposition which reveals an overwhelming revulsion from bloodshed and violence. Saros Cowasjee describes it as simply a work of disillusion: 'The Rising of 1916 completed his disillusion with revolutionary Republicanism. *The Plough and the Stars* is a vivid dramatisation of this disillusionment.' Thus Francis Mulhern depicts the play as no more than a demoralised reaction from an event which O'Casey could not artistically define:

O'Casey's *political* criticisms of the Dublin Rising of 1916 were profoundly at variance with his theatrical treatment of that event. In the first, he spoke as a revolutionary, condemning the fatal subordination of working-class interests to the ideals of the nationalist leadership; but his 'Dublin plays' present a *humanist* critique of all forms of political violence, counterposing the 'human' values of domesticity, compassion and so on to the destructive passions of public, political life. This position can hardly have been the formal political standpoint of one who had been active in the Irish Citizens' Army: it was in fact the ideological effect of the naturalistic theatrical modes which, at that time, he had not yet discarded. (*New Left Review*, May–June 1975)

In my opinion every word of that passage is untrue to the artistic facts of the case.

First we may point out that any work dealing with war, which is not quite unreal and inhuman, must be pacifist in the sense of depicting without palliation the hopeless cruelty, disaster and anguish of the situation. The passage from *Drums Under the Windows* stresses

O'Casey's humanist position, but in terms which seek to find the least murderous solution to the conflict. He wants guerrilla fighting, not an open challenge to Britain's vastly superior forces, which can only result in a maximum of slaughter and a bad defeat. That O'Casey has a fundamental humanism in his approach then proves nothing. The question is whether there is nothing else in his definition.

Certainly he defines in the play the IRB leadership in the same critical focus as that of *Drums*. He dramatises this key-point in the character of Jack Clitheroe, bricklayer. Clitheroe drops out of the Army when he thinks he has failed to get his expected promotion, but then eagerly returns when he finds that his wife Nora has destroyed the letter delivered a fortnight before from General Connolly. But though vanity plays an important part in bringing Clitheroe into the ranks of the uprising, he fights bravely and is killed. Nor is there any irony in the scene at the end of Act II where he and two other officers come into the bar. They speak romantically, but with complete conviction and devotion. The Act ends with Clitheroe's voice firmly issuing the command for action offstage: 'Dublin Battalion of the Irish Citizen Army, by th' right, quick march!'

It is true indeed that most of the characters remain aloof from the uprising, as did the mass of the Dubliners. The gap between their enthusiasms, their confused ideas and emotions, is the gap that actually existed between the IRB and the ordinary folk. The exit of Fluther and Rosie with her lewd song from the tavern just before the marching order is issued, explains with perfect dramatic concision why that order is futile and will lead to defeat. At the same time it provides a note of devious hope by juxtaposing the damn-all joy in life, 'dancin' a jig in th' bed', with the military order barren of all hope and directing the marchers to death.

Indeed the last twenty or so speeches of this Act, in a very brief and packed compass, bring vividly together the contrasting elements in the situation: shortsighted romantic devotion to an ideal that is worthy in itself, and the divigating forces of common life which are only superficially engaged in the conflict, ready the next moment to turn back in on themselves and to forget the devoted few who march off to death. One of these speeches is the last one given by the unseen Leader outside who is addressing the crowd from a raised platform and whose voice is heard on and off throughout the Act as he comes close to the window in his movements. Here is a dramatic device of the utmost brilliance. It enables O'Casey to bring the romantic rhetoric right into the heart of the action without letting the action be dominated by it as would happen if he showed us the meeting itself. At the same time the setting of the Voice of the Man outside the room

expresses perfectly the distance of the dreamer from the common
people. They share his aspirations enough to be moved by them when
they hear them enunciated, but the effect is transitory. Only when the
three officers come briefly in near the end of the Act, with the banner
of the Plough and the Stars, do we witness the direct effect on the
listening crowd. The trio are intoxicated by the words they have
heard. 'Their faces are flushed and their eyes sparkle; they speak
rapidly, as if unaware of the meaning of what they say. They have
been mesmerised by the fervency of the speeches.' Anything they can
drink in the bar will have no effect on them in their heightened state of
being; and in the midst of their exalted statements, which are given a
gnomic and heroic note, there comes the last passage from the speaker
outside: 'Our foes are strong, but strong as they are, they cannot undo
the miracles of God, who ripens in the hearts of young men the seeds
sown by the young men of a former generation . . .'

O'Casey did not himself compose the orator's speeches, so that he
could not be accused of inflating the rhetoric or belittling the
republican ideals. He based the speeches closely on those given by
Padraic Pearse, Commander of the Irish Volunteers in the uprising,
and used the most eloquent passages, typical in their passionate
sincerity and idealism. It is significant that the most important
passage employs religious imagery, alluding to the creed of transubstantiation and redemption through blood sacrifice.

The failure to draw the people in effectively is brought out by the
reactions of Fluther. Early in the Act, after the first time that the
Voice is heard, he comes in with Peter. Both of them are wild with
excitement, but Fluther expresses the mood of revolt most powerfully;
and after the Voice is heard a second time, he rushes out. 'Come on,
man; this is too good to be missed!' Peter follows him and on the way
bumps into his enemy, the sectarian socialist, the Covey. The latter
quickly deflates the excitement in the bar with his comment, aloofly
dogmatic, 'What's the use o' freedom, if it's not economic freedom?'
When he finally runs out to escape the prostitute Rosie, Fluther and
Peter return with Mrs Gogan. They have exhausted their response to
the situation, and in Mrs Gogan's comments on the green and gold
uniform of Peter as a Forester we meet in parodied form the theme of
romantic dressing-up.

Each of the four Acts ends with a song. We have noted the role of
Rosie's song in Act II; it expresses the delighted spirit of life which has
somehow got left out of the call of Pearse for a death-dedication to the
republican cause. The first and last Acts have songs of the English
soldiers at their closes. Act I has the soldiers singing 'It's a long way to
Tipperary' outside in the street. There is irony in the use of the Irish

place-name in the mouths of the oppressors; and the song is linked with the entry of Bessie, the street fruit-vendor, who has a son in the trenches of France. Bessie identifies herself with both the English soldiers dying in the mud for their bosses and the Irish slum-dwellers rotting in their tenements. As the soldiers' chorus dies away, she cries, 'There's th' men marchin' out into th' dhread dimness o' danger, while th' lice is crawlin' about feedin' on th' fatness of the land . . .' Near the end of Act IV she is shot by the English as she tries to save Nora at the window, and her death leads on to the entry of two soldiers who reply to their comrades singing 'Keep the home fires burning' outside on the barricade. Bessie thus in a sense links both sides tragically; she represents concretely the sense of brotherhood, without the least understanding of what the conflicts are all about, just as the Covey sets out theoretically and abstractly the question of international unity of the workers, without the least active connection with what is happening. The soldiers are singing as the general attack on the Post Office is being launched. 'They were summoned from the 'illside . . .' They, like the IRB, are playing their parts in a drama to which they have been called by forces they do not comprehend; and their reference to the Home Fires has its bitter links with the desperate efforts of the slum-dwellers, especially Nora, to build some sort of personal life. Here, it is true, O'Casey presents a humanist critique of the situation; but his humanism is merged at all points with the over-all judgement of the play, which involves equally the political critique.

The link and opposition of the English and the Irish is further brought out when the Covey tells Corporal Stoddart, 'An' it's all because of th' system we're livin' undher', and Stoddart replies, 'Ow, I know. I'm a Sowcialist moiself, but I 'as to do my dooty':

THE COVEY (*ironically*): Dooty. Th' only dooty of a Socialist is th' emancipation of th' workers.
CORPORAL STODDART: Ow, a man's a man, an' 'e 'as to foight for 'is country, 'asn't 'e?
FLUTHER (*aggressively*): You're not fighting for your counthry here, are you?
PETER (*anxiously, to Fluther*): Ay, ay, Fluther, none o' that, none o' that!

Then, as one of the soldiers outside is shot by a sniper, the momentary understanding between Fluther and the Corporal is broken down. The latter cries, 'Gawd, when we gets th' bloighter, we'll give 'im the cold steel, we will'. The nationalism of the English soldier is shown as perverting his socialism, and thus becomes a criticism of Irish nationalism, even though the latter is playing a progressive role and the former is a mask for oppression, as the comment of the Covey aptly brings out. Nationalism by itself, O'Casey is reminding us, is capable of all sorts of regressions.

At the end of Act III Fluther sings 'For he's a jolly good fellow', in praise of himself, together with the interpolation of 'Up th' rebels!' We here get the wild anarchic egoism of the lumpen-proletariat slum-dweller mingled with the equally wild and undisciplined response to the call for revolt; but while the egoism persists, the response to the call has no staying-power. Fluther has taken part in the looting, and his acclamation of the rebels is merged with his curse: 'th' whole city can topple home to hell'.

Fluther with his rambling talk, his veering moods, his capacity for self-intoxication and his readiness to respond to any stimulus without a sustained capacity for responsible action, is the key-figure for the broader meanings of the play, while the relations of Nora and her husband provide the main framework. Under a sudden impulse, or in some call based in the life which he feels part of him, Fluther can however show genuine courage and goodwill:

MRS GOGAN (to Fluther): I'll never forget what you done for me, Fluther, goin' round at th' risk of your life settlin' everything with th' undhertaker an' th' cemetery people. When all me own were afraid to put their noses out, you plunged like a good one through hummin' bullets, an' they knocking fire out o' th' road, tinklin' through th' frightened windows, an' splashin' themselves to pieces on th' walls! An' you'll find, that Mollser, in th' happy place she's gone to, won't forget to whisper, now an' again, th' name o' Fluther.

We see then that the full dialectics of the play is very complex. There is hardly a speech that does not contribute to bringing out one or other of the aspects I have mentioned. O'Casey expresses throughout the play the deep human aspiration to peace, happiness, brotherhood, and shows how it is ceaselessly confused, distorted, wrecked by the play of divisive forces, so that even the best impulses and hopes of men can turn out to be futile or destructive. The dream of the Citizen Army is foredoomed to failure, as every word of the play brings out; yet it is not simply pointless or misdirected. It is linked with the dream of happiness and freedom in the lost and exploited people, which is perpetually reborn despite all the setbacks. Fluther stands between the rebels whom he cannot join, and the Covey whom he cannot understand. Historically the gap cannot be closed, with the republican devotion and the socialist creed coming together in Fluther's thoughts and emotions; but the restless play of life, the something that is uncrushable in him as the symbol of the people, gives us all the while a conviction of the potentiality of a new unity, a new and more far-reaching resistance. We must remember that O'Casey is writing after the triumph of middle class Ireland, with all its extreme limitations, was already assured.

To the critic, then, who sees a humanist critique but not a political one, we can only reply: Could anyone have possibly written a play with all the values we have discussed, if he had not been deeply involved with the Citizen Army and had then seen beyond their limited aims? If he had not believed that the only final solution lay with socialism, yet had at the same time seen all too clearly and painfully the lack of a concrete basis for the socialist struggle? If he had not further believed that for all the aridity of the Coveys that struggle would in time emerge from the situation and the people he defined?

As for the suggestion that a naturalistic method has inhibited him from expressing just what he has expressed, we can only ask how the term naturalism can be applied to a work in which, as we have seen, every character, every speech, every event has its symbolic value. The play does not contain direct symbols (except in the title) but it is symbolic in the sense that everything said has overtones, significances beyond the literal content, and that the totality of the speeches adds up to the living aesthetic unity I have tried to portray. As a recent critic Alan Swingewood, in *The Novel and Revolution*, remarks: 'Naturalism differs from realism through the fateful workings of an invincible heredity combined with an oppressive external milieu; the subtle dialectic conjoining socio-historical forces and the problematic individual has been eliminated with a broadly non-problematical although critical structure.' The problematic aspects of the situation in O'Casey's play are not concentrated in a single character; but they appear all the while in the give-and-take between the various characters, especially in the utterances and angers of Fluther and the Covey. The rebels are doomed to failure, but the people remain undefeated. The heightened language is one of the ways in which O'Casey makes us feel that there are great forces in the people which have not yet been tapped but which are vitally present.

Finally, there is the title of the play, which is the name of the banner under which the rebels march. O'Casey uses it to express the gap between reality and the ideal, between the actual possibilities of the situation and the dream of freedom. In December 1923 he wrote:

The workers must come out of their one-room tenements and out of their dimly-minded Trade Unions – occasionally at least – to pull the plough a little nearer to the stars. They must learn that self-realisation is more important than class-consciousness . . . And this is the silent need of the workers: loss of ignorance and acquirement of culture. However the worker may shout for an increase in his wage, or protest against a reduction, be he at work, or waiting wearily in the Unemployment Exchange, his greatest need and most urgent claim is a share in the culture of the society of men.

He is not opposing class-consciousness to self-realisation, but insisting that the former is not enough by itself, as Lenin in a different relation said that Trade-Union consciousness was not enough. The worker must add to his immediate struggles a full awareness of all that is implied by human liberation; only then does the day-to-day struggle gain its final vindication and directive. (It is of interest that Lenin in his last days, as paralysis was closing in on him and as he saw that things were going wrong, made in his weakening efforts to grapple with the situation an impassioned demand for culture at all costs among the people, even a bit of bourgeois culture.) In the play it is the Covey who makes the point of the discrepancy between the banner's emblem and the aims of the uprising.

CLITHEROE: It'll be a treat to see him swankin' it at th' head of the Citizen Army carryin' th' flag of the Plough and the Stars . . .

THE COVEY: They're bringin' nice disgrace on that banner now.

CLITHEROE (*remonstratively*): How are they bringing disgrace on it?

THE COVEY (*snappily*): Because it's a Labour flag, an' was never meant for politics . . . What does th' design of th' field plough bearin' on it th' stars of th' heavenly plough, mean, if it's not Communism? It's a flag that should only be used when we're buildin' th' barricades to fight for a Workers' Republic!

PETER (*with a puff of derision*): P-phuh.

The title then seems to me to stress the points I have been making. However O'Casey might in one part of himself have been stirred by Easter 1916, he felt that the essential thing to stress was the tragic distance between the Plough and the Stars. By clarifying that point he hoped 'to pull the plough a little nearer to the stars', to lessen the gap between anarchic and romantic aspirations on one side and full consciousness of the terrible facts of human alienation on the other. To have pretended that the gap was not there and to have written a simple glorification of the uprising, with perhaps some peripheral criticisms, would have been to him the committing of an artistic and political sin.

SOURCE: article in the *Sean O'Casey Review*, II (1976), pp. 187–95.

SELECT BIBLIOGRAPHY

EDITIONS

The most handy text of the three plays is the Papermac edition simply entitled *Three Plays*, first published in this form in 1957 and frequently reprinted; from 1980 this edition has borne the Pan Books imprint. The Scholar's Library edition of *Juno and the Paycock* and *The Plough and the Stars* (in one volume), first issued by Macmillan in 1948 and often reissued since, has useful textual notes to both plays compiled by Guy Boas. Even more detailed notes are printed in *Seven Plays by Sean O'Casey*, edited by Ronald Ayling (London, 1985); all three of these plays are included in this edition designed for the use of college students. Most stage productions use the acting versions published by Samuel French Ltd (London & New York, 1932) and frequently reprinted; these versions, printed as three separate editions and prepared for publication by O'Casey himself, embody many minor changes, especially in the stage directions.

PLAYS

Two Plays: Juno and the Paycock and *The Shadow of a Gunman* (London & New York, 1925).
The Plough and the Stars (London & New York, 1926).
The Complete Plays of Sean O'Casey, 5 vols (London, 1984).

OCCASIONAL WRITINGS

Autobiographies, 2 vols (London, 1981).
The Letters of Sean O'Casey, 1910–41, vol. I, ed. David Krause (New York & London, 1975).

BOOKS AND ARTICLES ON O'CASEY

General
William A. Armstrong, *Sean O'Casey* (London, 1967).
Ronald Ayling, 'Sean O'Casey and the Abbey Theatre, Dublin', *Sean O'Casey: Centenary Essays*, ed. David Krause and Robert G. Lowery (Gerrards Cross, 1980), pp. 13–40.
—— and Michael J. Durkan, *Sean O'Casey: A Bibliography* (London, 1978; Seattle, 1979).
Thomas Kilroy (ed.), *Sean O'Casey: A Collection of Critical Essays* (Englewood Cliffs, N.J., 1975).
E. H. Mikhail, *Sean O'Casey: A Bibliography of Criticism* (London, 1972).
Eileen O'Casey, *Sean* (London, 1971; New York, 1972).

The Shadow of a Gunman
Paul Foley Casey, 'The Knocking Motif in Sean O'Casey's *The Shadow of a Gunman*', *Literatur in Wissenschaft und Unterricht*, XIII (1980), pp. 170–5.
Michael O'Maoláin, 'That Raid and What Went With It', *Essays on Sean O'Casey's Autobiographies*, ed. Robert G. Lowery (London & New York, 1981), pp. 103–22.

Katharine J. Worth, 'O'Casey, Synge and Yeats', *Irish University Review*, x (1980), pp. 103–17.

Juno and the Paycock

William A. Armstrong, 'The Integrity of *Juno and the Paycock*', *Modern Drama*, XVII (1974), pp. 1–9.

Ronald Ayling, '*Juno and the Paycock*: A Textual Study', *Modernist Studies*, II (1976), pp. 15–26.

James Coakley and Marvin Felheim, 'Thalia in Dublin: Some Suggestions about the Relationship between O'Casey and Classical Comedy', *Comparative Drama*, IV (1970), pp. 265–71.

Robert Fricker, 'Sean O'Casey: *Juno and the Paycock*', *Das moderne englische Drama: Interpretationen* (Berlin, 1966), pp. 181–200.

Heinz Kosok, 'Sean O'Casey, *Juno and the Paycock*', *Dramen des 20 Jahrhunderts für den Englisch unterricht in der Sekundarstufe II*, ed. Hans Weber (Frankfurt/M., 1982).

The Plough and the Stars

William A. Armstrong, 'The Sources and Themes of *The Plough and the Stars*', *Modern Drama*, IV (1961), pp. 234–42.

Ronald Ayling, 'History and Artistry in *The Plough and the Stars*', *Ariel*, VIII (1977), pp. 73–85.

David Krause, 'Some Truths and Jokes about the Easter Rising', *Sean O'Casey Review*, III (1976), pp. 3–23.

Roger McHugh (ed.), *Dublin 1916* (London, 1966).

Sean O'Casey, *The Story of the Irish Citizen Army* (Dublin & London, 1919).

Edward E. Pixley, '*The Plough and the Stars*: The Destructive Consequences of Human Folly', *Educational Theatre Journal*, XXII (1971), pp. 75–82.

Sean O'Casey Review, II (1976): *The Plough and the Stars* number.

NOTES ON CONTRIBUTORS

WILLIAM A. ARMSTRONG: retired in 1981 as Professor of English at Birkbeck College, London, having previously held chairs at Westfield College, London, and the University of Hull. Theatre consultant for the modern definitive edition of Pepys's Diaries, his publications include (in addition to his work on O'Casey) studies on the Elizabethan theatre (1958) and on Marlowe's *Tamburlaine* (1966), and a scholarly edition (1975) of Book I of Bacon's *The Advancement of Learning*.

RONALD AYLING: Professor of English in the University of Alberta, he is a graduate of the universities of Nottingham and Bristol. Literary adviser to the O'Casey estate, his publications include a posthumous collection of the playwright's writings (1967) and, in collaboration with Michael J. Durkan, *Sean O'Casey: A Bibliography* (1978). His edited and annotated volume *Seven Plays by Sean O'Casey* was published in 1985.

ERROL DURBACH: Associate Professor of English, University of British Columbia, specialising in Modern and Comparative Drama. His publications include studies on Ibsen, Synge and other dramatists, and the edited volume *Ibsen and the Theatre: The Dramatist in Production* (1980).

GABRIEL FALLON: a part-time member of the Abbey company in the early 1920s, appearing in each of O'Casey's plays staged by it; in later life he was on the theatre's Board of Directors (1959–74) and a Governor of the Royal Irish Academy of Music (1971–75). As well as his books on O'Casey (1965) and on the Abbey (1969), he wrote widely on drama subjects right up to his death in 1980.

HERBERT GOLDSTONE: Associate Professor of English, University of Connecticut. His publications include general critical studies; on drama, to his book on O'Casey (1972) he has added a study of John Osborne.

LADY GREGORY – *née* Isabella Augusta Persse (1852–1932): co-founder, with Yeats, of the Abbey Theatre and a prolific writer of plays and works of folk lore. Her *Our Irish Theatre* (1913) and, especially, her *Journals, 1916–1930* are central to an understanding of the Anglo-Irish literary movement. A new edition of the Journals is in preparation.

JOSEPH HOLLOWAY (1861–1944): an indefatigable theatre-goer in Dubin for sixty years and a conscientious (if often inconsequential) diarist. Deeply religious and strongly conservative, he was unsympathetic to much of the Abbey's innovative work and particularly hostile to Synge, Yeats and O'Casey.

MICHAEL W. KAUFMAN: formerly Assistant Professor of English in Cornell University, with interests embracing both Renaissance and Modern drama; his publications include articles on Shaw and Pinter as well as on O'Casey.

DAVID KRAUSE: Professor of English, Brown University (Rhode Island). His 1960 study of O'Casey (enlarged edition 1975) remains the definitive book on the subject, and his three-volume collection of the playwright's *Letters* is indispensable to students of O'Casey and his literary and political environment.

WILLIAM JOHN LAWRENCE (1862–1940): distinguished journalist and occasional lecturer, with a lifelong interest in theatrical lore. He is primarily regarded as a scholar of the Elizabethan stage, publishing several books between 1913 and 1937 in this area, dealing in particular with its physical conditions, conventions and prompt-books.

JACK LINDSAY: prolific poet, novelist, cultural historian and literary critic, member of an Australian family noted for its contribution to the arts. (He writes also as 'Richard Preston'.)

ROBERT G. LOWERY: editor of the *Newsletter* of the American Committee for Irish Studies and editor-publisher of the *Irish Literary Supplement*. Founder of the *Sean O'Casey Review* in 1974, in 1982 he became editor of Macmillan's *O'Casey Annual*.

JACK MITCHELL: a graduate of the University of London, he is currently lecturing in British and Irish literature at Humboldt University, East Berlin. With a special interest in proletarian literary work, he has written on Burns and on Robert Tressell as well as on O'Casey and Brecht.

P. S. O'HEGARTY: a noted Irish bibliographer and bibliophile, and author of studies on Irish history, politics and literature. At one time a member of the Supreme Council of the Irish Republican Brotherhood, he edited several nationalist journals during the campaign for an independent republic in Ireland.

BRIGID O'HIGGINS: a journalist in Dublin in the period when O'Casey was writing his early plays.

LAURENCE OLIVIER (Lord Olivier): outstanding English actor, and first Director of the National Theatre. Knighted in 1947, he was created a life peer in 1970.

ESMÉ STUART LENNOX ROBINSON (1886–1958): playwright, stage-director and member of the Abbey's Board of Directors from 1923 to his death; he directed the first productions in Dublin of both *The Shadow of a Gunman* and *The Plough and the Stars*. His autobiography, *Curtain Up* (1942), has a short account of O'Casey's dramatic apprenticeship at the Abbey.

RONALD G. ROLLINS: Professor of English, Ohio Wesleyan University. He has published widely on Anglo-Irish literature and modern drama, his studies including *Sean O'Casey's Drama: Verisimilitude and Vision* (1979).

BERNICE SCHRANK: a member of the staff of the English Department at the Memorial University of Newfoundland at St John's. In addition to studies on O'Casey's dramatic writings, she edited with Alison Feder *Literature and Folk Culture: Ireland and Newfoundland* (1977), a collection of papers sponsored by the Canadian Association of Irish Studies.

BOBBY L. SMITH: Professor of English, Kent State University, Ohio. His published writings are primarily concerned with modern Anglo-Irish literature, but he also has a special interest in the work of D. H. Lawrence.

WILLIAM IRWIN THOMPSON: a cultural historian who has taught at MIT, York University (Ontario) and Syracuse University (NY). In 1973 he founded the Lindisfarne Association (devoted to the study and realisation of a new planetary culture) and his most recent publications have mainly been concerned with urgent contemporary issues.

RAYMOND WILLIAMS: Professor of Drama in the University of Cambridge until his retirement in 1984. One of the best known of English Marxist critics, he has written widely on drama and film, and on English cultural traditions. Among his publications are *Drama from Ibsen to Eliot* (1952) – largely rewritten as *Drama from Ibsen to Brecht* (1968), with a considerably revised assessment of O'Casey – *Drama in Performance* (1954), *Culture and Society, 1780–1950* (1958), *The Long Revolution* (1961), *Communications* (1962), *Modern Tragedy* (1966), *The Country and the City* (1973) and *Keywords* (1976).

ACKNOWLEDGEMENTS

The editor and publishers wish to thank the following, who have given permission for the use of copyright material: William A. Armstrong, 'History, Autobiography and *The Shadow of a Gunman*', *Modern Drama*, II (1960); Errol Durbach, 'Peacocks and Mothers – Theme and Dramatic Metaphor in *Juno and the Paycock*, *Modern Drama*, xv (1972); Vincent C. de Baun, 'O'Casey and the Road to Expressionism', *Modern Drama*, IV (1961); Gabriel Fallon, extract from 'The House on the North Circular Road', *Modern Drama*, IV (1961); Herbert Goldstone, extracts from *In Search of Community: The Achievement of Sean O'Casey*, (Mercier Press, 1972); extracts from *Lady Gregory's Journals*, Colin Smythe Ltd on behalf of Anne de Winton and Catherine Kennedy; Joseph Holloway, extracts from his unpublished Journal, 'Impressions of a Dublin Playgoer' (1924), reproduced in Robert Hogan and Michael J. O'Neill (eds), *Joseph Holloway's Abbey Theatre* (Southern Illinois University Press, 1967); Michael W. Kaufman, 'Structural Design in *Juno and the Paycock*', *Quarterly Journal of Speech*, xVIII (1972); David Krause, 'Sean O'Casey's Anti-Heroic Vision' in *Sean O'Casey: The Man and His Work* (Macmillan New York 1960: revised and enlarged edn, Macmillan New York, 1975); Robert G. Lowery, 'Prelude to Year One: Sean O'Casey before 1916', *Sean O'Casey Review*, II (1976); Jack Lindsay, 'The Plough and the Stars Reconsidered', *Sean O'Casey Review*, II (1976); Jack Mitchell, extracts from *The Essential O'Casey* (Seven Seas Books, 1980); Programme Note from Cockermouth (Cumberland) Players Theatre Programme 1953, re *Juno and the Paycock* production, June 1953; Letter to Mrs Helen Kiok, 3 August 1955 – reproduced in *Sean O'Casey Review*, II (1976); Programme Note, Abbey Theatre production of *The Plough and the Stars* at London International Festival of Drama (27 April 1964 opening) by permission of Mrs Eileen O'Casey; P. S. O'Hegarty, extract from 'A Drama of Disillusionment', in the *Irish Statesman* (1924) by permission of Brighid ui Eigeartaigh on behalf of Cian o hEigeartaigh; Ronald G. Rollins, 'O'Casey and Synge – The Irish Hero as Playboy and Gunman', *Arizona Quarterly*, xxII (1966); Bernice Schrank, ' "You Needn't Say No More" – Language and the Problems of Communication in The Shadow of a Gunman', *Irish University Review*, VIII (1978); B. L. Smith, extracts from chapter 2, '*O'Casey's Satiric Vision*, (Kent State University Press, 1978); William Irwin Thompson, extract from *The Imagination of an Insurrection, Dublin, Easter 1916*, copyright © 1967 Oxford University Press Inc., reprinted by permission; Raymond Williams, extracts from *Drama from Ibsen to Brecht*, (Chatto and Windus Ltd, 1968): Penguin, Harmondsworth, 1973).

Every effort has been made to trace all the copyright holders but if any have been inadvertently overlooked the publishers will be pleased to make the necessary arrangement at the first opportunity.

INDEX

Page numbers in **bold type** denote extracts in this casebook. Entries in SMALL CAPS denote characters in plays. O'Casey's writings are listed under his name.

Abbey Theatre   8–13, 15–19, 24, 49–50, 83–5, 87, 135–8, 140
ADOLPHUS GRIGSON   69–71
Agate, James   24, 89n.
Allgood, Sara   16, 82–3, 88, 90, 133
Arden, John   9
Aristotle   87

Barzun, Jacques   144
Behan, Brendan   9
BESSIE BURGESS   16, 35, 133–4, 163–4, 167, 177–8, 182–7, 195
Bible   50, 56, 188n
Blythe, Earnest   135–6
Boyd, John   9
Brecht, Bertolt   20, 164–5, 172–5, 187; *Mother Courage and Her Children*   24
Burns, Robert   22

Canfield, Curtis   165
Carolan, P.J.   49
CHARLES BENTHAM   22, 100, 113, 119
Chekhov, Anton   91; *The Cherry Orchard*   119; *Uncle Vanya*   118
Clarke, Austin   154
Connolly, James   145–51, 155
THE COVEY   152–3, 156–7, 159, 198
Cowasjee, Saros   130n., 176–7, 192
Craig, May 49
Crowe, Eileen   17, 83, 132
Cusack, Cyril   89n.

De Baun, Vincent   **165–71**, 177–8
Delany, Maureen   83, 133

Dench, Judi   15
Dickens, Charles   88, 112
Dolan, Michael J.   88, 135
DONAL DAVOREN   29–31, 59–61, 63–6, 73–7

Easter Rising   29, 135, 139, 141–65, 176, 187n., 190–2
Eliot, T.S. The Waste Land   22
Expressionism   165–71, 187

Fallon, Gabriel   13, 19, 49, **133–4**, 144
Fitzgerald, Barry   83, 88, 132
FLUTHER GOOD   35, 39–40, 177–8, 182–4, 196
Ford, John   132
Fox, Ralph   146–7, 149

Galsworthy, John   *Strife*   33
Greaves, C. Desmond   149
Gregory, Lady Augusta   10, 13, 15–17, **49–50**, **84–6**, **134–8**, 140, 189–90

HARRY HEEGAN   177, 179–82
Hauptmann, Gerhart   *The Weavers*   33
Hayden, Christine   83
Higgins, F.R.   154
Hitchcock, Alfred   82
Hogan, Robert   130n.
Holloway, Joseph   10, 12, 16, 18, **49, 83**
Hunt, Hugh   10–11, 13
Hutchinson, Harry   90–2

Ibsen, Henrik *A Doll's house* 188–9
Irish Citizen Army 15, 139, 141, 145–53, 157, 191, 193, 196–7

JACK BOYLE 23, 36–9, 86, 88, 93, 97–8, 104–9, 112–13, 118–24, 126–7, 129–30, 173–4, 176–7
JACK CLITHEROE 156, 179–80, 196
JERRY DEVINE 91, 92n., 98, 100, 119
JOHNNY BOYLE 88, 95–8, 100–1, 125–6
JOXER DALY 22–3, 38, 86
Johnson, Lionel 138
Johnston, Denis 170–1
Jonson, Ben 112
Joyce, James 36, 60–1, 62, 66n.; *A Portrait of the Artist as a Young Man* 61
JUNO BOYLE 22, 24, 36, 39, 86, 93, 96–7, 108–10, 113–17, 119–24, 127–30

Kleiman, Carol 187n.
Krause, David 18, **29**, 121–2, 129, 176

Larkin, Jim 139, 145–8, 151–2
Lawrence, W.J. 13
Lenin, V.I. 144, 151, 197–8
Leonard, Hugh 15
Livings, Henry 9

MacArdle, Dorothy 94
Macaulay, Thomas Babington 22–3
McCormick, F.J. 19, 49, 83
MacDermott, Sean 149
MacDonagh, Thomas 149
MAISIE MADIGAN 14, 112
Malone, Andrew E. 54, 170
Markiewicz, Constance 146–8
MARY BOYLE 14, 94–6, 99–100, 119, 125–6, 128
Merriman, Brian 36
Milton, John 74

MINNIE POWELL 59–61, 77–9
Mooney, Ria 17
Moore, Thomas 22
Morgan, Sydney 90
Mulhern, Francis 192

NORA CLITHEROE 32, 156, 162–3, 179–81, 188–9, 196

O'Brien, George 17, 133, 135–7
O'Casey, Sean *Cathleen Listens In* 12, 139; *The Cooing of Doves* 15–16, 139–40; *The Crimson in the Tricolor* 49, 84–5; *Drums Under the Windows* 192–3; *The Easter Lily Aflame* 140; *The Frost in the Flower* 49; *Inishfallen, Fare Thee Well* 12–13, 54, 57–9, 62n.; *Juno and the Paycock* 10–11, 13–15, 22, 31, 42–3, 81–130, 142, 173–7, 180; *Nannie's Night Out* 15; *On the Run* 9, 55, 57; *The Plough and the Stars* 8, 15–20, 31–2, 34–5, 43–4, 115, 131–98; *The Shadow of a Gunman* 8, 10–12, 29–31, 41–2, 47–80, 88, 174, 180; *The Silver Tassie* 67, 90, 111, 165–6, 170, 174–5, 177, 179–82, 187, 188n.; *The Star Turns Red* 152–3; *The Story of the Irish Citizen Army* 148, 151; *The Story of Thomas Ashe* 151; *Two Plays* 14; *Within the Gates* 175, 177, 179
O'Faolain, Sean 146
O'Flaherty, Liam 154
O hAodha, Mícheál 13, 148
O'Hegarty, P.S. **52–3**, 112
Olivier, Sir Laurence 14–15, **90–2**
O'Neill, Maire 90
O'Regan, Kathleen 90
Orwell, George *1984* 97
Osborne, John 91

Pearse, Padraic 134, 145, 149–51, 155, 157–61, 167; *The Sovereign People* 150
Plunkett, Joseph 149
Pound, Ezra 22

Quinn, Tony   49

Radek, Karl   151
Redmond, John   147
Robertson, Tom   112; *Caste*   88
Robinson, Lennox   10–11, 16–17,
    51–2, 85, 133, 135–7, 140
ROSIE REDMOND   17–18, 136, 157–9,
    194
Russell, George (A.E.)   133–4, 154
Ryan, Desmond   149–50

Scott, Walter   22–3
SEUMAS SHIELDS   30–1, 59–61, 71–2
Shakespeare, William   20–1, 37–9,
    74, 138, 155, 163, 173–4, 190–1;
    Falstaff   37–9, 173, 176; *Hamlet*
    190–1; *Henry IV*   20, 173–4;
    Henry V   20; *Henry VI*   20;
    Lear   190; *Macbeth*   24; *Richard
    II*   20; *Richard III*   20
Shaw, George Bernard   62, 112,
    192; *Blanco Posnet*   50, 137; *The
    Doctor's Dilemma*   60; *John Bull's
    Other Island*   36, 63
Shelley, Percy Bysshe   10, 60–1, 74;
    Prometheus Unbound   77

Shields, Arthur   83
Sinclair, Arthur   90
Starkie, Walter   165
Styan, J.L.   130n.
Swingewood, Alan   197
Synge, John Millington   61, 87; *In
    the Shadow of the Glen*   18; *The
    Playboy of the Western World*   18,
    36, 41, 43, 57, 63–6, 113, 117,
    137; *Riders to the Sea*   43; *The
    Tinker's Wedding*   36

Toller, Ernst   165
Tolstoi, Leo   85
TOMMY OWENS   69–70

Ussher, Arland   62

Wesker, Arnold   9
Willett, John   172
Williams, Raymond   **41–5**, 80n.

Yeats, W.B.   10–11, 13, 16–17, 36,
    49, 50, 61, 83–5, 87, 111–12,
    133–7, 175, 188n.; *Countess
    Cathleen* 136–7; *A Vision*   120–1